The Writing Systems
of the World

THE LANGUAGE LIBRARY

EDITED BY DAVID CRYSTAL

The Articulate Computer	*Michael McTear*
The Artificial Language Movement	*Andrew Large*
Australian Aboriginal Languages	*Colin Yallop*
Children's Writing and Reading	*Katharine Perera*
A Child's Learning of English	*Paul Fletcher*
A Companion to Old and Middle English Studies	*A. C. Partridge*
A Dictionary of Literary Terms (revised)	*J. A. Cuddon*
Early English (revised)	*J. W. Clark*
Early Modern English	*Charles Barber*
English Dialects (revised)	*G. L. Brook*
A Dictionary of Linguistics and Phonetics (second edition)	*David Crystal*
The Foreign-Language Barrier	*J. A. Large*
A History of the English Language	*G. L. Brook*
A History of Foreign-Language Dictionaries	*R. L. Collison*
How Conversation Works	*Ronald Wardhaugh*
An Informal History of the German Language	*W. B. Lockwood*
John Donne: Language and Style	*A. C. Partridge*
Language and Class in Victorian England	*K. C. Phillipps*
The Language of 1984	*W. F. Bolton*
The Language of Walter Scott	*Graham Tulloch*
Language, Society and Identity	*John Edwards*
Languages of the British Isles: Past and Present	*W. B. Lockwood*
Languages in Competition	*Ronald Wardhaugh*
Modern Englishes: Pidgins and Creoles	*Loreto Todd*
Non-standard Language in English Literature	*N. F. Blake*
Puns	*Walter Redfern*
Scientific and Technical Translation	*Isadore Pinchuck*
Sense and Sense Development (revised)	*R. A. Waldron*
Speaking of Chinese	*R. Chang & M. Scrogin Chang*
The Study of Dialect	*K. M. Petyt*
A Survey of Structural Linguistics	*G. L. Lepschy*
Thomas Hardy's English	*Ralph W. V. Elliott*
The Treatment of Sounds in Language and Literature	*Raymond Chapman*
The Writing Systems of the World	*Florian Coulmas*

The Writing Systems of the World

FLORIAN COULMAS

Basil Blackwell

Copyright © Florian Coulmas 1989

First published 1989
Reprinted 1990

Basil Blackwell Ltd
108 Cowley Road, Oxford OX4 1JF, UK

Basil Blackwell, Inc.
3 Cambridge Center
Cambridge, Massachusetts 02142, USA

British Library Cataloguing in Publication Data

A CIP catalogue record for this book is available from
the British Library.

Library of Congress Cataloging in Publication Data

Coulmas, Florian.
The writing systems of the world/Florian Coulmas.
   p. cm. – (The Language library)
Bibliography: p.
Includes index.
ISBN 0–631–16513–4
1. Writing–History.   I. Title.   II. Series.
P211.C67 1989   88–25130
411–dc19   CIP

Typeset in 11 on 13 pt Garamond
by Joshua Associates Limited, Oxford
Printed in Great Britain by
T.J. Press Ltd, Padstow, Cornwall

Contents

Preface   viii

PART I   THEORETICAL PERSPECTIVES   1

1 What Writing Is all About   3
2 From Icon to Symbol: The General Trend of Evolution   17
3 Units of Speech and Units of Writing   37

PART II   WRITING SYSTEMS   55

4 Sacred Characters: The Theocratic Script of Egypt   57
5 From Word to Syllable I: Cuneiform Writing   72
6 An Alternative to the Alphabet: The Chinese
   Writing System   91
7 From Word to Syllable II: Chinese Characters
   for other Languages   111
8 Semitic Writing: Syllables or Consonants?   137
9 The Alphabet   158
10 Writing in India   179

PART III   PRACTICAL PROBLEMS   203

11 From Letter to Sound: Deciphering Written
   Languages   205
12 From Sound to Letter: Creating Alphabets   225
13 Writing Reform: Conditions and Implications   241

PART IV   CONCLUSION   265

14 What Writing Means for Linguistics   267

References   274
Appendix I   Ancient Near Eastern Chronology   290
Appendix II   Far Eastern Chronology   292
Index   295

Ein A B C für Ulysses

Preface

This book is one response to the disregard of writing prevalent in modern linguistics. Ever since de Saussure and Bloomfield, the two fathers of structural linguistics, presented powerful arguments for the primacy of speech, writing has been relegated to the final chapters of introductory textbooks. Most of these fail to acknowledge, let alone emphasize, the fact that linguistics itself would have been unthinkable without writing. Having been brought up in an alphabetic culture and trained by teachers who are used to looking at language through alphabetically tinted glasses, it took me a while to realize how utterly unsatisfactory and counterproductive the neglect of writing is for the study of language.

It was through my concern for non-alphabetically written languages that I began to see more clearly that languages are affected in various ways by the writing systems used for their visual materialization, and hence that writing should not only be accorded a proper place in linguistics as an object in its own right, but also be reckoned with as a factor of language change. To non-linguists and many non-Western linguists it is plainly evident that language attitudes and usage are influenced by the way a given language is written, and that, in the long run, through transmission from one generation to the next, the language itself is affected. What exactly it is that writing does to language is a question that linguists should try to answer (if anyone can). It is the contention underlying this book that a correct answer to this question depends on the nature of the writing system in question. Thus an attempt has been made here to present in some detail the major options of writing systems, past and present, and to demonstrate how they relate to language.

This book will have achieved its purpose if it helps students of linguistics to see that writing is more than a garment which hides the true nature of language and should thus be stripped away before linguistic investigation can begin. It is presented to the critical reader in the hope that it will stimulate further research into the intricate relationships between writing and language.

In the spring of 1987, I had the opportunity of teaching a course on 'Writing Systems of the World' at Georgetown University which, significantly, was the first course on this subject ever taught there. This book has been built on my lecture notes, and it has benefited much from the keen questions of my students. Among them Shay Auerbach, Alexandra Casimir, Dimitri Katsareas, Katherine A. Langan, Sumiko Nagasawa and Katalin Nyikos were particularly eager to challenge me for greater clarity and often contributed valuable observations of their own, thus helping to convince me that it was worth the effort of turning the lectures into a book. In this regard I was most intensely encouraged by two of my colleagues, Richard J. O'Brien of Georgetown University, and Danny D. Steinberg of Rikkyo University. They were both kind enough to read the manuscript. I owe them a great debt of gratitude for their many suggestions and pertinent advice which have played a significant role in improving this study. When I wrote this book I was a recipient of a Heisenberg Fellowship of the Deutsche Forschungsgemeinschaft (DFG) which is also gratefully acknowledged.

F.C.
Tokyo

PART I

Theoretical Perspectives

1

What Writing Is all About

Writing is the single most important sign system ever invented on our planet. A skeptic may disagree and point out that speech after all is a sign system, too, and one which is clearly more important than writing. Such an objection, however, misses the point. Whether or not speech is a product of nature or of the human mind has been a hotly debated question since antiquity, but there is general agreement that writing is an artefact. Many linguists believe that human beings are born to speak, a belief strongly supported by the fact that there is no society known which lacks speech. If ever one should be found, somewhere in the hills of New Guinea or in the rain forest of Brazil, having escaped the anthropologists' attention so far, then we would be forced to alter our conception of humanity drastically, or else to exclude that society from our species.

Some tragic cases have been reported occasionally of individuals growing up in isolation without ever getting a chance to acquire language; but those are exceptions. Wherever people associate they have speech to communicate with and thus are able to organize their social lives. Writing, on the other hand, is absent from many societies, and we do not consider this an abnormality or essential defect. Writing is a cultural achievement rather than a universal property and as such is much less important than speech for our self-understanding. Anything that is an invention might as well not be there, and writing, unlike speech, falls into this category. Of course it was not invented in the sense that one day somebody decided that writing was what was needed, and sat down at a desk to invent it. None the less, it is an invention and a very extraordinary one at that which, for all we know, happened only two or three times in the history of mankind. As a matter of fact, its invention created history in the technical sense. Historical knowledge, in other words, is closely linked with written records.[1]

A CULTURAL ACHIEVEMENT

It has often been said that writing is a very recent achievement which emerged late in cultural and societal history.[2] This is undoubtedly true although 'recent' is, of course, a relative notion. It is recent if compared with speech or the upright gait; recent in terms of the emergence of its earliest predecessors some 10,000 or maybe 12,000 years ago (Schmandt-Besserat 1978); and more recent still in terms of its almost universal spread in some societies (Oxenham 1980). Yet, despite its comparatively late advent, the invention of writing has had such pervasive effects on the development of civilization that for all of us who have grown up in a literate culture it is extremely difficult to imagine a world without writing.[3] Almost none of the familiar features of modern society would survive this test; there would be no books, no newspapers, no letters, no tax reports, no pay checks, no identity cards, no lecture notes, no street signs, no labels on commercial products, no advertisements, no medical prescriptions, no systematic education, no dictionaries or encyclopedias, no instruction manuals for radios, cars or computers, a very different kind of religion, a very different kind of law and no science in the proper sense of the word; there would be no linguistics either. A non-literate modern society is a contradiction in terms. Even though the dawn of the post-literate era has been proclaimed by scholars, such as McLuhan (1962) or Ong (1977), writing is, and will be for some time to come, one of the corner-stones of modern life. The entire civilization of the West as well as the East is unthinkable without it.

This is not to say that writing caused civilization, but the reverse is not the whole truth either. Rather, writing has to be seen as a result as well as a condition of civilization, as a product shaped by civilization and a tool shaping it. Writing was not invented for literary purposes, but its invention made literature possible – certain kinds of literature, anyway – and it also made possible a whole range of other complex communicative activities not found in non-literate societies. Why writing came into existence is a comprehensive question whose answer is shrouded in the mist of prehistory because, for obvious reasons, there are no written records about what life was like prior to the invention of writing. Since it is rather difficult to trace writing back to its historical origin, its achievement is often associated with myths and legends (Jensen 1925; Firth 1930). In India, for example, Ganesh (the elephant-faced god of wisdom) is credited with the invention of writing. He is said to have broken off one of his tusks to use as a pencil. In spite of the importance attached to orally transmitting the sacred Vedic texts from one generation to another, writing was highly esteemed in ancient India, as this legend tells us. Moreover, it was considered a feat quite beyond human capacities. It took a god to create writing. The Egyptians believed that the god Thoth was the inventor of writing for which their king Thamus, according to Plato (in *Phaedrus*), both praised and criticized him. In the Islamic tradition, too, God invented writing, while in the Northern Saga its invention is attributed to Odin.

The widespread belief in the divine character of writing reflects an important aspect of its origin and early history. Once they had been developed into fully-fledged systems, early scripts were rather complex. It took a long time to master them, and therefore they were quite beyond reach for the vast majority of the population. The training of scribes was prohibitively expensive and thus restricted to a small class or caste of privileged people. Very often they were priests. For the masses engaged in productive labor, writing was a mystery, a secret code in the literal sense of the word. Not only were they unable to read or write, to a large extent they were not even aware of the practical function that writing serves. Its association with the divine is thus twofold: (1) if it was too difficult for most people to learn, it could not possibly have been created by men, but must be god-given; (2) only – or mostly – those nearest to the gods could handle the secret code, and this meant the priests. It is interesting to note that beliefs of this kind are most prominent in cultures where writing remained the privilege of a small class of specialists. The ancient Near East knows many myths and legends about the divine origin of writing. In Greece, on the other hand, where for the first time in history writing was made available to a large part of the population, such myths are conspicuously absent.

To those who cannot read and write, a book or any other written document manifestly demonstrates their own ignorance and powerlessness; of which fact the educated few can and, of course, do take advantage. One of the crucial consequences of the invention of writing becomes apparent here: it is a powerful instrument of social control.

Writing establishes the great divide between those who have and those who do not have access to knowledge in objectified form. In oral societies, knowledge can be acquired only by experience or direct instruction by another individual. Literate culture, on the other hand, makes possible the storage and transmission of knowledge independent of the human individual who can verbalize it upon request. This was recognized by the earliest scribes who guarded their privilege jealously. Rather than promoting widespread literacy they stressed the divine character of writing, which was not meant for ordinary human beings. The skills of reading and writing provide access to knowledge, and knowledge is power.

While mass literacy may be regarded as a necessary prerequisite for building a modern society in our days, it was perceived as an acute threat to authority as late as the eighteenth century by those who were in power. In 1807 the president of the Royal Society in Britain argued against general literacy which, he said, would: 'teach [the poor] to despise their lot in life, instead of making them good servants in agriculture, and other laborious employment to which their rank in society had destined them; . . . it would enable them to read seditious pamphlets, vicious books, and publications against Christianity; it would render them insolent' (Oxenham 1980: 68).

However, from the invention of writing to the mere conception of mass literacy there was a gap of several thousand years. James Breasted, an ancient historian and Orientalist, once wrote in a frequently quoted passage of his book *The Conquest of Civilization* (1926: 53ff): 'The invention of writing and of a convenient system of records on paper has had a greater influence in uplifting the human race than any other intellectual achievement in the career of man.' While this is hardly an exaggeration, a more specific assessment of the consequences of writing for the civilization of humankind is by no means easy. We can start out by noticing that writing is present wherever societies develop an organization of moderate complexity, while it is absent in societies of lower complexity. This is not to say that higher or more complex forms of civilization were brought about by writing, but rather that they emerged concurrent with writing. And this cannot very well be a coincidence. It is no doubt true that societies which lack the technique of writing can none the less develop highly sophisticated social customs and beliefs, and therefore it is perhaps commendable that among cultural anthropologists they are no longer called 'primitive'.[4] Eventually, however, this is only a terminological quibble. Euphemisms such as 'traditional culture' or, more obviously yet, 'oral culture' essentially mean the same thing: cultures that do not exhibit the typical features of complex societies. The only virtue of abolishing the term 'primitive' is that it carries certain negative connotations in ordinary usage. But so does 'dialect', and that does not hinder dialectologists from continuing to use the term 'dialect'. But whatever these societies are called, it is conspicuous that they fail to develop complex forms of industry, commerce, administration, technology, science and art. Those only emerge together with, or in the wake of, writing.

The most obvious function of writing is that it greatly enlarges the range of communication and, consequently, power. The communicative range of speech is severely limited. A message can be conveyed reliably only to those within earshot. The unaided human voice does not carry very far; more people than can gather in the market place of a hamlet cannot usually be reached. To be sure, messengers can be sent to other places, but they are hardly as reliable as direct face-to-face communication. The messenger may get killed *en route* or suffer from loss of memory. This may seem like a rather remote possibility, but the point is that the message is bound to the messenger if it is to be conveyed orally. Once it becomes possible to convey a message in writing, it is in principle separated from the messenger. The spoken message depends on the messenger, the written does not. Language itself is thus liberated from the spatio-temporal constraints of its ephemeral materialization in speech. The written message may be carried over thousands of miles by messengers who have no idea what the message is all about and who need not even understand the language in which it is phrased. Thus the message becomes an object which has very little to do with the message carrier. In terms of content an oral message, too, may have little or nothing to do with the messenger. However, its material realization or retrieval is bound to that person's physical existence.

Typically, communication in oral societies is face to face, which implies that the difference between oral and literate societies is, among other things, a difference in dimension. The city as a form of social organization is unknown in oral cultures.[5] The intricate social network and division of labor that emerges where masses of people settle in the same place brings with it and/or presupposes a means of recording information in an objective way: that is, independent of the message carrier. In those oral societies which have survived until the present time cities do not exist and, for all we know, no big cities ever existed in any oral society. Just as the communicative range of the human voice is limited, so is the size of oral societies. The great empires of Persia, Greece and Rome are unthinkable without writing (Jensen 1969: 9). To exercise power over a distance of thousands of miles, to rule *in absentia* and to establish uniform standards of administration and law in an area stretching from the Peloponnese to the Indus valley would have been quite impossible without writing. Writing is a means of social control, and it creates social coherence.

What this means is easily understood if we compare the multiplicity and fragmentation of native American cultures with the unity of the Chinese empire which joins together hundreds of millions of people for whom a common writing system serves as a unifying bond. To fulfil this function not everybody, not even the majority of the population, needs to be literate (DeFrancis 1984). An administrative infrastructure can be built on a small number of scribes who set up a system of recording commercial transactions, credits, loans, prices and stocks. Thus more complex forms of economic exchange become possible.

CONSEQUENCES OF WRITING

The interdependence of the development of writing and modern civilization is well documented for the priestly city states of Mesopotamia in the third millennium BC.[6] They developed around the construction of great temples under the supervision of priests who organized the import of building materials, the employment of artisans and slaves for construction work and the agriculture that generated the surplus necessary to feed those who were engaged in the construction. These tasks called for a novel method of keeping records and transmitting human experience. Also, administering the wealth of the temple corporations made it necessary to give an account of receipts and expenses. In this way writing 'gradually emerged from accountancy' (Bernal 1954: 119). The priests were held responsible by their colleagues. Their records had to be accurate and intelligible and not simply to the official who made them. A private system of reminders like knots in handkerchiefs would not do. They had to be noted in symbols which not only reminded the official who was in charge of the transaction in question of time, place, quantity, etc., but which meant the same to colleagues or successors. What was needed was a set of signs, the meanings of which were agreed upon by the consensus of all who used them. In speech this happens naturally as a child grows up in a community where signs with conventional meanings are in use. However, for those who were faced with the task of designing record keeping means of this kind, it was of course not at all clear that what they should, and eventually would, do was to link visual symbols for record keeping with *language*. That is why the invention of writing was such a marvelous feat.

The step from simple mnemonic devices such as tally sticks to the first conventional system of writing capable of recording information on clay tablets was immeasurably greater than all subsequent steps combined leading up to the modern technology of recording information on microchips. Basically, microchips are merely a technical improvement over clay tablets. The invention of writing, however, was the *invention of an entirely new technology*, 'the technology of the intellect', as Goody (Goody and Watt 1968) likes to call it. The complexity of this task cannot be appreciated if we look at it from our present point of view; that is, from the point of view of a literate society. It is difficult for us to conceive of life without writing, but to assume ignorance of *what writing is* is an even greater stretch of our imagination. But that was the state of affairs before the invention of writing. The invention of writing, in other words, was not a clearly defined problem such as, for instance, the construction of a digital code for computerized word processing. Rather, there were a number of practical problems (such as record keeping, accounting, conveying messages indirectly, etc.) whose common solution lay in a conventional system for visually manifesting language. This was not a clearly defined problem in the sense that there was no method for its solution. An understanding of what the actual task was only developed gradually, together with its gradual solution.

At the outset, people were hardly aware that the solution had to be found collectively. Agreement had to be reached on the meanings to be attached to visual signs by the society using them for its common ends. A convention had to be established. The establishment of a convention is a kind of *social problem solving* (Ehlich 1983), and that is what the invention of writing amounts to. Writing is a collectively created tool, a means of production whose invention answered certain needs and made possible a whole range of novel activities and modes of production, as well as kinds of societal communication and economic exchange.

Although this assessment is hardly an exaggeration, the overall contribution of writing to civilization and historical progress is a matter of controversy. Recently a view has gained prominence, largely through Goody's work, that literacy is *the* decisive factor for the 'domestication of the savage mind', to use a phrase which is the title of his 1977 book. Writing, he claims, is closely connected to, or even enforces the development of, logical reasoning (Goody 1977), the distinction of myth from history and the emergence of complex social institutions and scientific thought (Goody and Watt 1968: 43).[7] Goody has repeatedly stated that his point of view is not deterministic. He does not want to argue that writing made all these things happen, but rather notices their concurrence with writing, a fact which needs to be accounted for by any theory of civilization. Yet he goes so far as replacing the traditional distinction between 'primitive' and 'modern' culture with the distinction between 'literate' and 'non-literate'. By thus stressing the importance of writing he lays himself open to the criticism of those who challenge 'the literacy myth', to use the title of a book by one of his opponents, Harvey Graff (1979), a social historian who favors a more socially based view of literacy. Literacy, he contends, should not be seen in isolation, and it should not be assumed that literacy of itself will lead to social improvement, civilization and cultural development.

This is particularly important with respect to literacy campaigns carried out nowadays in Third World countries (Coulmas 1984b) or, for that matter, in impoverished parts of industrialized countries like the US or UK (Street 1984). It would be cynical rather than just naïve to maintain that literacy education can overcome the social problems of race and class conflicts. The achievement of literacy cannot be correctly appreciated if it is seen as a mere technical skill. Its potential and consequences have to be assessed in the context of other social practices that determine how literacy is put to use. An isolated approach to literacy is more likely than not to produce a distorted picture of its historical significance and to raise unwarranted expectations of the effect of present day literacy campaigns.

It seems premature to venture a general answer to the question of how and how much literacy of and by itself shaped history and can help to shape social development now. However, this is not the place to resolve this issue. To put writing into perspective, it will have to suffice in the present context to register the fact that the invention of writing was a cultural achievement of fundamental importance, and that its social possession can make a great difference for societal institutions, customs and socialization practices. Writing is a tool which, like any other tool, serves as a means of extending the power of people over nature and their fellow human beings. Its invention answered certain social needs and made possible a whole range of novel activities and modes of production, as well as kinds of social communication and economic exchange. The availability of this tool does not, however, imply that all its potential is made use of in every given society. It is well known that, for a long time, the Chinese knew of gunpowder without using it to kill each other. Similarly, within a society the use of writing may be restricted to certain functions. The Tuareg, for instance, of North Africa have known of writing for a long time, but have used it for little else but love letters, charms and occasional poems (Friedrich 1966: 94ff). It is quite possible, as this example shows, that the introduction of writing does not affect the culture and social organization of a people in such a dramatic way as would be suggested by its enormous importance in our society. It seems, therefore, that writing is a necessary but not a sufficient condition of higher forms of social organization. Once it is widely used, however, it fulfils a number of functions that make a difference for society, culture and also for language. What we have to keep in mind here is that writing, by meeting certain functional requirements, may at the same time bring about certain effects which go quite beyond the initial requirements.

FUNCTIONS OF WRITING

Consider now some of the more important functions of writing that can be deduced from the way it is used in modern literate societies.

1   Maybe the most obvious function of writing is memory supportive (Goody 1977: 78; Ong 1982: 96). I call this function the *mnemonic function*. Cultural anthropologists always marvel at the memory of non-literate people of traditional cultures. They are able to recite from memory long genealogies and legends that would fill several volumes. This is remarkable, indeed, but none the less hardly comparable with a mnemonic device such as, say, the catalogue of a university library. For the development of writing its mnemonic function was most important. Lists[8] played a major role as a device extending the human memory which is vast but also limited. What happens here and now can be remembered for some time, and such memories may even be passed on

to the next generation, but that is where legend and memory become indistinguishable. If an event is recorded in writing, however, it can be 'recalled', more or less exactly, for ever. Almost everything we know about the Sumerians, the Hittites, the ancient Chinese or the Greeks is through information that they themselves committed to writing. History becomes possible thanks to the mnemonic function of writing, as well as the accumulation of knowledge.

2   A related function is that of expanding the communicative range, as mentioned earlier. Communicating in speech requires the presence together of speaker and listener. Writing, by contrast, enables communication over any distance in space or time (Street 1984: 20). This function will therefore be referred to as the *distancing function*. The written message read by the receiver 10,000 miles away or two millennia later can be the very same document produced by the sender, and it can also be reproduced exactly, word for word, phrase by phrase. The three essential components of linguistic communication – the speaker, the listener and the utterance – can be spatially and temporally separated from each other. The conceiver can thus become the receiver of his or her own message, and the same message can be received by many in different places and at different times. Writing is a distancing medium not only with respect to sender and receiver, but also as regards the sender and the message.

3   By distancing the message from the sender and making it available to others or the originator at a later time, the *medium* of transmission comes to the fore. More obviously than its oral counterpart, which disappears as soon as it materializes, the written message assumes the qualities of an object. This function may be called the *reifying function* of writing. The spoken word is ephemeral and spontaneous in its very essence. In writing, on the other hand, words become stable and tangible. As objects in their own right they become, moreover, depersonalized.

   The interpretation of a spoken utterance is first and foremost the interpretation of the speaker's intended meaning. The focal question is *what* **the speaker** *means by the utterance*. Once words are engraved in stone or clay tablets, inscribed on parchment and paper and thus given a stable physical presence, the focal question about their interpretation becomes *what do* **the words** *mean*. The meaning no longer resides in the speaker but in the text. This point has sometimes been overdrawn, especially by Olson (1977). However, it can hardly be doubted that strategies for interpreting written and spoken utterances differ on several counts. Written words possess meaning by virtue of the conventional relationship between linguistic forms and meanings. This is, of course, also true of spoken words. But their interpretation depends to a much greater extent on both context of situation and the assumed intentions of the speaker. Speech is bound to the 'here', 'now' and 'I' (that is, to a specific deictic center, relative to which it is to be interpreted). The written word, on the other hand, is subsequently detached from the 'here', 'now' and 'I' of its production. In order to be fully interpretable, it must therefore be self-sufficient and explicit. All the information that can be inferred from reference to a common deictic field in speech has to be made explicit in writing. Reification thus means that a linguistic message becomes interpretable as detached from, and independent of, its conceiver. It also means that the code itself becomes an object. Language becomes visible, and as such assumes a physical existence which can be investigated and consciously regulated. In speech language is in flux; in writing it is stable. To study language without analysis and record is quite impossible. Writing provides the means of analyzing language because it turns language into an object.

4   Another aspect of the permanence of writing is its potential for regulating social conduct (Lévi-Strauss 1955: 354ff).[9] This is the *social control function*. The notions of law and right, of standard and correctness, are closely linked with writing. It is, after all, *the letter of the law*. By committing laws to writing they are given a depersonalized authority in their own right.[10] (Notice, incidentally, that the words *author* and *authority* have the same etymology.)

Other socially important forms of written communication include government decrees and announcements, and inter-individual contracts. 'Can I have this in writing?' (Stubbs 1983), is an expression that very clearly testifies to the fact that people – in Western cultures – tend to trust the written word more than the spoken. Social control is exercised through writing because the 'letter-craft' has always been carried by privileged elites who could refer to written documents as seemingly objective standards of human conduct. Even in a fully literate society many more people read than write, and the naïve credence of what is written in books is still widespread.

Writing also serves as a means of social control in a very concrete and technical sense through registering the members of a community for purposes of taxation, military draft and voting. One's identity is certified in writing. To a large extent one's entire social existence depends on written records.

Yet another side of the social control function of writing is related to language. Language behavior is a part of social conduct. The elites who write obviously write their variety of the language in question. By virtue of their social position and of the permanence of written documents this variety is strongly favored over others which, in many cases, leads to its establishment as the standard. Writing may thus become a model of speech. That a standard language has important ramifications for society is generally recognized. The part that writing plays in its making is manifold and complex (Coulmas 1987c). At this point, we cannot go into it in more depth, but we will come back to it occasionally.

5 A somewhat derived function of writing is *interactional*. By liberating linguistic communication from the constraints of speech, writing makes possible novel kinds of coordinated action. Letters and wills are directed at particular addressees whose behavior is influenced by the message they convey. Similarly, instruction manuals, recipes, style sheets, etc., directed at an unspecified readership, serve to regulate behavior. Whereas coordinating interaction by means of speech presupposes the presence together of speaker and listener(s), it may be mediated and achieved indirectly where writing is available.

6 Finally, the *aesthetic function* of writing should be mentioned. The very word *literature* is self-explanatory in that it refers to the medium of verbal art (Ong 1982: 10ff). There is, admittedly, oral poetry, and recently much attention has been paid to its peculiarities and distinctions as compared with literature proper (Duggan 1975). The question of the orality of Homer is hotly debated,[11] and there can be no doubt that the aesthetic function of language is realized in oral as well as in literate cultures. Yet some *genres*, such as novel and drama, and certain kinds of poetry, too, are quite unthinkable without writing. Moreover, the medium itself is cultivated and can be turned into the highly sophisticated art of calligraphy which, by making a verbal message beautiful to look at, appeals both to the intellect and the sense of visual beauty.

CONCLUSION

More could be said about the aesthetic function of writing and about the others as well. This sketchy overview is, however, enough for present purposes to put writing into perspective and to illustrate that it is one of the major signs of civilization. Everywhere in the ancient world, writing was the invariable accompaniment of certain sociocultural conditions that led to higher forms of civilization. Outstanding among these conditions are: the development of government; the division of labor; the appearance of specialized professions in agriculture, industry, commerce and transportation; the domestication of animals; the production of goods for a market; the growth of cities and empires. Wherever these conditions develop writing is always present. Complex civilizations cannot exist without writing. As pointed out earlier, the invention of writing can be seen as a kind of social problem solving, and any writing system as the common solution of a number of related problems.

An important feature of such solutions is their *conventional character*. This implies that there is a variety of solutions. The main purpose of this book is to give an overview of the most important and most interesting such solutions. It presents an introduction to the great multiformity of writing systems, scripts and orthographies, and then goes on to investigate their relative merits and demerits and to discuss the question of whether and how criteria can be defined for the evaluation of writing systems, scripts and orthographies. In so doing it focuses on the systematic make-up of writing systems. One of the central questions to be pursued is how the various writing systems relate to language. How far are they adapted to particular languages, and how do they differ as regards their suitability for representing that language? In some cases it will be necessary to go into rather technical details to see how writing systems work. In the context of this book this question is of interest, however, only inasmuch as it enhances our understanding of how writing represents language, and whether and how it affects language.

NOTES

1 'Writing . . . ushers in *civilization* and initiates the historical record' (Childe 1982: 31). 'Looked at in the perspective of time, man's biological evolution

shades into prehistory when he becomes a language-using animal; add writing, and history proper begins' (Goody and Watt 1968: 27).

2 'All writing, in fact, is a relatively recent invention, and has remained, almost to our day, the property of only a chosen few' (Bloomfield 1933: 13). The same point is repeated in Hockett (1963: 7).

3 Bernal (1954: 119) calls writing 'that greatest of human manual–intellectual inventions'.

4 Goody (1977) is, for the most part, a discussion of the 'great divide' between societies that have been variously labeled as 'primitive' v. 'advanced', 'traditional' v. 'modern', 'hot' v. 'cold' or 'oral' v. 'literate'.

5 Childe (1982: 31) thus called writing 'a necessary by-product of [the] urban revolution' and refers to the oldest 'historical' cities as those 'in which legible written documents occur' (1982: 98).

6 Cf. Chiera (1938), still a classic; Kramer (1981); Oppenheim (1964); Green (1981).

7 Cf. also Feldbusch (1985: 285ff, *passim*). 'Written language provides the opportunity to plan the language–thought process exactly and subject it to critical control' (Feldbusch 1985: 285).

8 Lists were at the beginning of scientific inquiry. Von Soden (1936) introduced the term *Listenwissenschaft* in his treatment of Babylonian science. Cf. also Goody (1977, chapter 5).

9 'La lutte contre l'analphabétisme se confond ainsi avec le renforcement du contrôle des citoyens par le Pouvoir. Car il faut que tous sachent lire pour que ce dernier puisse dire: nul n'est censé ignorer la loi' (Lévi-Strauss 1955: 355).

10 Stratton (1980) explores the impact of writing on the concepts of 'law' and 'justice' in Greek society. He offers the interesting hypothesis that writing so strongly affected Greek society because it was perceived in Greece without any religious overtones, and was not guarded as a privilege by the powerful.

I would like to suggest that one of the most important reasons for the rapid flowering of written Greek thought was the early lack of governmental control of literacy. As a result of this lack, the Athenian government, in spite of all its late attempts, was unable to stop the rapid development of moral and ethical debates which were directly related to the increasing secularisation of the idea of social order. This, in turn, led to the rapid development of an idea of law based on control and therefore on exercised power. (Stratton 1980: 117ff)

11 Ong (1982) provides an overview of the work by Parry, Lord, Havelock and others.

2

From Icon to Symbol:
The General Trend of Evolution

Instead of giving a formal definition of writing, let us discuss three of its fundamental characteristics:

1 it consists of artificial graphical marks on a durable surface;
2 its purpose is to communicate something;
3 this purpose is achieved by virtue of the marks' conventional relation to language.[1]

Given these characteristics, we can identify forerunners of writing which have some but not all of them. We know of quite a few such precursors whose analysis has contributed greatly to our understanding of the history of writing because they provide essential clues to the question of where writing came from.

PRECURSORS OF WRITING

Even in the most restricted culture, people had to do some communicating with others who were beyond the range of hearing. They needed some means of transcending the spatio-temporal confines of the face-to-face speech act. This could be achieved in several different ways. Signs of a non-graphical nature can be found in all cultures. A rock placed on a grave somehow means something, be it as a reminder of a deceased person or as a precaution to ward off that person's return to the living. Places can be marked for other purposes too; a branch placed in a certain way can indicate the direction of one's path, or stones may claim ownership of a piece of land. Such marks are erected for the purpose of communication, but do not exhibit the other two features of writing: the marks consist of natural objects and they do not relate to language.

Similarly, tally sticks fail to qualify as writing proper, because the signs that are incised on them, while being produced artificially, have no linguistic reference. They are signs, nevertheless, but the semiotic relation they exemplify is a rather simple one holding between a sign and an object. Tallies, or notched sticks, are known in many parts of the world, in Australia as well as in pre-colonial America, in Africa, in Europe and in China too. They were used for counting cattle or for economic transactions such as the recording of debts, or simply for taking stock. An interesting interactional aspect is seen in those notched sticks that are split in half so as to provide each party of a loan or delivery transaction with an identical record of the agreement in question. Any attempt at changing the record would be discovered when the halves are held together. The custom of carving notches in rifle butts is another analogue of the tally stick, if a rather gruesome one. A somewhat elaborate version relates to the messenger sticks that were commonly used among the aborigines of Australia, where every notch or line carved into the stick referred to a part of a message. The message, however, could not be 'read' by the receiver. Rather it had to be conveyed to him by the messenger for whom the stick was a memory aid. The messenger stick does not relate to language, however, and thus cannot be considered as writing.

A similar but more complicated mnemonic device is the knot-string notation that was used by the Incas, apparently the only forerunner of writing developed in the Andean region (Prem and Riese 1983). These *quipus*, or looped ropes, as they are called, were used as a rather complicated system of accounting and recording. The length and color and the number of knots of a string were given a particular significance. Some scholars have claimed that quipus were used as memory aids for legends and even laws, and certainly for 'propositional contents' rather than objects, while others insist that they served statistical purposes only. The issue seems to be unresolved.

Other objects are reported to have been used as mnemonic devices, such as pebbles or cowrie mussels. Usually they relate in a simple and straightforward way to the things for which they stand: ten pebbles for ten goats and so on. Also common is the method of communicating meaning by indexical signs – that is, signs that bear a contiguity relation to the objects for which they stand – such as a few grains of rice for food, a feather for fowl, etc. An interesting case of transmitting messages by objects is reported from the Yoruba in Nigeria (Gelb 1963: 5). It involves cowrie mussels and language and a purely linguistic relation, namely the homonymy of certain number words. The Yoruba word *efa*, for instance, means 'six' but also 'attracted', and the word *eyo* means both 'eight' and 'agreed'. Thus, by sending someone six cowries, you can convey the message that you are attracted, and the receipt of eight cowries as a reply would indicate 'OK, let's have an affair.' The interesting point here is that there is no intrinsic relation between the sign and its referent. For anyone who does not speak Yoruba, the relationship between eight cowrie mussels and the notion of 'agreement' is quite impossible to guess by virtue of the perceptible features of the sign. It cannot be decoded without linguistic mediation. None the less, for several reasons, this peculiar usage of signs does not constitute writing. The signs are natural objects rather than artefacts. They are used for the purpose of communicating, and this purpose is achieved through linguistic mediation, but the linguistic relation exploited here is rather coincidental and cannot be extended systematically. To say that six cowries are used to write the word *efa* which means 'attracted' would be rather misleading.

Writing is done by engraving or drawing, scratching or incising surrogational signs[2] by motor action of the hand. In this sense, too, the exchange of objects, even if they are surrogates for other objects or ideas, does not constitute writing. It is impractical and can hardly be elaborated into a full-fledged system. The etymology of various words for 'write', such as Greek *gráfein* (to carve) and Latin *scribere* (hence German *schreiben*, English *scribe*, *inscribe*) among others testify to the physical origin of writing. In Semitic languages relations between the words for 'write' and 'cut' or 'excavate' are apparent by common roots. The root *shf* in South Semitic languages, for instance, meant both 'to write' and 'to hollow'.

Another way of communicating messages visually which resembles writing in some respects is by drawing pictures. Where this is done in a more or less systematic and iconographic way, the term 'picture writing' has been used to describe it. The American Indians have used this method extensively. Mallery (1893) has collected many samples, such as the Cheyenne 'letter' reproduced in figure 2.1.

This composition consists of a number of hand-drawn signs on paper and serves the purpose of communicating an explicit message. The

2.1 A Cheyenne Indian letter (from Mallery 1893: 364)

message is as follows: Turtle-Following-His-Wife, a Cheyenne Indian, wants his son, Little Man, to come home. To pay for the trip, he sends $53.00. Apparently, the recipient of the letter, Little Man, had no trouble understanding it. Two of our three conditions are met by this document: it consists of artificial graphical marks, and its purpose is to communicate something. However, if there is any relation to language at all, it is very loose. Any message can, of course, be put into words, but that does not mean that any message is linguistically coded. The 'letter' cannot be read. Not just anyone can look at it and say 'Aha, what this letter says is this: "Dear Son, please come home. I am sending $53.00 for your travel expenses. Your father."' This is the content of the message, but it is not transmitted linguistically. Even though we have a case here of a specific message being communicated by graphical means, this is not writing. It is interesting, in this connection, that a message with a propositional content can be conveyed by graphical means, but non-linguistically.

Pictures were also used as memory aids. The Ewe of Togo, for example, used to record proverbs by means of pictures. These pictures do relate to language; their purpose is to communicate something; and they consist of artificially produced graphical marks. In the literature these and similar signs have therefore sometimes been called *sentence writing* (Meinhof 1911; Friedrich 1966: 12). This terminology has been criticized, rightly, by Gelb (1963: 50) as being inappropriate and misleading. Why is this, and why are we reluctant to call pictures of this kind writing? The reason is that they stand for the respective proverbs only in the sense that they remind someone who already knows the proverbs. There is no way to decipher the message for someone who does not, because there is no systematic relation between parts or aspects of the graph and parts of the sentence. Moreover, the signs are not conventional. Their primary semiotic function is iconic: that is, they depict certain concrete objects which are also referred to by the proverb. The semiotic relation is from sign to object to sentence rather than the other way round. Also, proverbs are proverbially oral being fixed in form and memorized as units of speech.

There are many iconic signs in present-day use for a variety of purposes, such as shop signs: a picture of a book for a book shop; a pair of glasses for an optician; a brush for a paint shop; and so on. In public places, especially where many foreigners are expected such as airports or hotels, fairs and expositions, we find many iconic signs, such as little figures with trousers or skirts; pictures of drinking fountains, little running figures for indicating escape routes, or partly iconic signs such as pictures of crossed-out dogs indicating that a store or a room is off-limits for dogs (see figure 2.2); pictures of flames to warn the illiterate that a container holds inflammable liquid, or pictures of a glass used as a label on packages communicating the message 'handle with care!' Recently, the use of such icons has increased. An interesting question that poses itself in this regard is whether this increase is a reflection of the fact that illiteracy seems to be a growing phenomenon in industrialized countries (Copperman 1980; Street 1984).

2.2 An example of a partly iconic sign

Mass tourism has also contributed to the spread of modern pictorial symbols. More people than ever come to places where they cannot read what is written, or cannot speak the language of the country. International expositions, sport competitions and so on are places where one can find an abundance of such icons. They can tell us something about the difference between pictorial signs and writing proper. We could, of course, say with some justification that ♟ means 'handle with care' and should therefore be read as such. The whole point of this sign, however, is that it can be understood – or at least is meant to be understood – not only by speakers of English but by speakers of all languages. Its *raison d'être* is that it is *language independent*. When the parcel arrives in Paris, ♟ should neither be taken to mean something like *à votre santé*, nor should it stand for an English phrase incomprehensible to the Algerian who works at the post office there. Thus its meaning should be fixed, but its being fixed must not depend on its conventional relationship to a linguistic expression of a given language. There is both an element of conventionality and language independence. The sign is iconic in the sense that it designates an object by means of depicting its actual physical appearance. However, no intrinsic feature of the picture forces us to interpret it as meaning 'handle with care!', or 'don't throw!' A glass could mean several different things. What meaning the pictogram actually has is thus a matter of convention.

Conventions can be established by conscious decision and agreement, as is nowadays the practice of international terminology committees. People can decide, for instance, that a camera with through-the-lens focusing and a range of movements of the lens plane should be called a *land camera*. In ancient times, however, terminology committees did not exist. Conventions developed naturally and nowadays, too, new conventions come into existence without any formal procedures. It does not seem likely that the sign of the glass was first introduced by mutual agreement. That it assumed a conventional meaning as a sign to be careful or attentive has to do with the *context of situation* in which it was first used. As a label on a parcel an interpretation such as 'glass, handle with care!' or anything to this effect is much more likely than, say, 'glass, have a drink!' The same label may be put on parcels not actually containing glass but other fragile things. It bears no iconic relation any more to its referent, then, and assumes a derived character which is entirely conventional, the meaning being reduced to 'careful!'

This is still not writing in the strict sense, but it comes close, and it will be useful to keep in mind the two decisive factors of the making of this sign: its introduction in a particular context of situation, and its becoming conventionalized. Also important for signs of this sort as well as for writing is the fact that they become graphically stylized. While at the outset the iconicity of the sign (that is, its resemblance with the referent) is the most important feature of the sign by virtue of which it conveys a certain meaning, the stylized form becomes the most important aspect once the meaning has become fixed and conventionalized.

Graphical conventionalization is a process quite analogous to the historical development of words and phrases (Coulmas 1981a). In the beginning it was quite important that a particular meaning was conveyed with the phrase (*May*) *God be with you*. Eventually, however, it became a conventional and formally fixed formula for a particular communicative function. It was generally understood what this function was, and it was also understood that the phrase 'God be with you' was the appropriate means for fulfilling this function. To indicate one's willingness to fulfil this function gradually became more important than the verbatim meaning of the phrase which, therefore, became ever more stylized and cursivized. Nowadays, few people remember that *goodbye* was originally a wish referring to the benevolence of a superior being. Similarly, in many cases of the development of written symbols out of pictorial signs, the pictures became linearized, stylized and conventionally associated with a particular meaning whereby the iconic meaning was supplanted. Thus we can observe a gradual transition from icon to symbol.

TOKENS AND IMPRESSIONS

At the basis of all writing, it is often said (for example, Gelb 1963: 27), stands the picture, and this is certainly a reasonable assumption. However, recent research has shed light on yet another possibility. In 1978, Schmandt-Besserat published an article entitled, 'The Earliest Precursors of Writing'. It is the result of a meticulous study of certain artefacts that were used for accounting throughout Asia Minor as much as 10,000 years ago. Those objects were little stones and pieces of baked clay of various different shapes, as can be seen in figure 2.3.

Initially these tokens or counters, as they are commonly called, were used for computation and record keeping. The semiotic relation between sign and referent was a very simple one, one token for one

Token type I		II		III		IV		V	
Sphere		Disk		Cone		Tetrahedron		Biconoid	
Tokens	Sumerian pictographs	Tokens	Sumerian pictographs	Tokens	Sumerian pictographs	Tokens	Sumerian pictographs	Tokens	Sumerian pictographs
○	○ Numeral 10	⊕	⊖ Seat	▽.	⊅ Numeral 1	◇	◁	◇	◇ Good sweet
◐	⊸ Numeral 10	⊕	⊖ Garment, cloth	◡	◖ Numeral 60	◈	◁	◈	Legal decision, trial, peace

2.3 *Tokens matched with earliest Sumerian characters (from Schmandt-Besserat 1978. Copyright© 1978 by Scientific American, Inc. All rights reserved)*

object. However, differently shaped tokens were used for different kinds of objects. Furthermore, to avoid confusion and to systematize the inventory, the tokens were put into little clay containers, called *bullae* (Schmandt-Besserat 1980). These containers could then be used to convey messages, either to the successor of a record keeper or to the other party in a commercial transaction by sending the container. The problem with the containers, of course, was that items could be added or taken away from them. Presumably for this reason, people started to seal the containers[3] which brought about another disadvantage, however: once sealed, one had to break them in order to check the contents. The solution to this problem was most likely of enormous consequence for the development of writing.[4] By impressing the tokens on the shell of the container before it was sealed and while the clay was still wet, it was possible to indicate on the outside what was contained inside and thus check the record without breaking the container.

The important point here is that, all of a sudden, a new semiotic relation was introduced into the method of record keeping. The relationship between the impressions of the tokens on the outside of the containers and the objects was an indirect one. While the tokens themselves stood in a direct relation to their referents, the clay impressions referred to the objects only by virtue of representing the tokens. They were *signs of signs*, in other words. This novel semiotic relation was not necessarily recognized immediately in its full significance by those who first used this technique of representing objects indirectly. However, it proved to be of major importance for the development of writing because gradually the impressions on the outside of the containers assumed the function of the primary signs, the tokens, which in turn became less and less important. Thus a direct relation developed between the impressions and the objects. The transformation of the relation between sign and referent can be depicted schematically as shown in figure 2.4.

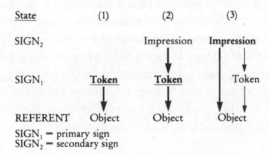

2.4 *The relation between a token and an object is superseded by the relation between the impression of the token and the object*

The crucial point of Schmandt-Besserat's work is the discovery that the impressions of the tokens are graphically identical with the earliest pictograms of what would become the most important script of Asia Minor, the Sumerian cuneiform writing.[5] If her analysis is correct, and the available evidence is quite convincing, many Sumerian pictograms are direct descendants of the impressions of the tokens. A technical innovation thus led to a semiotically more complex system of record keeping, namely a system of secondary signs. This device was used for several thousand years (approximately from 9000–2000 BC). At the same time, the Sumerians developed a numerical system, also used for accounting (Schmandt-Besserat 1981). 'Count stones' were used to represent numerical values. A numerical system is a major intellectual achievement because numbers are totally abstract entities. They cannot be perceived as such in the physical world; rather they have to be deduced from perceptible sets of objects. The representation of numbers thus transcends the representation of physical objects. Interestingly, the abstractness of numbers is reflected in the non-iconic shapes of the 'count stones' that had a numerical denotation: spheres, cylinders, cubes, etc.

Number signs are also more complex than simple icons representing physical objects. They can be justly called *ideograms*, because what they stand for are ideas; abstractions, that is, of sets of things. That these ideas came to be represented by means of graphical marks was again mediated through the process of impressing the abstract 'count stones' on the outside of the bullae. It is likely that the Sumerians also had number words at this stage, but there was no necessary connection between the number words and the graphical figures with the same numerical value. In this sense too the number signs were truly ideographic (Schmandt-Besserat 1981: 341). They could be manipulated and calculated without any direct relation to language. It was, however, more likely that through calculating and accounting a link was established between the graphical number sign and the corresponding linguistic sign. In the beginning, people were not necessarily aware of this linkage which was a result of the identity of the signs' referent, but gradually it became fixed and the ideographic sign developed into a linguistic sign of secondary order.

THE MISSING LINK

By the same token, so to speak, the graphical signs of objects, originally derived from the impression of tokens with concrete referents, came to be associated with the linguistic signs of the same objects. This process is called *phonetization*.[6] The visual sign of the object acquires a linguistic interpretation. In the case of count stones, or rather the graphical representations of them that stood for concrete objects such as cattle, dogs, lions, beds, pots, etc., this was most obviously a word. The establishment of the missing link in the semiotic relation between object, graphical sign and linguistic sign constitutes the beginning of writing proper.

Notice that Feldbusch (1985: 126, 139ff) interprets Schmandt-Besserat's findings quite differently, emphasizing the language-independent origin of the system of graphic signs constituted by the impressions of the tokens. While Feldbusch relies on the Sumerian tokens and their impressions as key witnesses in making a case for the non-derived nature of written language,[7] Schmandt-Besserat (1981: 341) takes a more pragmatic position. Whether or not the earliest impressed signs constitute writing, according to her, 'depends upon the definition of writing adopted. Some scholars place the dividing line between pre-writing systems and writing when the signs take a *phonetic* value, others at the emergence of *graphic* symbols.'

Schmandt-Besserat is probably right about the beginning of writing proper being basically a question of definition and one should not, therefore, belabor it too much. As stated at the beginning of this chapter, a conventional relation between graphical sign and linguistic unit is considered crucial for writing. The reasons for this assumption are as follows. Language is the most elaborate symbolic system that human beings control. While it may be possible, in principle, for a group of people to develop a graphical code which is independent of their language and which reaches the same complexity and expressive power as a natural language and would thus be a genuine written language, it is highly unlikely that any group of people would engage in such an uneconomical endeavor (developing, as it were, language again from scratch). Sooner or later any system of visible signs that grows into a writing system must therefore be assumed to be provided with a linguistic interpretation: that is, with a conventional, structurally motivated link with a language.

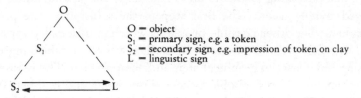

2.5 The relation between an object, its primary and secondary sign and its linguistic sign

The important point here is that 'the missing link' is a mutual mapping relation, as shown in figure 2.5. The representation S_2 is recognizable as a representation of the object O by virtue of its visual features. Its association with the linguistic sign L (the word designating O) makes S_2 in a fundamental sense *readable*. The inverse relation – that is, that between L and S_2 – also holds and is equally important, because on account of it the spoken word becomes *writable*. Only where the mutual relation has been firmly established can we speak of writing in the strict sense of the term.

FROM MEANING TO SOUND

There is no reason to believe that phonetization was achieved suddenly. It seems more likely that it only gradually supplanted the use of pictorial ideograms for record keeping and accounting. People continued to represent *objects* by means of graphical marks, and it must have taken many generations to accomplish the shift from object representation to word representation. Once this was done, important consequences quite beyond accounting and calculating followed. The transmission of societal knowledge, which so far had been a mental operation (memory) relying on the use of particular language forms being taught by one generation to the next, became objectified and could be handled as the transmission of material goods. Language could be engraved in stone or clay and handed over to subsequent generations, thus defying the volatility of the individual speech event.

However, when graphical marks were first used to represent linguistic signs rather than their material referents, the change from an oral to a literate tradition was only a potential awaiting realization. The novel technique of writing linguistic units had yet to be expanded into a full-fledged *writing system*. The first step of the solution of the problem brought with it other possible problems which in turn called for a solution. The first step, as pointed out earlier, was the establishing of the missing link between graphical sign and acoustic sign. The referents of these signs were physical objects on the one hand, and numbers on the other hand. The corresponding language unit was a name: that is, a *word*. The written sign thus created visualizes the basic relation constituting a linguistic sign in the Saussurean sense: namely, the relation between a *sound image* and an *idea*, as represented in figure 2.6 (de Saussure 1972: 99).[8] This was a straightforward solution for those linguistic signs referring to material objects.

Material objects could be readily represented by graphical means. At this point in the development of writing what has been achieved is *word-*

2.6 *De Saussure's linguistic sign*

picture writing, or *ideographic writing* as it is sometimes called because of the close relation the written sign has to the meaning which it still represents iconically. Indeed, if we look at the written signs of this stage, the relation between sign and meaning is more obvious and hence stronger than that between sign and sound image; or, to put it differently, the sign body bears no intrinsic relation to the form of its linguistic correlate (its phonetic shape), but it does relate directly, by virtue of its graphical shape, to the meaning side. There is no equilibrium of the two sides of the Saussurean sign, because the written sign continues to have iconic features with respect to the represented object while the relation to the word is totally arbitrary, the relation between the word and the object itself being arbitrary. The details of the graphical shape do relate to parts of the referent, but they do not relate to parts of the acoustic shape of the linguistic sign which is represented only as a totality.

The primary use of writing in the early stages of development was for economic purposes (Powell 1981), therefore, and also, in the interest of clarity and reliability, conventionalized and stylized signs were preferred. In many cases, this meant abstraction and a consequential reduction of iconicity. The Sumerian ideograms, for example, were reduced to abstract symbols as early as 2500 BC, almost all of them having lost their iconic features. To the extent that visual iconicity was reduced, the relation of the sign to its linguistic form attained equal weight. Gradually the graphical sign thus came to stand for a linguistic sound unit (Green 1981). Initially, this unit was a word, and the words which could thus be visualized were restricted to those having a concrete referent, such as *ox*, *grain*, *fish*, *mat*, *bird*, *donkey*, etc. For the most important practical purposes of writing this was quite enough. But words with more abstract meanings, such as *brother*, *go* or *dear* were still impossible to write. Generally speaking, properties, movements, states of affairs, events and relations could not be represented easily by means of pictorial signs. Hence the system was severely limited and could not yet unfold its full potential for handing down societal knowledge from generation to generation.

However, phonetization coupled with graphical abstraction opened the path to a solution of this problem too. As the relation between graphical sign and phonic word form became more stable and prominent, it became conceivable to use graphical marks for sound configurations only, irrespective of their meanings, because the meanings were no longer self-evident by the icon. In Sumerian (Chiera 1938: 63) as well as in Chinese,[9] at the time of the beginning of writing, most words consisted of few syllables only, and many were monosyllabic. This implies in a rather strict mathematical sense that there were many homonymous words. As the graphical signs stood for word forms, they could be used to write one word as well as another identical in form but different in meaning. Graphically, the process which led to this kind of representation (known as 'rebus sign') can be represented as shown in figure 2.7.

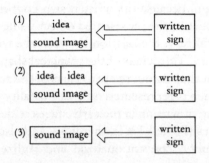

2.7 The transition from (1), word writing resting on a unique relation between word form, word meaning and written sign, via (2), rebus writing based on homophony, to (3), sound writing

Gradually, the meaning side of the linguistic sign as a denotatum of the written sign was canceled out. Thus phonetization progressed one step further. The primary value of the written sign had become a sound. It had been transformed from icon to symbol.

Among the reasons that made phonetization necessary was the demand for signs representing proper names to which no meaning could be assigned (foreign names of kings or other dignitaries fall into this category). A phonetic device was needed for their written representation. Names were very early recognized as words of a special kind, as magical aspects were attributed to them. Knowing the name of a thing or a person was to have some power over the thing or the person. Replacing names by definite descriptions, such as 'the king of so-and-so', was no satisfactory substitute for the names themselves. The obvious strategy for doing so was to use word signs with a similar sound value. This strategy has been employed in all word writing systems, in Sumer and Egypt as well as in China, and even in the hieroglyphic system of the Aztecs in Mexico.

THE REBUS PRINCIPLE

The Aztec system is a picture-word writing system in which the initial steps towards phonetization had been accomplished, but which never developed into a full-fledged system, however. It remained at the threshold of writing proper. The same may be said of the Maya writing system. In both systems we find a marked contrast between graphic complexity and sophistication and low systematic development. It is easier to talk about the Aztec system, as the Maya hieroglyphs are only poorly understood. Nevertheless, most scholars agree that neither of them are fully developed phonetic systems (Thompson 1968; Vollemaere 1971; Prem and Riese 1983). The Aztecs had a rich stock of inscriptions on stone, hide and even on a kind of paper, but most of it was destroyed by the Spanish conquerors. Most of the remaining texts are written in ideographic picture writing which can be understood, given the appropriate context of situation, without linguistic mediation. Most of the time the pictures speak for themselves. There are, however, also word signs which are occasionally used in rebus fashion for representing meaningless sound configurations, and this combination of both strategies is the typical case. Consider an example from the often quoted Codex Boturini (figure 2.8).

It tells about the migration of the Aztecs (Jensen 1969: 222). Four Aztec tribes come to a sacred place to bid farewell to their kinsmen of eight related tribes. The names of the former are indicated by symbols over the heads of the four figures on the left. The names of the latter, however, are given in 'phonetic' writing. Word signs in combination

2.8 Aztec writing from the Codex Boturini

with the sign for 'house' give a hint as to the pronunciation of the names. Thus, the word sign for *matla-tl* which means 'net' (the one on the right) refers to the *Matlazinco* tribe; the word sign for *te-tl*, 'stone' (second from right) refers to the *Tepaneca*, etc. In principle, this procedure of using word signs for their phonetic value only, if systematically applied, can lead to the development of a fully phonetic system. The pre-Columbian systems did not reach this stage, however.

Applying the rebus principle to foreign proper names or words is likely to bring about new problems to be mastered. Without difficulties it can be applied only to words of a language with a very similar phonetic structure as that for whose representation the writing system is used. We will have occasion to come back to this problem more than once. At this point, consider for illustration an example of the Aztec script (figure 2.9).

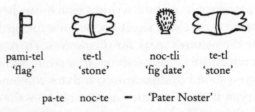

pami-tel	te-tl	noc-tli	te-tl
'flag'	'stone'	'fig date'	'stone'

pa-te   noc-te — 'Pater Noster'

2.9 The beginning of the Pater Noster *in Aztec writing*

Spanish missionaries were very active in Mexico. As Christianity is a book religion, they felt the need not only to convey their spiritual message to the poor native heathens but also to teach them the very words of the Latin bible. Presumably, in lieu of some magical formula, they wanted the converts to read the Lord's prayer in Latin. Thus they used Aztec word signs to write Latin. The native language of the Aztecs is, however, quite different from Latin in its phonological make-up, and therefore this was not an easy task. It has, for instance, none of the phonemes /f/, /g/, /r/ and /d/. Rebus writing of Latin with the Aztec script could at best be a rough approximation. Consider the example. Only the beginnings of the Aztec words – that is, their initial syllables – are functional in the transcription. Reading it requires some ingenuity on the part of the reader. This particular use of word signs employed by missionaries did not develop systematically in Aztec writing, and is usually called the 'acrophonic principle' (Jensen 1969: 46, 250),[10] whereby a word sign acquires the phonetic value of the beginning of the whole word for whose writing it was originally used. For the transition from word to syllable writing it was of some importance. The Aztec system, however, never reached that stage.[11] To put it differently, the relation between graphical symbol and the phonetic side of the linguistic sign remained rather loose, because to a large extent meaning was conveyed by more or less iconic or allegorical signs. In so far as an association between graphical sign and linguistic sound was established it illustrates the important point that phonetic writing is language specific. 'Phonetic' is not used here in a technically specific sense but rather in the general sense of 'sound-based'. For the development of writing in general and for the adaptation of writing systems the language specificity of writing systems is very significant, as will become clear in several particular cases.

Proper names, especially foreign names, are words whose graphical representation enhances the phonetization of a word script. This can be observed in the Aztec systems as well as in Sumerian or Chinese. They play a similar role for the converse process of deciphering a script whose tradition has been interrupted or, rather, broken off by the destruction of a culture such as the Egyptian, Sumerian or Hittite. Deciphering an unknown script is rightly recognized as a profound achievement of scholarship (cf. chapter 11), but it is no more than an intellectual pastime if compared with the collective intellectual achievement of writing as a novel technique which had not previously existed.

CONCLUSION

The decisive step in the development of writing is *phonetization*: that is, the transition from pictorial icon to phonetic symbol. The ultimate consequence of phonetization is the alphabet, which is often praised as the finest and most highly developed writing system.[12] From an abstract point of view it would seem that it is a natural consequence of phonetization. This viewpoint, however, pays too little attention to two important points; (1) that writing systems are artificially created historical constructs (in technical terms artefacts, rather than naturally developed objects); and (2) that every writing is language specific in the sense that phonetization means to create systematic relations between graphical signs and the sound pattern of a given language. Phonetic writing was not developed to represent speech sounds in general but to represent the sounds of a particular language.

There is, no doubt, an internal logic in the development from the earliest iconic precursors of writing over increasingly more stylized and abstract pictograms to purely arbitrary phonetic symbols that has to do with simplicity and flexibility. However, for the very reason that writing systems are artificially created by people, there is always an element that interferes with this internal logic. More than that of language, the development of writing is subject to conscious interference as well as dependent upon the ingenuity of the creator.

The general tendency of development is roughly from pictogram to alphabet via word writing first and then syllable writing. Because of the history of writing there is, however, no natural law causing every attempt to write to go through every one of these phases and to complete the evolutionary scale to its logical conclusion. Language specific as they are, various writing systems have terminated the evolutionary process at transitory stages somewhere in between to be further elaborated, systematized and standardized on the achieved level.

Returning now to the three characteristics of writing stated at the outset of this chapter, it is clear that they are of a rather general kind and open to more specific interpretation. What kind of information is felt to be necessary to communicate in writing depends on the general level of cultural development. For simple listings a rather crude system is sufficient; the graphical marks' conventional relation to language can be held at a coarse-grained level. Committing every linguistic expression to writing requires a more refined system whose units relate more minutely to the units of language.[13] The writing systems of the world present a variety of solutions to this problem, most of which are of a systematically mixed rather than pure kind. The details of the relations between units of speech and units of writing are discussed in the next chapter.

NOTES

1 Most definitions of writing encompass the same elements while varying with respect to the emphasis attributed to them. Gelb's (1963: 12) definition of writing is as follows: 'a system of human intercommunication by means of conventional visible marks'. Jensen (1969: 17) singles out two features of writing proper: (1) its production by means of drawing or scratching on a

hard surface, and (2) the purpose of communication. Friedrich (1966: 11) states: 'Writing may be characterized as a medium of communication which people use in order to bridge spatial and temporal distance by means of readily understandable or agreed upon signs' [my translation].

2 The view that written signs are surrogational signs has a long tradition which can be traced back to Aristotle (McIntosh 1956; Ludwig 1983). Recently, this tradition has been attacked zealously by Feldbusch (1985). I have myself argued against the surrogationalist position in so far as it has obscured the view on fundamental differences between *spoken* and *written language* (Coulmas 1981b). However, I do not think that Feldbusch is right in considering the conventional relation of the written sign with the speech sign as a contingent feature of writing (Feldbusch 1985: 384, *passim*). Even if they did not come into existence as such, most written signs that are elements of full-blown writing systems are surrogates of spoken signs, but this does not imply that written language is a surrogate of spoken language.

3 The practice of putting tokens into containers which is attested for the fourth millennium, later developed into enclosing clay tablets in envelopes for safe keeping with identical texts inscribed on the outside. Cf. Chiera (1938: 70ff).

4 Schmandt-Besserat (1981: 322) credits Jordan (1932) with first realizing that imprints on clay tablets and their envelopes were the first step in the evolution of writing.

5 In this way Schmandt-Besserat's work is a specific reconfirmation of Speiser's (1939) flamboyant remark that writing was 'the by-product of a strong sense of private property'.

6 Although the definitions of writing cited in note 1 make no overt reference to language, phonetization is generally considered a critical criterion for recognizing a system as writing proper. Cf. Chiera (1938: 57), Gelb (1963: 64ff), Friedrich (1966: 17), Jensen (1969: 44) and Sampson (1985: 31).

7 Cf. my review of Feldbusch's book (Coulmas 1987b) for a more detailed argument about why she does not succeed in exploiting what is known of the Mesopotamian development for her attack against what she calls the 'dependency dogma'.

8 I use de Saussure's notion of a linguistic sign here, but I do not want to suggest that it was used in a similar way in de Saussure's analysis of writing, which is quite different.

9 The question of the often stressed monosyllabism of classical Chinese is discussed in more detail in chapter 6.

10 Gelb (1963: 111, 141) rejects the acrophonic principle as a productive mechanism in the development of writing.

11 The Zapotec, whose culture occupied a prominent position in Mezzo-America between 500 BC and 700 AD, are said to have possessed a true form

of writing. Marcus (1980: 46) claims that their 'glyphs were at least indirectly related to a spoken language'. So far very little is known about this
system, however.

12 E.g. Diringer (1943: 77). Powell (1981: 419) argues 'that cuneiform was not
as difficult as usually assumed' and 'that the superiority of the alphabet over
cuneiform has been exaggerated'. I have made a similar point with respect to
the often claimed superiority of the alphabet over Japanese writing
(Coulmas 1981b, 1987a).

13 Of course, writing systems can go beyond that by developing expressive
possibilities unparalleled in speech. Such possibilities are discussed occasionally, and especially in the context of Chinese writing.

3

Units of Speech and Units of Writing

As far as is known, no graphical system of communication ever developed that was independent of, and more powerful than, speech. In this sense writing is derived from speech although, as pointed out in chapter 2, historically it is not. The present chapter deals with the question of *how writing represents language*. To this end it is necessary to take a systematic look at units of speech and units of writing.

To begin with, some terminological definitions are in order. Terms such as 'writing', 'writing system', 'script', etc., are often used rather loosely. Henceforth, the term 'writing system' will be used to differentiate systems depicting linguistic units of different structural levels. These units are words, syllables, and phonemes. Accordingly it makes little sense, prima facie at least, to talk about the 'English writing system' or the 'Dutch writing system'. Dutch writing and English writing make use of the same system: that is, the alphabetic writing system. They also use the same *script*, namely the *Roman alphabet*. Scripts are thus graphical instantiations of writing systems. The alphabetic writing system is instantiated by several different scripts, such as the Roman alphabet, the Greek alphabet or the Russian alphabet, each of which may be used for writing several different languages. Moreover, they may be used in various ways to write one and the same language. The Roman alphabet is used to write English, for example. However, the rules for applying it vary (W. Haas 1969). Thus we have a British English *orthography* and an American English *orthography*. Similarly, the rules for writing the German language in Switzerland deviate slightly from standard German orthography. Chinese is written rather differently in Taiwan and in China, although the same writing system and the same script are used in both countries. Orthographies are always language specific, writing systems less so and in a different way.

The term 'script' is often used as if scripts were inherently related to a given language, which is partly true. Thus some people would talk about the Balinese script, the Arabic script or the Cambodian script. In some cases no confusion arises, because some scripts just happen to be used for one, and only one, language. Such is the case with the Korean *Han'gul*. No other language is written with Han'gul. Many other scripts, however, are used for several different languages such as, for instance, the *Devanagari script* which is used for a variety of languages of India. To avoid confusion, it is important to differentiate those aspects of writing concerning individual languages from those that are independent from any particular language while relating to language in general on a more abstract level. Words, syllables and phonemes are units of every language. The corresponding types of writing systems are independent, therefore, of particular languages.

Scripts are more than simply the material forms of writing systems. Not all scripts of the same systemic type are isomorphic. This is because they were not developed in the laboratory but in the context of a language for whose writing they were and are employed. 'Word writing', 'syllable writing' and 'phoneme writing' are thus very general terms. 'Script' is more specific, and 'orthography' is more specific yet. Orthographies are language specific, but they can be even more specific than that. Like languages they are, in principle, subject to historical change and geographical variation. What this means for the relationship of writing and speech will become clear as we discuss several specific instances.

For the purposes of discussing the relationships between writing and speech, a threefold distinction will be observed: *writing system*, *script* and *orthography*. The relationships between them can be stated as follows.

Proto-writing	Picture writing
	Idea writing
Writing system	Word writing
	Morpheme writing
Every writing system makes a selection of	Syllable writing
the linguistic units to be graphically repre-	Phoneme writing
sented (not language specific)	Phonetic writing

Script

Every script makes a specific selection of the possibilities of a given system in accordance with the structural conditions of a given language	Chinese script Arabic script Greek script

Orthography

Every orthography makes a specific selection of the possibilities of a script for writing a particular language in a uniform and standardized way	Chinese/Taiwanese
	  orthography
	Standard German/
	  Swiss-German
	  orthography

STRUCTURE MAPPED OR STRUCTURE IMPOSED?

To say that a script makes a selection of the possibilities of a writing system, or that a writing system makes a selection of linguistic units to be represented, is, of course, a purely analytic statement which disregards the fact that the objects which are 'selected' are not necessarily given. To some extent, they are also created. Writing, in other words, not only maps, but also imposes structure. Part of the general problem of defining linguistic categories and units is that often no proper attention is paid to the important differences between spoken language and written language.

Fries (1952), for instance, collected 200 different definitions of *sentence*. Several scholars have commented on the obvious dependency of the notion of a sentence on written language, especially in the Western grammatical tradition (for example, O'Donnell 1974; Harris 1980: 18; Linell 1982: 63ff),[1] and called into question its applicability to the analysis of speech (Chafe 1979; Beaugrande and Dressler 1981; Pawley and Syder 1983).[2] In the Eastern tradition, too, the sentence must be considered an artefact of writing (Kindaichi 1957: 181).

The notion *word* poses similar problems. A very simple and seemingly naïve definition of the notion *word* is 'a part of speech which is separated by two spaces from other such parts when written down'.[3] Non-linguists would not find such a definition all that strange because as members of a literate culture they know where to turn to in matters of language: dictionaries, grammar books and other written sources (Harris

1980). Any attempt to use such a definition when faced with the problem of selecting the units of a language to be written with a word writing system is, however, futile because of obvious circularity: the major criterion of the definition is the written form of a word. A more useful notion of *word* is, however, rather difficult to construct. Not only laymen's conceptions of what a word is depend to a considerable degree on language as it is written; as Linell (1982: 83) points out, 'it is hardly a mere coincidence that the notion of the morphological word corresponds well with the unit of conventional writing, ... a sequence of letters surrounded by empty spaces but containing no internal spaces.'[4] Bierwisch (1972) tries to deal with the problem of a consistent definition of *word* by suggesting that there are several non-congruent notions: that is, the orthographic word, the phonetic word and the semantic word. Further evidence for the dependency of the notion *word* on written language is provided in Goody (1977: 115), where he observes that there are no words for 'word' in LoDagaa or Gonja, two West African languages without a literary tradition.[5]

The phoneme, too, is a precarious unit of linguistic analysis, as it is determined by contrast only. Individual realizations of phonemes are both contextually and articulatorily so variable that there is no physical basis for class formation. It is not altogether unreasonable to argue, as Lüdtke (1969) does, that phonological theory is an offshoot of alphabetic writing rather than the other way round.[6] The notion 'phoneme', in other words, is modeled on the letters of the alphabet which, in turn, are the results of historical coincidences rather than systematic analysis. Without pursuing this line of thought any further, it can be stated here (1) that the independent existence of the units supposedly depicted by a given writing system cannot be taken for granted, and (2) that in mapping language, writing systems, scripts and orthographies are as much based on analytic perceptions as they form them and the resulting conceptualizations of the structural units of language. It is important to note, furthermore, that the alphabet is no less prone to imposing structure and determining language awareness than other more coarse-grained systems.

ANALYTIC DEPTH

The historical development from pictogram to alphabet has been described as a process of increasing abstractions of graphical signs concurrent with an advance in the analytic penetration of language.[7] Pictures are very concrete and convey meaning directly; letters, on the other hand, are very abstract entities conveying meaning indirectly: that is, through mediation of sound or sound image. Every writing system is based on an implicit analysis according to which language is segmented into units of different size. Differences between writing systems are thus differences between the underlying analyses, differences about what is and what is not represented of the segmental units and how they are graphically mapped (W. Haas 1976). The segmental unit of the alphabet is smaller, and its analytic level higher and more abstract than that of a word writing system. These differences reflect differences in analytical depth, on the one hand, and typological differences between languages, on the other.

Syllables are clearly more abstract and more difficult to conceive of than words, and accordingly syllabic writing appears historically later than word writing. The conditions for the transition from word writing to syllabic writing also differ from one language to another. Syllabic systems are not equally well suited for representing every language, because syllable structures vary considerably across languages.

A consistent syllabic script has the syllable as its basic unit and is capable of representing a given language without too much distortion and without leaving too much unrepresented. A syllabary is like a grid. Those parts that do not fit cannot be represented. Therefore the inventory of necessary signs varies with the syllabic structure of the language to be written: the more complex the syllable structure, the greater the number of necessary elements. Some languages have a very simple syllable structure, but others are highly complex in this regard. Consider a language with syllables as complex as these: CCVCC (where C stands for consonant and V for vowel), as in /grips/ or /knaks/; CCCVCC as in /strumf/, or even CCVCCCC as in /krankst/. Those are monosyllabic German words. It is clear that a syllabic writing system for a language that allows for syllables of such high complexity would have to be very intricate indeed. The advantages of a syllabic script over a word script would not be nearly as great for German as for a language with a less complex syllable structure. The chief advantage of syllabic writing over word writing is the reduction of the number of necessary elements.

In every language, the number of words is far greater than the number of syllables. Synchronically, the latter is fixed, while the former is open.

At any one time only the structurally possible syllables can be used productively, whereas the potential to create new words by composition and derivation is part of the synchronic grammar of a language. Even the words in current usage in a given language at a given time by far out-number the syllables of that language; but the relation between both varies from one language to another. The syllable structure of Japanese is very simple. A system of less than 50 basic syllable signs plus a few dia-critical marks can represent the language quite faithfully in writing. The cuneiform syllabary comprised about 100 signs, still a manageable number. For writing German with a syllabary, however, the number of necessary signs would have to be much greater than that. If there have to be signs for syllables with an internal complexity as high as that of *krankst* (CCVCCCC), it is obvious that many hundreds of signs would be needed. Such a calculation is based on the assumption that a genuinely syllabic script is one where the syllable is the smallest unit of analysis and every syllable is given its sign.

On the other hand, the advantage of replacing a syllabary with an alphabetic orthography may be very minor for a language with a simple syllable structure such as Japanese, whereas a language with a complex syllable structure would make this advantage very noticeable.

LANGUAGE DEPENDENCY

The fact that writing systems reflect structural differences between the respective languages in whose context they developed is most obvious when we consider what happens when a script is adapted to another language. Typically, certain modifications ensue in accordance with structural features of the new language. The biggest problem, for instance, of adapting the Sumerian cuneiform script to Hittite was repre-senting consonant clusters. In Sumerian and Akkadian simple sequences of vowels and consonants prevailed, and therefore the application of the syllabary that was developed for these languages to Hittite made it unavoidable to write vowels which were not there. Conversely, the adaptation of the Arabic script for writing Persian, Urdu and Malay led to the creation of new letters.

Borrowing the script from another language is a process which has happened many times in history. It is a rather difficult operation pre-supposing a clear understanding of the nature of writing, at least in so far as writing and language (or rather *a* script and *a* language) are recognized as two different and, in principle, independent things. This is by no means self-evident. Whenever illiterate peoples wanted to write, they usually borrowed the written language of a neighboring people. Only gradually did bilingual individuals grasp the possibility of writing their own mother tongue, too. Thus the Hittites in their first written documents around the beginning of the second millennium BC used the Sumerian and the Akkadian languages from which the cuneiform script was subsequently borrowed, and they continued to write in these languages even after Hittite had become a written language also. Very similar conditions accompanied the adaptation of the Chinese script for writing Korean, Annamese and Japanese. The first written documents produced in Japan were in Chinese, and for a long time a peculiar mixture of Chinese and Japanese was typical of the written language in Japan which makes it very difficult to read.

A syllable is an abstract linguistic unit, and obviously the same such unit may occur in many different languages. If a graphical sign is available for a given syllable it can be represented, no matter to what language it belongs. Simple as this insight may seem from our point of view, it was not so obvious to those who first applied a fully developed script to a hitherto unwritten language. For the intellectuals who would eventually carry out the adaptation of a script to their mother tongue, writing must have been intimately linked with language, if only because the first time they ever learned the art of reading and writing it was through, and together with, another language. Borrowing the script only and adapting it to the respective native language might have been more trouble than borrowing the script *and* the language for whose writing it was used in the first place. In any event, the technical problems of adapting a script to another language were considerable, and the solutions not always satisfactory.

It is unlikely that the systematic make-up of the earliest scripts was clearly understood by those who used them (Gelb 1963: 110); after all, only few people understand the systematic make-up of alphabetic orthographies nowadays. More often than not, solutions to adaptation problems therefore had a makeshift character. Systematic coherence was never in itself important. It is noteworthy, for instance, that none of the Mesopotamian syllabaries are complete in the sense that they contain signs for all possible syllables in the language for which they were used. They do not even provide signs for all actually occurring syllables, a number which is smaller than that of the phonologically possible ones, since languages do not usually exhaust all the structural possibilities of their phonological systems. The representation of the phonetic shape of a language by means of a cuneiform syllabary was, therefore, invariably incomplete or redundant. Solutions tended to develop naturally, not by conscious design.

STANDARDS OF EXCELLENCE

In the ancient Near East the general development was from word to syllable writing and further to consonant writing and eventually to phonemic writing. Abstractions increased, and at the same time the inventory of necessary elements was drastically reduced. The alphabet has fewer elements than any syllabary, and syllabaries have fewer elements than word writing systems. Therefore, according to a common argument (Diringer 1943; Gelb 1963: 72, *passim*; McLuhan 1962), the alphabet is superior to syllabic scripts and the latter are, in turn, superior to logographic scripts (Pulgram 1976: 15). The logic behind this is straightforward enough, but it is also somewhat simplistic. Surely it cannot explain why the great alternative to the alphabet, the Chinese script, has not been replaced by a simple system long ago. There must be rival standards of excellence that favor the Chinese script. 'What is a good script?' is a very intricate question with many different aspects, and any simple and uniform answer is almost certainly wrong.[8]

ECONOMY, SIMPLICITY, UNEQUIVOCALITY

In principle, the alphabet is the most economical system. However, it cannot be applied to all languages equally well. Unlike Greek or the Semitic languages, Annamese, for example, is a tone language, and tones are phonemic. In an alphabetic representation of this language the tones cannot, therefore, be ignored. Significant modifications were thus necessary for adapting the Latin alphabet to Annamese. The letters ⟨f⟩, ⟨j⟩, ⟨w⟩ and ⟨z⟩ were deleted because there are no corresponding phonemes. The letters ⟨â⟩, ⟨ă⟩, ⟨đ⟩, ⟨ê⟩, ⟨ô⟩ and ⟨u'⟩, on the other hand, were added. Furthermore, an adequate representation of the rather complex tones made the introduction of another five diacritical marks necessary: o', ồ, ố, õ, ọ.

They are used in various combinations with each other and with the new letters to produce a great many derived signs. The letter ⟨a⟩, for instance, appears in 18 different variants. The paucity of vowel signs in the alphabet bears witness to its Semito-Greek origin, a fact which is often played down by those who emphasize the universality of the alphabet.

The application of a given writing system to a new language always bears the risk of badly adjusted scripts, because typically scripts are borrowed in a process of 'natural' adaptation rather than on the grounds of linguistic analysis. Moreover, languages are subject to historical change, and therefore a script that was once a faithful mapping may become gradually distorted unless it is changed accordingly.

Writing systems are only rarely the result of conscious linguistic analysis,[9] yet they are the expression and materialization of linguistic consciousness. In writing, linguistic utterances are detached from their source and must stand for themselves. Written language, therefore, has to be (and usually is) more explicit than its spoken counterpart. For example, in speech, the sentences

> *Elle se lève toujours a cette heure,*
> [She always gets up at this time]

and

> *Elle se lève toujours a sept heures,*
> [She always gets up at seven o'clock]

are indistinguishable; in writing they are disambiguated. Disambiguation is achieved by virtue of the analysis implicit in the written representation. Clearly it is desirable that we have clarity as to whether the time referred to is 'this hour' or 'seven o'clock', especially in writing when we may not be able to ask for reconfirmation. However, the price to be paid for clarity here is reduction of economy. There can be no doubt that economy and simplicity are virtues of writing systems and can thus serve as a standard of comparison. Then again, writing systems are abstract entities. Applying their underlying principles in specific scripts for writing specific languages invariably leads to corruptions. Also it must be noted that several different criteria of goodness compete with each other. Economy is one, simplicity is another and unequivocality a third.

Economy means that the number of necessary signs is kept small. *Simplicity* means, among other things, that the relation between the signs and their values is simple and straightforward. *Unequivocality* means that the meaning of a written expression is determined by its form. It seems that maximizing one of these criteria to some extent is always at the expense of the others. It is not economical or simple to have different graphic representations for units of identical sound shape. *Cette heure* and *sept heures* are homophonous and could both be written like this /sɛt‖ œ:r/, which is very economical and very simple, but ambiguous. By giving up a little economy, we can disambiguate the expression as in standard French orthography. Simplicity is also reduced, because we no longer have a system where one sound is represented by one and only one graph:[10] that is, the principle of sound writing is undermined, and a little bit of word writing creeps in with a direct relation between graph and meaning.

In word writing the criterion of unequivocality can be carried to its extreme: every word is assigned a distinct graphical sign. Take an expression, such as *his book*. In Chinese this is *ta de shu*. In speech this phrase is ambiguous as it also means *her book* or *its book*. In writing the ambiguity disappears because the gender of the pronoun is graphically differentiated:

他 的 书   她 的 书   它 的 书

It is well known that homophony is pervasive in Chinese. Owing to the phonetic poverty of the language, there are large numbers of homophonous morphemes, the three words /shēn/, for instance, meaning 'to extend', 'body' and 'deep'. These meanings preclude an analysis of one word with three readings. In Chinese writing this is absolutely clear as the words are graphically distinct: 伸, 身, 深. This is both simple and unambiguous, but it is not economical as one sound configuration corresponds to several different graphs.

Economy has to be measured on different levels. Relative to the level of a logographic system a one-to-one correspondence between words and graphs is economical, but the logographic system itself is not economical if compared with more abstract writing systems.

ABSTRACTNESS

Every writing system is an abstraction to a certain degree, because what their units represent is not concrete objects but abstract classes of objects. Written symbols stand for types rather than tokens of linguistic units. The abstractness of writing is possible and functional because the typical reader – that is, the reader for whom the script is made – knows the language in which the written message is coded, and can thus rely on the redundancies of the language as an aid for deciphering (reading) written expressions which represent speech only incompletely or vaguely. Therefore it is possible, for example, to leave the tones of Tibetan unrepresented in the Tibetan script, or the vowels in Semitic scripts. The alphabet is the logical conclusion of a development of ever-increasing abstraction. As its units are minute and highly abstract it is, in principle, universally applicable.

FAITHFUL MAPPING

It is a generally accepted view that the alphabet is the teleological goal of the history of writing. That alphabetic writing was never achieved in a number of cultures in spite of their long literary tradition must be due, according to this view, to external factors which interfered with the natural course of evolution. This evolution, where it took its predetermined course, allows us to infer a regular correlation: the more abstract the elements of a system, the fewer their number. Moreover, accuracy of mapping increases with fineness of segmentation: the smaller the segment, the more flexible the system; or, to put it the other way round, 'the more minute the level which is reflected in a script, the more constrained the script by the spoken language' (Henderson 1982: 54). The alphabet, therefore, appears to be the simplest, the most abstract and the most efficient system. This seems to be an obvious enough statement, but actually it is a gross simplification.

The underlying assumption which is taken for granted is that a good writing system is an isomorphic mapping of speech. This is, however, a very daring proposition, to say the least. It ignores three important things, namely (1) that this ideal has never been achieved for any script, and it is doubtful that it ever will be; (2) that the requirements that an ordinary user puts on a writing system are not the same as those of the linguist who needs an instrument of precision; and (3) that an orthography is a normative device. Also, the script user is not necessarily interested in isomorphism. Faithful mapping is not the user's primary concern. For the user writing is a medium or a mode of communication which follows rules partly different from those of speech. This is too often ignored, and therefore it is easily taken for granted both that the economy of the inventory of signs is an absolute measure of goodness; and also that the optimal writing system consists of symbols standing for sounds which are concatenated in such a way that the relation between written sign and meaning is always mediated by sound (Klima 1972).

These presuppositions rest on the familiar belief that the human brain is better at combining than storing units. To put it differently, it is assumed that minimizing the mnemotechnic load while at the same time maximizing the combinatorial complexity is what makes a writing system good. As a matter of fact, no existing script works in accordance with this abstract principle. Minimizing the inventory of signs is valid only as a relative criterion of goodness. The Morse code consists of only three basic signs – a dot, a dash and a space – but it is hardly superior to the alphabet.

It is also noteworthy in this connection that the letters of the alphabet stand for phonemes in a broad sense. Alphabetic scripts do not usually go further in the analysis towards representing distinctive features. This is quite unnecessary for the reason already mentioned: typical readers are already familiar with the particular sound qualities of the units of their own language. It is easy to conceive of a system that is sensitive to the phonetic peculiarities of a language. IPA, the international phonetic alphabet, is such a system; but as an orthography such a system is impractical because it is highly redundant. Thus both economy and faithfulness are relative virtues only. A script cannot be called superior because it maps a phonetic feature which in another is easily inferred, or because it has ten signs less than another.

However, there can be no denying that a word script makes use of an inventory of signs of an altogether different magnitude as it operates on an open-ended level. Again, this is a rather general statement, because word writing systems have usually made use of homophony and other systematic features which make it unnecessary to provide original signs for every lexical item; that is, they tend to assume certain properties of sound-based systems.

It should be obvious from the foregoing observations that scripts do not embody writing systems in a pure form, but are often distorted and of a mixed character with respect to their systemic levels.[11] There are no pure word writing scripts, or syllabic scripts or phonemic scripts.

Usually information on more than one level is made use of (W. Haas 1970). *Word writing*, *syllable writing* and *phoneme writing* are thus very abstract categories. Scripts can be assigned to these categories, but this does not mean that their application in writing a particular language makes use consistently of only one unit of segmentation and structural principle.

THE LEVEL OF A SCRIPT[12]

There are only a very few distinct levels to which a given script can belong. Basically, four levels of analysis can be distinguished: the lexemic level, the morphemic level, the syllabic level and the phonemic/phonetic level. These four levels can be assigned to just two types, as there is an obvious difference between the first two which operate on the level of sense-determinative (that is, meaningful) elements, and the second two which operate on the level of sense-discriminative elements. With terms borrowed from Hjelmslev, W. Haas (1983) calls the former 'pleremic' and the latter 'cenemic'.[13]

As the difference between elements that carry meaning and elements that distinguish meaning is well motivated, there seems to be nothing contentious with such a division. Nevertheless it is a non-trivial question, and sometimes a matter of dispute, as to what level a given script belongs. Haas, one of the few modern linguists who has always recognized writing as an important object of linguistic theorizing, has tackled this question in several of his many works. His major point (W. Haas 1983) is that the level of a script cannot be determined by simply looking at its elements because linguistic units often belong to more than one level. In *a book*, /əbuk/, for example, /ə/ is a phoneme, a syllable, a morpheme and a word; in *books*, /buks/, /s/ is a phoneme as well as a morpheme. In the French example above, /sɛt/ is two morphemes and two words which are graphically distinguished. If we look at Chinese and make a list of all Chinese morphemes, it appears that almost every one is a syllable and many are words. Should we conclude from these observations that in English, French and Chinese we have mixed systems?

Two issues must be distinguished here: (1) the level of the basic operational unit of a given system; and (2) the information that is conveyed, by design or accident, about units of other levels. For (1) it is decisive to discover the rules by which units of a certain level are assigned their graphic symbols. Although certain units, such as, the /ə/ in /əbuk/ or the /s/ in /buks/ may be units on more than one level, the rules by which they are assigned a graphical symbol do not operate on more than one level. /ə/ in /əbuk/ is assigned the letter ⟨a⟩ according to phoneme-grapheme correspondence rules. The fact that /ə/ also happens to be a morpheme and a word written with the letter ⟨a⟩ does not interfere with these rules, and cannot justify the assumption that English writing is pleremic. Similarly, the fact that (1) most Chinese morphemes are mono-syllabic and (2) Chinese characters are occasionally used for their syllabic value which is partly predictable on the basis of certain graphical elements does not make the Chinese script a syllabic script. The Chinese script is not cenemic because it is morphemes rather than syllables which are assigned characters.

SOME PRACTICAL ISSUES

Let us consider, briefly, how the signs of cenemic and pleremic writing systems are employed. The rules relating linguistic units and written symbols are bidirectional. They are rules for writing down (that is, assigning to a linguistic unit a written symbol), and rules for reading aloud (that is, for assigning to a graphic unit a spoken unit). The latter are easier than the former, which is only to say that reading is easier than writing. Still, from a systematic point of view, it is no simple task to show how the written symbols of a script are to be pronounced (that is, phonologically interpreted).

First, we have to identify the basic written units, a task which is not as trivial as it may seem. In a pleremic script the basic pattern is as follows:

$$\text{grapheme} \rightarrow \text{morpheme} \rightarrow \text{phonetic form}$$

for example,   笔   → (bi) brush → /bi/

For a skilled reader, however, this simple mapping relation may be supplemented as follows:

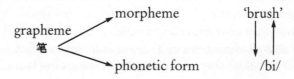

There may be a direct link between grapheme and phonetic form, but none the less the basic operative relation is that where the phonetic form is determined by a morphemic unit.

In cenemic scripts the fundamental relation is the other way round:

grapheme ----› phonetic form ----› morpheme (meaning)

The units of cenemic scripts are smaller than those of pleremic scripts, and therefore the above is only a very general picture. Meaning is accessible by a combination of cenemic units only. The phonetic interpretation of the symbols of a cenemic script works basically like this:

grapheme ----› phoneme/phonetic form

What is the fundamental unit of a cenemic script? In syllabic scripts it is a syllabic sign, but the mapping function between syllabic signs and syllables is not usually one to one because most syllabic scripts (such as Akkadian or Japanese) consist of fewer signs than the number of syllables of the language for which they are or were used.

In alphabetic writing the basic graphemic unit is, obviously enough, the letter. The fundamental correspondence is between a letter and a phoneme.

grapheme   t a n k

phoneme   /t//æ//ŋ//k/

But this is an ideal case, not at all typical of the rules governing the relation between graphemes and phonemes in alphabetic scripts. Consider next the word *thank*. Here the relation we have observed for *tank* does not hold any more.

grapheme   t h a n k
phoneme   /θ//æ//ŋ//k/

In the English orthography the letter combination ⟨th⟩ is a digraph. It is obviously made up of two elements, ⟨t⟩ and ⟨h⟩, which may each correspond to a different phoneme, for instance in *hat*, /h/, /æ/, /t/. The letters ⟨t⟩ and ⟨h⟩ will have to be listed therefore as different graphemes. But in *thank* no separate phonemes correspond to ⟨t⟩ and ⟨h⟩; rather in combination they correspond to the phoneme /θ/. There is no systematic reason of course why there should not be a letter for /θ/, but for historical reasons there is none. A digraph fulfils the function of a letter here instead. This is another example of the contamination of a simple principle and the difficulty of identifying the basic units of a cenemic script. ⟨h⟩, ⟨t⟩ and ⟨th⟩ have to be included into the list of elementary graphical signs of English writing, and contextual rules have to be given that determine when ⟨t⟩ is to be treated by itself and assigned the phoneme /t/ and when, on the other hand, it has to be treated as part of the digraph. Unfortunately it is not sufficient to state that ⟨t⟩ is to be treated as part of the digraph whenever it occurs in combination with (that is, before) ⟨h⟩ because that would give us *θailænd* and *θɔmɔs* and the like. In all probability, the cases where ⟨th⟩ is not to be treated as the digraph for /Θ/ or /θ/ have to be enumerated in a list of exceptions. The source of such inconsistencies is usually historical. Alphabetic scripts differ greatly as regards the simplcity of the mapping relations between letters and phonemes, and the faithfulness of the mapping.

The examples discussed here are sufficient to show that the relative economy of sign inventory is only one characteristic feature distinguishing writing systems of different structural levels which by itself cannot serve as a measure of goodness. The system with the fewest elements is not necessarily the simplest and the best, because the number of necessary elements says nothing about the complexity of the mapping relation between graphical sign and linguistic unit. What an ideal system of writing would be like is a multifarious question whose answer must be more specific in so far as it has to state 'ideal for what?'

Those features that make a system good for a learner are not necessarily ideal for the user. To be sure, an alphabet of 25 odd letters is easier to learn than a system consisting of several thousand signs such as the Chinese. But the information load of a sign that is one out of several thousand distinct signs is much higher than that of a sign or even a combination of signs belonging to a very small inventory. Therefore reading Chinese is much faster than reading English for those who know both systems equally well (Chao 1968: 111ff).

From the point of view of reading it is quite impractical that the sound stream of speech is broken up into units corresponding only in a complex way to phonemes, because the skilled reader of an alphabetically written text does not read letter by letter anyway but by larger units (F. Smith 1973; Frith 1980; Henderson 1982). A morphemic or word-sign system can be processed faster than a system operating on a cenemic level of smaller units. Because of its higher information load, a Chinese character sticks out on a page and is easily detected if looked for. An alphabetically written word is not so prominent because of the uniformity of the letters. It is, of course, another question as to whether it is worth the great effort of learning an uneconomical system such as the Chinese for the benefit of eventually more convenient use. From the point of view of writing, on the other hand, a logographic system such as the Chinese asks much more of its users than a rational and regular cenemic orthography.

To conclude, the merits and demerits of scripts of different levels must be specified relative to different purposes. Readers and writers, native and foreign language users, dialect and standard speakers, linguists and poets do not all have the same needs, and their respective demands on a suitable writing system are sometimes in conflict. To some extent all writing systems appeal to the linguistic knowledge of the user. How this is done, what aspects of linguistic knowledge are employed most intensely in cenemic and pleremic systems and how they differ in this regard is to be shown by examining some examples of every type in greater detail.

NOTES

1 Akinnaso (1982) and Bieber (1986) provide the most comprehensive over-views of recent research on differences between spoken and written language. The latter presents a carefully worked out 'multi-dimension' approach, making possible a better appreciation of earlier findings.

2 Lyons, while pointing out that there are 'important grammatical and lexical differences between [spoken and written languages]' (1977: 69), neverthe-less maintains that the term 'complete sentence' which 'for written English is reasonably clear, . . . can be made applicable in essentially the same sense to the spoken language' (Lyons 1977: 29).

3 Notice Cowgill's (1963: 120) self-critical remark concerning his inter-pretation of Modern Greek data: 'In the matter of word boundaries I have probably been over-influenced by whether or not a space was left between letters by the editor of the text I was using.'

4 Cf. G. A. Miller and Johnson-Laird (1976: 3) who discuss from a psycho-linguistic point of view the problem of furnishing a definition of *word* that is better than 'a textual unit consisting of consecutive letters bounded at both ends by spaces'.

5 Similarly, it is obvious in Beck's (1964: 156) discussion of the problem of word division in some East African Bantu languages that the word is partly

an artefact: 'We will have to be careful that words do not become confusingly long, but we should on the other hand be free from the misunderstanding that a multitude of partial words, some of them not amounting to more than one letter, are easier to read than fewer words which are a little longer.'

6 Morais et al. (1979) contend that familiarity with alphabetic writing induces more analytical awareness of phonological contrasts.

7 'In the beginning, then, was not the word but speech ... Writing changes this situation; at the cultural level, it enables people to analyse, break down, dissect, and build up speech into parts and wholes, into types and categories, which already existed but which, when brought into the area of consciousness, have a feedback effect on speech itself' (Goody 1977: 115).

8 'A broadly phonetic ("phonemic") transcription is regarded as the ideal alphabet. Any orthography, established or proposed, is judged against this standard of excellence. This view has rarely been challenged; but it is, to say the least, a gross oversimplification' (W. Haas 1970: 3). While Haas deals with alphabetic orthographies only, the point he makes can be extended to a comparison between the alphabet and other writing systems where the former is usually taken as the yardstick. Cf. also Sampson's discussion of evaluating writing systems, especially his account of the readability of logographic versus phonographic systems (Sampson 1985: 163f).

9 The Indic Brahmi script and the Korean Han'gul are exceptions in this regard, as their set-up testifies to great systematic insight into the phonetic systems of the respective languages.

10 W. Haas (1970: 4) makes it very clear that economy cannot be the only criterion of goodness: 'though ... "phono-graphic divergence" must distract from the script's economy, it need not constitute a flaw in its overall efficiency'; and 'there seems to be no simple scale for measuring the disadvantages of phono-graphic divergence'.

11 Sampson (1985: 42) also notes that many writing systems are not pure exemplars of the two basic types he distinguishes, that is, logographic and phonographic systems.

12 In this section I draw heavily on W. Haas (1970) and (1983).

13 Sampson (1985: 31), who like Haas (1983) argues that the basis for classification of a writing system should be the linguistic units mapped by its graphic units, makes a similar distinction between 'semasiographic writing' and 'glottographic writing'.

PART II

Writing Systems

4

Sacred Characters: The Theocratic
Script of Egypt

Genuine creations of writing happened only a few times in the history of humankind. The most important developments originated early in the third millennium BC in two Near Eastern river valley civilizations, Egypt at the Nile, and Sumer in the two-river valley of Mesopotamia. The only other independent development of a full-fledged writing system happened in the Far East, in China. Any historical consideration of writing, therefore, has to start out with the genuine creations of the ancient Near East: the Sumerian cuneiform and the Egyptian hieroglyphs.

Sumerian writing is now generally thought to be slightly older than Egyptian. However, temporal precedence does not necessarily imply developmental precedence. The relationship between Sumerian and Egyptian writing is rather complex and, for reasons to be discussed, both have to be regarded as genuine developments (Friedrich 1966), even if there were certain contacts between the two cultures at the time of the origin of writing. We will discuss the Egyptian solution first, because the historical development is less complicated than that of cuneiform writing where several different languages were involved. Egyptian hieroglyphs were employed, over a period of more than 3,000 years, for writing the Egyptian language before it finally fell into disuse.

FOR WHAT PURPOSE DID THE EGYPTIANS NEED WRITING?

As a result of their magnificent pictorial beauty, the hieroglyphs have fascinated scholars since antiquity. Herodotus, the Greek historian who traveled widely in the fifth century BC, thought that these signs must be something sacred and thus speaks of ἱερα γράμματα, 'holy signs', and Clemens Alexandrinus eventually coined the term ἱερογλυφικὰ γράμματα in 210 BC, thus giving expression to the belief that writing was used chiefly by the Egyptians for sacred purposes, and that the material they used was stone. (ἱερός means 'sacred', and γλύφειν 'to incise', namely on stone; γράμματα obviously means 'letters'.) Both of these conceptions were misleading. The material used by the Egyptians was not primarily stone, and the religious cult was not the chief purpose of writing. Thus a reinterpretation of the sacredness of the sacred characters is in order. Let us start by considering the question of why and for what purpose the Egyptians needed writing.

A rather naïve but none the less widespread view is that writing develops 'naturally'; that is, following a natural law which brings about writing whenever the appropriate conditions obtain.[1] It is assumed that similar conditions and similar needs necessarily result in the invention of writing. To specify these conditions and needs, leading Egyptologists have suggested three main factors which contributed to the invention of hieroglyphic writing in Egypt: (1) the need to record events as a result of an 'awakening historical consciousness'; (2) the need to record economic transactions as a result of a more complex social infrastructure; and (3) a religious need.

As for the first point, the need to record events, some of the earliest documents indeed refer to historical events. Hence it seems quite plausible to assume a relationship between historical consciousness and writing. However, the assumption of a causal relationship between historical consciousness and the invention is scarcely justified by these documents. Rather, it is hard to imagine, or find any evidence for the supposition, that the desire to record historical events led to the invention of writing. The reverse may be more likely. An important event in the history of Egypt was the unification of upper and lower Egypt early in the third millennium. After that time it became customary to record important events on little year tablets. This can be taken as an indication of historical consciousness. However, this practice only evolved at least 150 years after the initial introduction of writing in Egypt. It cannot have been its cause, then, but must have been a by-product.

Turning now to the second factor, the need to record economic transactions, it is safe to say that the development of the hieroglyphs would not have been so rapid and so complete had there not been economic utility of the new invention.[2] If economic necessities were not the original cause of the invention, they were certainly a driving force of its further development. A great many of the documents that have been preserved are of an economic nature.

Interestingly, the bulk of these documents are intimately related to the third domain which is assumed to be of importance for the invention of writing in Egypt: cult. Lists of gifts and offerings were used as substitutes for real objects and were recovered from individual tombs and necropoles. There can be no doubt that cult played a central role in the life of Egyptian high culture from the very earliest times, and that writing was used for purposes of cult very early. But is this enough to prove the sacred origin of the hieroglyphs? In order to answer this question, we have to evaluate the significance of the contacts between Egypt and Sumer around the turn of the fourth millennium. Furthermore, we have to investigate the development of the form of the hieroglyphs as well as their systematic relation to structural levels of language and linguistic units.

THE GENERAL PATTERN OF DEVELOPMENT

Let us first recapitulate the general pattern of the abstract development of writing and then see how far the hieroglyphs conform to it. In the abstract, steps and levels may be distinguished which in the course of history actually concurred (cf. Schenkel 1983).

Level I: word writing (pleremic)
1 Words referring to representable objects are 'written' by drawing the objects in question; a representation of the object stands for a representation of its name.
2 Common nouns are represented by a drawing of a typical member of the species, such as a particular bird for the species of birds.
3 Words of any kind can be represented by symbols: that is, arbitrarily assigned signs. For example, the number word 'one' can be represented by a single stroke which does not stand for 'one stroke' but for the number word 'one'.

Level II: sound writing based on rebus principle (cenemic)
1 A word is represented by drawing an object whose name sounds like the word in question; for instance, ☼ for *son*.

2 A part of a word is represented by drawing an object whose name sounds like the part of the word in question; for instance, 🏃 for *man* in *mandate*, and 🌴 for *date*.

3 Instead of looking for a suitable rebus whenever one is needed, a set of suitable signs for all sound forms in the language is agreed upon and thus conventionalized. All the words not written in accordance with the principles of level I are written with the signs of this set, a syllabary (or alphabet).

4 Point 3 provides a solution for writing every sound of the language, but does not preclude the possibility of more than one representation of a given sound or combination of sounds. The next step is a reduction of the sign inventory.

5 The final step is regularizing the use of the signs of the conventional inventory: that is, the establishing of an orthographic norm.

The above is an analytic scheme and must not be read as a temporal sequence depicting the historical development of Egyptian hieroglyphs. One of the puzzles of the Egyptian documents is that what in the abstract model appear to be subsequent steps are all present in the earliest records. Documents dating from the beginning of the dynastic era (about 3000 BC) exhibit all features of pleremic writing and also contain cenemic signs created in accordance with the rebus principle of level II. No conventionalized set of syllabic signs had been established at that time, but rebus signs were used both for words and parts of words. This state of affairs represents a high level of development suggesting that writing had been in use then for some time. This opens up the possibility that Egyptian writing was developed independent of the achievements of Sumer.[3]

A set of suitable signs for all sound forms was available in Egypt early in the second dynasty at the latest (that is, at about 2700 BC). The earliest Sumerian documents[4] of the time before writing can be attested in Egypt also exhibit the typical features of level I. Rebus writing, however, is extremely rare, let alone a full set of conventionalized phonograms. This was only achieved in the early twenty-fifth century BC, at a time when Egyptian writing already had a complete set of phonograms.

Contact between Egypt and Sumer early in the third millennium is an undeniable fact. But if this contact brought Egypt the art of writing, it must have been in an embryonic state. It is conceivable that the

Egyptians only took the idea of writing on the pleremic level from Sumer. They were the first to make the third step on the cenemic level, establishing as they did a set of suitable signs for all relevant sounds of their language. However, while progress in these matters has been impressive, the exact dating of the earliest forms of writing is still a matter of conjecture. Also, the question of historical priority may not be that important in the end. After all, writing was not invented overnight, and neither was it created in accordance with one particular systematic principle. Both the Near Eastern writing systems are based on a mixture of principles which were discovered at different times and developed to different degrees. While the Sumerians were quick to design symbols for representing non-concrete phenomena, the Egyptians discovered and developed quite early the rebus principle. The development of writing in the ancient Near East was thus a complex process which took place in both countries.

THE EGYPTIAN SYSTEM: ITS INNER FORM

Before its successful decipherment in the second decade of the nineteenth century by Champollion (Andrews 1981), the nature of Egyptian writing was misunderstood. It was generally assumed that hieroglyphs had no phonetic value and that they did not even relate to language. This idea had been expressed already by Plotinus, a Greek philosopher who was born and raised in Egypt in the third century AD:

When [the wise men of Egypt] wanted to express their meaning philosophically they did not go through the whole business of letters, words, and sentences. They did not employ devices to copy the sounds of a proposition and how it is pronounced. Instead, in their sacred writings, they drew signs, a separate sign for each idea, so as to express its whole meaning at once. Each separate sign is in itself a piece of knowledge, a piece of wisdom, a piece of reality, immediately present. There is no process of reasoning involved, no laborious elucidation. (Pope 1975: 21)

Plotinus' mistaken ideas were handed down through the centuries practically unchanged until it was finally understood that the hieroglyphs were not signs of ideas or concepts, but were used to write the Egyptian language. As pointed out already, the script contains word signs of level I and rebus signs of level II. Graphically all of the glyphs exhibit a vivid imagery; functionally different signs were not formally distinguished: the same signs were used for words and for syllables (see p. 66). Obviously, this was a major obstacle for the decipherment of the hieroglyphs, but it must also have created enormous difficulties for reading a text. How was one to know whether a glyph stood for a word symbolizing its meaning by virtue of the imagery, or for a part of another word? The system was not perfect, so it was hardly possible just to read the sound and thus arrive at a meaning.

Word signs, or logograms, are sometimes called 'ideograms', suggesting that they stand for concepts rather than words. Bloomfield (1933: 285) criticized this notion, rightly, as misleading because 'the important thing about writing is precisely this, that the characters represent not features of the practical world ("ideas"), but features of the writers' language'. Gelb (1963: 74) pointed out that, while the hieroglyphs were graphically very elaborate and stylized, Egyptian writing disregarded 'entirely the main object of full writing, which is to reproduce language in its normal word order'. This feature of early Egyptian writing may account for the persistent reference to 'ideograms'. It is important to note that Egyptian writing in its fully developed form is not ideographic. Rather, it was a word-syllable system: that is, a system operating on both the pleremic and cenemic levels. Word signs were used for concrete nouns or verbs signifying perceptible actions or movements as illustrated in figure 4.1.

| soldier | eye | giraffe | horn | swallow |

| angel | mountain | sun | flower | scarab |

| hit | fly | eat | walk |

4.1 Logograms for concrete objects and actions

Phonograms are of various kinds: one word may stand for another which is homophonous or similar in sound (level II.1): *wr*, 'swallow', is used for *wr*, 'big'; *hprr*, 'beetle', is used for *hpr*, 'to become'. For reasons to be discussed presently, the vowels between these consonants were ignored and left unrepresented. Phonograms were also used to represent parts of words (level II.2). For instance, the word *msdr*, 'ear', was a combination of the signs ⋔ *ms*, 'fan', and ⊟ *dr*, 'basket'. Several of these biconsonantal signs came into conventionalized use as phonograms only. In many cases it is not clear, however, whether they stood for one or for two syllables: that is, it is not certain whether the word for 'fan' was m^*s or m^*s^*, where '*' stands for whatever vowel was appropriate.

Some words must have been monosyllabic containing one consonant only, and a selected set of them became used as phonograms also. Gelb (1963: 77) calls the set of monoconsonantal phonograms 'the Egyptian uniconsonantal syllabary', a term which is not uncontroversial because of its theoretical implications. Other scholars (such as Friedrich 1966; Jensen 1969; Andrews 1981) refer to the inventory of monoconsonantal hieroglyphs as 'the hieroglyphic alphabet' given in figure 4.2.

Some of the signs listed in figure 4.2 were bifunctional, being used both as pleremic word signs and cenemic sound signs. It is a peculiar feature of Egyptian writing that pleremic and cenemic signs are used side by side and freely mixed. To make matters more difficult yet, but actually for reasons of clarification, a third kind of sign is used in combination with the other two. These are called 'determinatives', and are employed to specify the meaning of words that are spelled out phonetically. They are silent and serve the purpose of indicating a semantic field. For example, the words for 'thirst' (verb) and 'little goat' are both spelled with the monoconsonantal signs for *j* and *b*. To distinguish them, the first is supplemented with a determinative showing a man holding a hand to his mouth, and the second with the sign of a little goat as a determinative. The sign for 'house', *pr*, may stand for either 'house' or 'to leave'. To distinguish the latter from the former, two walking feet are attached to the verb as a determinative. Some other examples of determinatives may be found in figure 4.3.

The determinatives play an important role in Egyptian writing, although they are often redundant and at times their use was excessive. Their invention testifies to a keen awareness of the two planes of linguistic structure, sound and meaning. Although they do not constitute a complete list of semantic categories – which would be expecting too

Sign	Transcription	Sound value
	(vulture) *3*	glottal stop (as in 'bottle' when pronounced by a Cockney)
	(flowering reed) *ỉ*	I
	(two flowering reeds) *y*	Y
	(oblique strokes) *y*	Y
	(forearm and hand) *ʿ*	Ayin of the Semitic languages
	(quail chick) *w*	W
	(cursive development of) *w*	W
	(foot) *b*	B
	(stool) *p*	P
	(horned viper) *f*	F
	(owl) *m*	M
	(water) *n*	N
	(mouth) *r*	R
	(reed shelter) *h*	H
	(wick of twisted flax) *ḥ*	slightly guttural *h*
	(placenta?) *ḫ*	CH (as in loch)
	(animal's belly) *h̲*	slightly softer than *h*
	(door bolt) *s*	S
	(folded cloth) *s*	S
	(pool) *š*	SH
	(hill) *ḳ*	Q
	(basket with handle) *k*	K
	(jar-stand) *g*	G (as in goat)
	(loaf) *t*	T
	(tethering rope) *ṯ*	Tj
	(hand) *d*	D
	(snake) *ḏ*	Dj

4.2 The hieroglyphic alphabet with sound values in English orthography (adapted from Andrews 1981)

much, as nobody has yet produced one – they do cover a number of very general concepts testifying to what was important in ancient Egypt. Thus there are determinatives for 'man' and 'woman', for 'fire' and 'water', for 'desert' and 'irrigated land', for 'minerals' and 'plants' and 'mammals', as well as for certain actions such as 'walk', 'cut' or 'bind' and 'action' in general. A very interesting determinative signifies 'abstract objects', itself a very abstract notion.

When and how the determinatives came into existence is hard to tell because they are already present in the earliest documents. Clearly their existence is bound to cenemic writing of level II, and if from a systematic

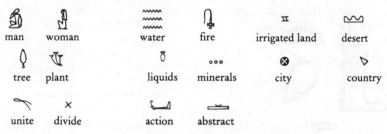

man	woman	water	fire	irrigated land	desert
tree	plant	liquids	minerals	city	country
unite	divide	action	abstract		

4.3 Egyptian determinatives

point of view level II is a more advanced state of the development of writing, then the determinatives appear to be a regression because they belong to the pleremic level I. What the determinatives seem to indicate is that the advantage of sound writing was not immediately recognized because of its makeshift character which relied entirely on the rebus principle. As determinatives have no sound value of their own, they might be regarded as elements of truly ideographic writing. The two most plausible reasons for their coming into existence are as follows.

1 In the earliest stages, Egyptian writing may not have been used for, and may not have been capable of, writing a running text (Friedrich 1966: 36). The reader could thus not readily rely on contextual information for disambiguating a rebus sign. In a running text of cenemic writing most ambiguities can be eliminated simply by referring to what makes sense. However, individual words or phrases, such as titles of kings or gods, are not so easily understood out of context. Determinatives would help to disambiguate.

2 Phonograms are not formally distinguishable from word signs. Putting a determinative next to a rebus sign or other sound sign thus fulfils a double function: first, it indicates that the sign in question *is* a phonogram, and second, it indicates the semantic domain of the target word.

The problem with the pleremic determinatives is that they too are pictographs: that is, they are not graphically distinct from the other two classes. Mixing three classes of functionally different but formally indistinguishable signs not surprisingly resulted in a writing which was rather hard to penetrate. Figure 4.4 illustrates how the system works. It is an inscription of the second millennium, a time when the use of

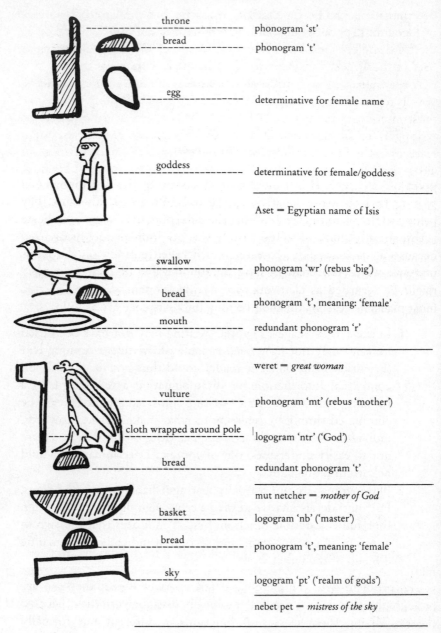

throne	phonogram 'st'
bread	phonogram 't'
egg	determinative for female name
goddess	determinative for female/goddess
	Aset ⁼ Egyptian name of Isis
swallow	phonogram 'wr' (rebus 'big')
bread	phonogram 't', meaning: 'female'
mouth	redundant phonogram 'r'
	weret ⁼ *great woman*
vulture	phonogram 'mt' (rebus 'mother')
cloth wrapped around pole	logogram 'ntr' ('God')
bread	redundant phonogram 't'
	mut netcher ⁼ *mother of God*
basket	logogram 'nb' ('master')
bread	phonogram 't', meaning: 'female'
sky	logogram 'pt' ('realm of gods')
	nebet pet ⁼ *mistress of the sky*

Aset weret mut netcher nebet pet ⁼ Isis, great woman, mother of God, mistress of the sky

4.4 Hieroglyphic inscription of the thirteenth century

determinatives had become rather pleonastic, but similar combinations of logograms, phonograms and determinatives are attested already in the third millennium. The inscription identifies the goddess known as 'Isis' in the Greek, and 'Aset' or 'Eset' in the Egyptian pantheon.

A very conspicuous feature of the phonograms is that they disregard vowels representing consonants only. From a linguistic point of view the most interesting point here is that this particular feature of Egyptian writing is to be understood as a consequence of certain structural features in the Egyptian language. The origin of ancient Egyptian is not altogether clear, but it is clear that it belongs to the group of Hamito-Semitic languages[5] (Gardiner 1957; Cohen 1969). At least 300 Semitic and 100 Hamitic words have been identified in Egyptian, too many to be explained as the result of commercial contacts. Table 4.1 shows some examples. Like the Semitic languages Egyptian exhibits a word structure with consonant roots; its morphology consists mainly in altering vowels while retaining the consonantal frame of words. The semantic nucleus of the word is hence expressed in its consonants. Vowels, on the other hand, serve to indicate noun and verb inflections.

TABLE 4.1   *Connections between Egyptian, Semitic and Hamitic words*

Egyptian	Semitic	Hamitic
m(w)t	mwth (Hebrew) 'die'	
djb'	isba' (Arabic) 'finger'	
hsb	hasaba (Arabic) 'count'	
sms		simis (Bedja) 'follow'
nfr		nefir (Bedja) 'good'
gm		egmi (Touareg) 'find'

As pointed out above, the consonant signs of the Egyptian script are a matter of controversy. Basically there are two positions as to their systematic evaluation. One is that monoconsonant signs stand for individual consonants, a selected group of which gradually assumed the function of standard phonograms in accordance with level II.3. The 25 signs of this group (figure 4.2) are recognized by Jensen (1969) and Friedrich (1966) as the Egyptian (forerunner of the) alphabet. The other position is Gelb's (1963), opposing the traditional view and maintaining that the monoconsonant signs must be considered to have syllabic values.

Jensen's argument is based on the documents which have been preserved. He assumes that while the monoconsonant signs once had a definite vowel value, this must have faded away gradually so that the sign came to be used irrespective of the vowel which followed in the word to be written. A syllabic sign containing one consonant only can only be either CV or VC. If the vowel is not expressed any more, the syllable ceases to be a syllable. Hence, Jensen (1969: 60ff) argues, the monoconsonant signs must be interpreted as having a consonantal value only. Additional evidence for this view is found in the practice of 'syllabic writing' which developed early in the second millennium (W. F. Albright 1934). 'Syllabic writing' in this sense means that certain consonant signs are used to indicate a vowel which, in combination with another consonant, then constitutes a syllable. This practice seems to suggest that the latter stood for a consonant only (cf. also Friedrich 1966: 41).

For Gelb, by contrast, all Egyptian writing was always syllabic. His argument for this assumption is theoretical, having to do with what he considers the natural and necessary development of writing systems. A development that proceeds from logographic units to consonantal units cannot be accommodated in his theory. Thus he argues: 'The Egyptian phonetic, non-semantic writing cannot be consonantal, because the development from a logographic to a consonantal writing, as generally accepted by the Egyptologists, is unknown and unthinkable in the history of writing, and because the only development known and attested in dozens of various systems is that from a logographic to a syllabic writing' (Gelb 1963: 78ff). This argument is clearly based on a *petitio principii* and is therefore hard to accept. Gelb does not deny that the monoconsonant signs have no definite vowel value yet he argues that they are syllabic, having a structure like $C*$ or $*C$, where $*$ is a variable that can be any vowel. The question that Gelb cannot answer is this: is there any difference between a sign for a consonant-plus-unspecified-vowel-syllable and a sign for a consonant? Egyptian writing does not indicate vowels, except in the syllabic writing referred to above. The syllabic nature of monoconsonant signs, therefore, looks very much like a stipulation for the sake of a developmental theory.

The disagreement between the two positions is not trivial. It indicates, most of all, that the available evidence allows for widely different interpretations. In the absence of native speakers of Egyptian, it does not seem likely that more evidence will be forthcoming to settle the issue.

THE EGYPTIAN SYSTEM: ITS OUTER FORM

Hieroglyphs were not the only form of Egyptian writing; rather they were reserved for monument inscriptions and other formal usage. They remained almost unchanged from the earliest documents in the third millennium until the third century AD, when the last documents were written with them. In everyday use, the glyphs became more cursivized and gradually lost their pictorial character. Out of this less ceremonial use a new script evolved which, however, never replaced the hieroglyphs. As early as the middle of the second millennium, a very beautiful book script was fully developed in which the pictograms were already highly stylized. This form of writing is known as 'hieratic', a designation which came into use only much later. It results from the fact that this script, which was originally used for secular purposes, was replaced in the seventh century BC by a yet more cursivized variety and came to be used for religious purposes only. The new script was called 'demotic' by

Hieroglyphic					Hieroglyphic book-script	Hieratic			Demotic
2900–2800 BC	2700–2600 BC	2000–1800 BC	c. 1500 BC	500–100 BC	c. 1500 BC	c. 1900 BC	c. 1300 BC	c. 200 BC	400–100 BC

4.5 *Cursivization of the outer form*

Herodotus: that is, a popular script. The three varieties which were then used side by side are illustrated in figure 4.5.

CONCLUSION

Structurally Egyptian hieroglyphic writing makes use of pictorial signs with three different functions: word signs, phonetic signs and determinatives. It is generally recognized that the Egyptians, although they had all the elements of an alphabet, did not make the final step to alphabetic writing. The imperfectly phonetic method of writing continued with little change for many centuries. Despite the analytic insight underlying cenemic signs, some 500 pleremic word signs remained in use, making the system hard to learn and the privilege of an elite group. Naturally this group, the clerks and priests of the royal household of the pharaoh, had no desire to endanger their status. 'Put writing in your heart that you may protect yourself from hard labour of any kind' (Childe 1941: 187). Such was the advice of an Egyptian in the fifteenth century BC; advice that was only reasonable where writing was the privilege of a few. It was in the best interest of these few to guard their privilege and make sure that writing was complicated and not readily available for everybody.[6] In this sense, Egyptian writing was rightly called 'theocratic' (Diringer 1968). Indirectly the social privilege of writing may well have contributed to the stability and conservatism of the Egyptian script whose development stopped short of the alphabet.

The latest documents recorded in the hieratic script date from the third century AD. Demotic writing continued until the fifth century when, under the influence of Christianity, Egyptian came to be written with Greek letters. The sacred characters were discarded, and what they represented remained a secret until the nineteenth century. How the enigma of Egyptian writing was solved is discussed in chapter 11.

NOTES

1 Cf., for instance, Sethe (1939). This treatise on the origin of Egyptian writing has long been regarded as authoritative.
2 As Childe (1982: 126) puts it, for 'administering the enormous revenues of Egypt it too required a script to record receipts and expenditures'.

3 Gelb (1963) advocates the monogenesis theory, arguing that at least the idea of writing must have come to Egypt from Sumer. Cf. chapter 5.

4 It is generally acknowledged now that precursors of writing – that is, 'count stones' and their impressions – were used much earlier in Mesopotamia (cf. Schmandt-Besserat 1979). However, the use of writing proper is not assumed prior to the turn of the fourth to the third millennium.

5 The successor of Old Egyptian, Coptic, was used as a vernacular in Egypt at least until the seventeenth century AD, when it was replaced by Arabic. As a church language, however, it has survived until the present. The word *Coptic* is derived from the Greek *aigyptios* and thus means 'Egyptian'. The insight that Coptic was actually Egyptian was instrumental to deciphering the hieroglyphs (see chapter 11).

6 The question of how far social conditions of this kind have contributed to the preservation of Chinese writing until the present time is discussed in chapter 6.

5

From Word to Syllable I:
Cuneiform Writing

HISTORICAL BACKGROUND

The origin of the cuneiform (from *cuneus* = Latin 'wedge') script is well known and better documented than that of Egyptian hieroglyphics. The credit for the invention of cuneiform goes to the Sumerians,[1] a people of unknown descent whose language seems to be isolated.[2] The excavations from Uruk – the city of Gilgamesh[3] – Jemdet Nasr, Ur, Babylon and many other places in the 'land of the two rivers' brought to light the traces of a civilization of the highest order. The findings included tens of thousands of documents written in cuneiform.

Unlike the Egyptian hieroglyphs, the cuneiform script was used to write more than one language of several different language families, reflecting the varied history of the ancient Near East over a period of some 3,000 years: Sumerian, Akkadian, Babylonian and Assyrian, as well as Ugaritic or Syrian, Elamite, Hurrian, Old Persian and Hittite. This widespread adaptation and use of the cuneiform script testifies to its enormous importance in the ancient world. The first documents of cuneiform writing proper date from about 3000 BC, and Babylonian astronomers still used it in the middle of the first century AD (Falkenstein 1964: 13).

By the end of the fourth millennium, Sumerian civilization had reached a level where inventions such as the wheel and the plow had raised food production above subsistence supply (Speiser 1939; Oppenheim 1964). Production for a market became possible and with it greater division of labor, planned agriculture, irrigation and taxation. The economy was centered about the temple where community projects were planned and commercial transactions carried out. More complex economic transactions called for sophisticated recording systems. There can be no doubt that in Sumer it was economic necessity that led to the development of writing (Chiera 1938).[4] More than 75 per cent of the 150,000 cuneiform inscriptions excavated in Mesopotamia are administrative and economic documents including legal documents, deeds of sale and purchase, contracts concerning loans, adoption, marriage, wills, ledgers and memoranda of merchants, as well as census and tax returns. Especially among the earliest documents economic records form the vast majority. Many of the documents are lists, such as inventories of objects and persons, stock, itemizations of goods for trade, payments to officials, food rations for slaves and work requirements. Other lists were intended for study or practice, such as classificatory lists of plants and animals and also the earliest dictionaries: that is, word lists where word signs were ordered for (1) pronunciation, (2) sign form, and (3) meaning (Wieseman 1970). Recently, cookbooks have been added as a new genre of cuneiform literature. Tablets dating from the eighteenth century before our era were found to contain what is probably the most time-tested collection of recipes (Bottéro 1987). However, on the whole, the cuneiform literature is a clear indication of the fact that writing came into existence in Mesopotamia in response to an economic necessity and was developed by the Sumerians as a tool of a highly sophisticated bureaucratic organization that controlled the distribution of goods, services and social privilege (Jacobson 1970).

THE CONSTRUCTION OF THE SUMERIAN SYSTEM

The most archaic stage of fully developed Sumerian writing is represented by the tablets of Uruk (Jordan 1932) and Jemdet Nasr.[5] At this stage the writing system contained an extensive sign inventory. Approximately 1,200 signs are known, but it is assumed that as many as 2,000 signs were in use (Falkenstein 1964: 11). However, a gradual reduction of this numerous set of signs began during the archaic period. The tablets of Shuruppak (2700–2350) exhibit a character inventory of some 800 signs, and by 2000 BC the set was reduced to some 500 word signs in common use.

In contradistinction to the magnificent beauty of the Egyptian hieroglyphs, the imagery of early Sumerian pictograms is rather simple. Clay, the writing material of the Sumerians, makes it difficult to draw curved lines. Accordingly, the early pictograms are linear, consisting almost entirely of straight lines. Stylization set in early and was very important, because the scribes had to be able to produce and recognize such a large number of different signs. Thus 'the standard gestalt of each sign is fixed, with only limited variation permitted' (Green 1981: 356). However, that the pictorial character of cuneiform signs was lost completely at an early stage has to do with the technical side of the practice of writing on clay. The earliest clay tablets were rather small and square, and writing was from top to bottom. Later, bigger rectangular tablets were used, which

Original pictograph	Pictograph in position of later cuneiform	Early Babylonian	Assyrian	Original or derived meaning
				bird
				fish
				donkey
				ox
				sun day
				grain
				orchard
				to plow to till
				boomerang to throw to throw down
				to stand to go

5.1 Rotation and loss of iconicity of some Sumerian signs

presumably forced the scribes to change the position of their left hand in which the tablets were held while being written. As a result, the written signs were rotated 90° counterclockwise and thus lost their iconic quality.[6] From around the middle of the second millennium, clay tablets were written and read from left to right in horizontal lines. The process of rotation and loss of iconicity is illustrated in figure 5.1.

The stylization of the signs set in early, which was necessary because the scribes had to be able to distinguish such a great number of signs, and also because clay is a rather inflexible surface for drawing pictures. It is much easier, faster and cleaner to make impressions on such a surface than to draw lines. Impressions were made with a stylus that was cut from reed in such a way that it had a triangular tip. Every line ended in a triangle; hence the wedge. The wedge thus became the elementary building block of all signs. Once the script was fully developed, a writing convention emerged, and only a few types of wedges were permissible for the composition of more complex signs: vertical (Υ), horizontal ($\vdash$), oblique from upper left to lower right ($\prec$) or from lower left to upper right ($\checkmark$), plus a wedge that looks like two superimposed wedges one of which is turned 90° in relation to the other ($\prec$). All complex signs had to be composed of these elements.

Loss of iconicity affected the further development of the signs in several ways. While for pictograms it was important to preserve certain features that were critical for recognizing the depicted object, the most important consideration regarding the non-iconic symbol was its distinctness: that is, that it was sufficiently different from other such symbols. Pictorial similarity no longer imposed restrictions on graphical variation. Over the centuries, the signs underwent great changes, although simple signs remained remarkably constant. Figure 5.2 illustrates the stylization and simplification of the sign for 'sky' (or 'God') from the most archaic version of Uruk (IV) to the modern one of New Babylonian.

Every sign is a configuration of wedges of the permissible types. This formation principle implies that simple signs form parts of more complex ones. However, complex signs are not to be interpreted as compounds of constituent configurations. In other words, the articulation on the level of graphical form is independent of the articulation on the level of values or referents. For example, the graphs which (in Akkadian) are read PA and IB in combination do not yield a graph PA + IB but the graph for SAB.[7] It is important to realize this because, while

Uruk	Jemdet Nasr	Sumerian	Old Akkadian
(3200)	(2900)	linear cuneiform	(2200)
		(2400)	

Old Assyrian	Old Babylonian	New Assyrian	New Babylonian
(1900)	(1700)	(700)	(600)

5.2 The gradual stylization and simplification of the signs for 'sky', an, and 'God',
dingir

some signs were originally formed by combining already existing signs (see below), the constituents of a graph have no systematic relation to the constituents of the morphophonetic referent.

Typically, cuneiform texts were written in horizontal lines progressing from left to right. Whenever different records had to be made on one tablet, the lines were arranged in columns also running from left to right and separated by vertical lines. The back of the tablet was also used for writing. Here columns were in reverse order, progressing from right to left.

THE INNER FORM

As early Sumerian writing functioned as a device to record commercial and bureaucratic transactions, the written language of that time is very restricted. Falkenstein (1964: 11) calls it 'a sentenceless language'. This is not to be understood as a language that fails to reproduce the sentences[8] of the spoken language, but rather as the absence of any continuous utterances or an attempt to create any segments larger than the word or lexeme. Early Sumerian writing can thus be considered word writing in the sense that graphs represented words and words only. Falkenstein

(1964) also points out that it was quite a long time before the script was made available for other purposes by providing for the representation of grammatical rather than purely lexical elements.

The expressive power of pure word writing is obviously very limited. In the beginning only concrete visible objects were represented with pictograms. The expressive power of the system was expanded somewhat when new signs were formed on the basis of combining others by virtue of their meaning. For example, the sign for 'mistress' was formed by combining into one the signs for 'woman' and 'dress'. The combination of 'ox' and 'mountain' yielded a new sign for 'wild ox', and 'mouth' plus 'bread' came to be used for the verb 'to eat'. Figure 5.3 illustrates this.

Another strategy for increasing the expressive power of the system consisted in metaphorical or metonymic expansion of the meaning of given word signs. The sign for 'plow' came to be used for 'to plow', even though both words were unrelated in Sumerian (*apin*, 'plow', and *uru*, 'to plow'). Eventually it was even used for 'plowman'. Using the sign of '(rising) sun' for 'white' and that of 'night' for 'black' is another example of metaphorical extension.

The breakthrough came with the exploitation of phonetic similarities of words and the cenemic use of signs motivated by their sound values rather than by their meanings. The scribes discovered the rebus principle

woman + dress → mistress

ox + mountain → wild ox

mouth + bread → to eat

5.3 The graphical composition of new signs

realizing, for instance, that the sign for 'arrow', *ti*, could be used for writing the Sumerian word for 'life', *ti(l)* (Friedrich 1966: 46). While this kind of sign transfer operates still within the confines of word writing, it is clearly the first step toward the development of syllabic signs.

Gradually the sound value of the signs became increasingly important and their meanings receded into the background. The transfer was always from one content word to others first, and then to function words. For example, the sign for *mu*, 'plant', was first transferred to *mu*, 'year' and *mu*, 'name', before it was used also for the enclitic *mu*, 'my' and the third person masculine prefix *mu*. Eventually, the original sign for 'plant' came to be used for any syllable *mu*. Thus a syllabary came into existence whose elements, like Egyptian hieroglyphs with syllabic values, are formally indistinguishable from logograms. Unlike the Egyptian glyphs, however, Sumerian syllabic signs identify both consonants and vowels. The syllable structure of Sumerian is relatively simple, consisting of the following possibilities: V, CV, VC and CVC.

The strategies of rebus and syllabic writing greatly increased the range of words that could be expressed, but they had the obvious drawback of introducing a lot of ambiguity into the system because many signs became polyfunctional, having several different meanings as well as uses for their syllabic value only. In order to remedy this undesired side effect of the achievement of greater expressive power, it became necessary to devise a means that would make an unequivocal interpretation possible. The solution at which the Sumerian scribes arrived was very similar to that of their Egyptian colleagues: they introduced determinatives. Word signs for generic terms such as 'man', 'God', 'land', 'city', 'wood', 'stone', 'copper', 'plant', 'meat', etc., were placed in front of – or, less frequently, behind – a word sign in order to specify its meaning. The sign for 'wood' put in front of that for 'plow' made it clear that the intended meaning was the tool rather than the activity. 'Man' instead of 'wood' in the same context, on the other hand, could only be interpreted as 'plowman' (cf. Falkenstein 1964: 10). Determinatives were also used to specify the meaning of syllabically written words and later, when cuneiform was used for writing Akkadian, for indicating the pronunciation and grammatical ending of a given word sign.

With three kinds of signs, word signs (pleremic with sound value), syllable signs (cenemic) and determinatives (pleremic without sound value), the cuneiform system was fully developed. Graphically all three were indistinguishable, being composed of the standard wedges. However, later on certain signs came to be used as determinatives only. Further developments of the cuneiform system were triggered by its application to other languages.

THE LANGUAGES WRITTEN

As pointed out above, the cuneiform script was used for a number of different languages. Sumerian was most probably the first and, therefore, in certain respects the most important one.

Sumerian

Sumerian is a language without inflections which belongs to the agglutinative type. Grammatical relations are expressed by means of affixes. Nouns and verbs are morphologically indistinguishable. Most of them are monosyllabic, but words with two or more syllables are also attested. Grammatical cases are mostly indicated by postpositions which are, however, often left out in old documents, especially in economic records of the archaic period.

Sumerian is a triumph of artificial selection, being as it is a prime example of the success of a written language. While the original speakers of this language had disappeared as a people by 1900 BC at the latest, having been absorbed by the Akkadian invaders, their language continued to be cultivated until the end of the cuneiform tradition. Even though it had lost its population of native speakers, Sumerian survived as a medium of the cult and other literary functions for more than a thousand years.

This is particularly noteworthy because Sumerian was spoken in the rather small area between the rivers Euphrates and Tigris south of present-day Baghdad. According to Falkenstein (1964: 17), the language area was too small for the speakers to develop significantly different dialects; yet the documents exhibit a lot of variation testifying to local writing traditions, on the one hand, and to consciously cultivated and functionally specific styles. The metalinguistic terminology indicates a high level of linguistic awareness. In addition to *eme-si-sá*, 'normal language', the Sumerians distinguished a number of different varieties such as *eme-gal*, 'big language', *eme-sukud*, 'high language', *eme-suh*, 'select language' and *eme-te-na*, 'oblique language', all of which were used for literary functions. Other terms were available for 'languages for special purposes', such as *eme-má-lah-a*, 'the language of navigators' or *eme-udula*, 'the language of herdsmen'.

A variety of special sociolinguistic interest is attested in early Old Babylonian literature (about 2000 BC), the so-called *eme-sal*, a gender-specific style used for dialogue parts of female characters. Male characters and narrator's parts were usually written in normal language. Normal language and *eme-sal* are distinguished by a number of phonological and morphological, as well as lexical, differences, which seems to indicate that there were pronounced gender-specific differences in the Sumerian speech community. In any event, it is obvious that language was an object of refined cultivation in Sumer, and that writing played a most significant part in language cultivation.

Akkadian and other Semitic languages

When the Akkadians first gained political influence in Mesopotamia, after about 2800, a situation of language contact and bilingualism with diglossia (cf. chapter 10, pp. 193–8ff) came into existence in the ethnically mixed population of the region. Akkadian was widely spoken, but for centuries Sumerian remained the written language. Tentative attempts at writing Akkadian with the Sumerian script first began around the middle of the third millennium, but extensive literature in Akkadian is attested only since Sargon I (about 2350). Akkadian was used in writing roughly until 100 AD. Its history as a spoken language is a matter of debate, as other Semitic languages and dialects were competing with it. Babylonian and Assyrian are considered Akkadian dialects by some and separate languages by others (cf. Reiner 1966: 20ff). The latter are further classified in terms of Old, Middle and Neo-periods. Regional and chronological divisions overlap. However, the dialect classification of Akkadian does not concern us here. More important for the present discussion are the far-reaching consequences of adapting the Sumerian script for writing Akkadian.

Akkadian is a language unrelated to, and typologically different from, Sumerian. Using the Sumerian script for writing it was, therefore, quite difficult and brought about important changes in the system. Most significantly, the ratio between the three kinds of signs shifted drastically. Civil (1973: 26) provides figures summarized in table 5.1 showing the relative frequency of cenemic and pleremic signs in various Sumerian

TABLE 5.1   *Pleremic versus cenemic signs in cuneiform writing of Sumerian and Akkadian texts*

Signs	Sumerian (%)	Akkadian (%)
Logograms	60.3–42.8	6.5–3.5
Syllabograms	36.4–54.3	85.6–95.7
Determinatives	3.1–2.9	7.6–0.7

and Akkadian texts. The variation indicated by maximal and minimal percentages is across different kinds of texts.

Generally speaking, the figures in table 5.1 indicate a shift from pleremic to cenemic writing. Although syllabograms occupy a significant position in Sumerian writing already, they clearly play a much more important part in Akkadian writing. This is hardly surprising because logograms are more cumbersome for an inflecting language, such as Akkadian, than for a language without inflections. There are thus two factors that contribute to the shift towards cenemic writing, (1) efficiency and (2) linguistic structure.

First, there is an increasing preference for using signs for their sound value rather than for their meaning for, in principle, a system of signs which maps sounds regardless of meanings can be more efficient than one whose elements are also differentiated with respect to meaning. However, the Akkadians adopted the majority of the Sumerian logograms and continued to use them as such. Hence another explanation must be sought for the great relative increase of cenemic signs in Akkadian writing. The chief reason for the increase is that the syllable structure of Akkadian is quite different from that of Sumerian so that the set of Sumerian syllabograms was insufficient for writing Akkadian. The Akkadians, therefore, reduced adapted logograms to new syllable signs. The proportion of syllabograms increased furthermore because, for the sake of unequivocal representation, the Akkadians developed a rather pleonastic way of writing, often representing a single syllable with more than one sign. A word such as *šadu*, 'mountain', for instance, would be spelled out like *ša-du-u*. Finally, syllabic signs came to be used in Akkadian as complements of logograms, indicating their proper pronunciation and/or form.

The three kinds of Sumerian signs were adapted to Akkadian as follows.

Logograms   The adaptation of logograms was the first and easiest step in the process of applying the Sumerian system to the Akkadian language: the word signs were simply associated with the Akkadian equivalents of the Sumerian words for which they stood. For example, the logogram ⸾ which in Sumerian has the value *dingir*, 'god', was used to write the Akkadian word *ilu* which also means 'god'; or ⸾, the sign for Sumerian *lugal*, 'king', was used for Akkadian *šarru*, 'king'. While this was a simple strategy, it produced a very complex result because many logograms already polyvalent in Sumerian became even more so in Akkadian.

Together with the script, and owing to the intensive language contact, the Akkadians adopted many Sumerian loan words. In writing, these loan words were naturally represented in the same way as in the Sumerian texts. However, most of the logograms with which Sumerian loan words were written were also adapted to Akkadian and given an Akkadian word value. As if this was not difficult enough, many of the Sumerian logograms had more than one word value in Sumerian already. The above mentioned logogram ⸾ for *dingir*, 'god', for example, also stands for Sumerian *an*, 'sky'. Since it was borrowed to write the Akkadian words for both 'god' (*ilu*) and 'sky' (*šamu*), it eventually had four different values in Akkadian writing: *dingir/ilu* ('god') and *an/šamu* ('sky'). A substantial number of Sumerian logograms became polyvalent in Akkadian writing in a similar way.

Determinatives   The system of determinatives in Sumerian was quite simple, consisting of a small set of mute signs used as graphic affixes to indicate the semantic range of meaning of a given sign and thus determine its reading. The Sumerians used noun determinatives only (Falkenstein 1964: 21). Obviously determinatives are particularly important for reading polyvalent signs. This may partly explain the greater frequency of determinatives in Akkadian compared with Sumerian texts.

The Sumerian semantic noun determinatives were adopted part and parcel for Akkadian, but in Akkadian a parallel system of phonetic determinatives developed consisting of syllabic signs which specified the reading of a given sign by referring the reader to the terminal sound of the verb (form) in question rather than to its meaning. These phonetic determinatives or phonetic complements (Reiner 1973) were essential for disambiguating polyvalent Sumerian logograms, because semantic determinatives could not indicate whether a Sumerian or Akkadian reading was intended. Thus for *šamu*, 'sky', the Akkadians wrote *šamu-u*; the final vowel is not pronounced but only indicates Akkadian rather than Sumerian reading. Also logograms in Akkadian could not represent inflections. The sign 𒈗, 'king', could stand for the nominative form *šarru*, for the genitive *šarri* or for the accusative *šarra*. Phonetic complements, usually consisting of the final consonant of the Akkadian word and a vowel, were therefore used to represent the paradigmatic ending of the word required by the syntactic environment. For the skilled reader who knows the language this device provided enough linguistic information to enable an unequivocal interpretation of Akkadian texts. The problem for the reader whose knowledge of the language is not first-hand but mediated through writing is that phonetic complements, like the semantic determinatives, are not graphically distinguished from logograms or syllabic signs.

Syllabic signs Syllabic signs were adapted as they were. Unlike Egyptian phonetic signs, Sumerian syllabograms indicated both consonants and vowels, and the Sumerian syllabic values were adapted to Akkadian unchanged. Thus Sumerian *mu*, *ti*, *an*, *šu*, etc., were also *mu*, *ti*, *an*, *šu*, etc., in Akkadian writing. However, as pointed out above, the inventory of Sumerian syllabograms was insufficient for representing all Akkadian syllables. To augment their syllabary, the Akkadians created new syllabograms by using word signs for their sound value only. For example, the Sumerian word sign 𒋗 for *šu*, 'hand', was first used to write Akkadian *qatu*, 'hand', and was then given the syllabic value *qat*, because the Sumerian syllabary did not provide a sign with this value.

The adaptation of the Sumerian script for Akkadian resulted in a great increase of frequency and relative proportion of syllabic signs. This is due to the creation of new syllabograms as well as to the introduction of phonetic complements for indicating inflectional endings. A third reason is a change in writing conventions. In Akkadian CVC syllables were written either as one or broken up into two parts. The syllable *šar*, for example, could be represented by a single sign or by the two signs for *ša* and *ar*. Similarly, *lum* was often represented as *lu-um*, or *gir* as *gi-ir*. Obviously this practice greatly contributes to the relative frequency of syllable signs in running text.

As compared with Sumerian, Akkadian texts represent a shift from pleremic to cenemic writing; yet Akkadian cuneiform is a very involved system consisting as it does of polyvalent signs that are not graphically distinguished. To illustrate, the sign ⟨ᶻ⟩ was used as a logogram for both *šadu*, 'mountain', and *matu*, 'country', as a determinative for names of mountains and countries and also as a syllabic sign with as many as five different values, *kur*, *mat*, *šat*, *nat* and *gin*.

A question that has intrigued many scholars, therefore, is why the Akkadians did not simplify their system and discard the polyvalent word signs in order to reduce it to a syllabary of some 100 signs.[9] That they did not make any further changes seems to indicate that the system was considered to be efficient. Also it must be taken into account that wherever writing systems have been established in a more or less standardized way and widely used, changes have been slow and strongly opposed by those who have mastered the complex system.

Elamite

The land of Elam in south-west Iran had contact with Sumer already in the third millennium. Cuneiform writing was imported early, but for a long time it was used only as the medium of Akkadian. As in many other instances, the written language was borrowed rather than the writing system only. Writing was so strongly associated with the language for which it was used that it was by no means evident that another language could be written as well. In the case of Elamite its isolated position, being neither a Semitic nor Indo-European language, must have contributed to this difficulty (Friedrich 1966: 52).

During the first half of the second millennium the Elamites began to write their own language with Sumerian/Akkadian cuneiform. The new adaptation of cuneiform again led to far-reaching changes of the system. The shift toward sound writing continued, leading to predominantly syllabic writing in the Middle Elamite period. The royal inscriptions of the thirteenth century BC are almost completely syllabic (König 1965). The total inventory of cuneiform characters was reduced to 113 different signs; writing had thus become almost completely cenemic. The general principle of writing Elamite was to use the Sumerian/Akkadian cuneiform signs for their syllabic value, although in Elamite some of the signs assumed a different value. Only 25 signs were also used as logograms for very frequent words including some Sumerograms: that is,

Sumerian loan words written with their original signs (Jensen 1969: 98). The number of determinatives was greatly reduced to only seven which were, however, used extensively. A single horizontal and, later, a perpendicular wedge was used as a determinative for place names and other nouns. In late inscriptions it is so frequent that it can be regarded as a word boundary marker (Friedrich 1966: 52).

In sum, under the hands of the Elamites, the cuneiform script became a manageable system consisting of little more than 100, mostly cenemic, signs.

Hittite

Yet another language written with cuneiform signs was that of the Indo-European Hittites.[10] Hittite cuneiform is attested in eastern Asia Minor since the beginning of the second millennium when the Hittites borrowed the script from the Akkadians. Again the transfer to another language caused certain difficulties because of structural differences. While the syllable structure of Akkadian exhibits a relatively regular alternation of consonants and vowels, Hittite has many consonant clusters which were hard to represent with the available syllable signs. The introduction of several new syllable signs did not result in a well-adjusted system. Vowels were often inserted in consonant clusters. For example, *tar-ri-ja-na-al-li* stood for what must have been **trijanalli*, 'third', in speech (the * indicates that this is a reconstructed form), or *li-in-kat-ta* for **linkt* 'he pledged'. It was difficult, therefore, to reconstruct spoken Hittite on the basis of the written documents, and some uncertainties remain (Friedrich 1966: 53).

Unlike Elamite, Hittite cuneiform texts contain a relatively high proportion of pleremic signs. Many Sumerograms are used which are, however, thought to have been read with Hittite pronunciation, sometimes indicated by syllabic complements. As the Hittites also borrowed a substantial amount of Akkadian words, Hittite texts exhibit a rather mixed character (Rüster 1972).

Old Persian

The Old Persian script is the simplest and the latest cuneiform variety, and the first to be deciphered. With the exception of Hittite, which is sometimes considered to be a mixed language, Old Persian is the only

Indo-European language written with a cuneiform script. Most written records date from the time between the sixth and the fourth centuries BC. Monumental inscriptions, the most important one of which is the trilingual (Old Persian, Elamite and Neo-Babylonian) inscription of King Darius at the rocks of Bīsōthum, have preserved Old Persian cuneiform for posterity and provided the key for the decipherment of other cuneiform systems (Cottrell 1971) as well as the reconstruction of the languages written. While scholars in the field, therefore, agree about attributing special importance to Old Persian cuneiform, their treatment of it varies.

In the Bīsōthum inscription just mentioned Darius claims credit for the invention of Old Persian cuneiform. Gelb (1963) ignores this testimony, considering the Old Persian script as a necessary step in the development from word writing to letter writing. Friedrich (1964: 100), on the other hand, takes the possibility of the invention of the Old Persian system by Darius or his scribes seriously. Jensen (1969: 98ff) also assumes an *ad hoc* invention for, while the outer form of Old Persian cuneiform bears witness to its origin, its inner form is radically different from its predecessors. Obviously the Persian scribes knew and were inspired by the Mesopotamian and Elamite scripts, but the changes they carried out for applying cuneiform to their language were so drastic that only the outer form remained while the underlying system is completely different.

Consisting of only 41 signs, the Old Persian system is at the threshold of alphabetic writing. It cannot be considered a genuine alphabet because the signs can have both syllabic and phonemic interpretations. Jensen (1969: 101) and Friedrich (1966: 98) thus call Old Persian cuneiform 'half syllabic, half letter writing'. In any event, the system is virtually completely cenemic, making use of only four logograms in addition to the 36 syllabic/phonemic signs listed in figure 5.4.

When Old Persian cuneiform came into existence, the Persian scribes could have been influenced by a variety of different systems in addition to Babylonian cuneiform. In particular, it is likely that they knew West Semitic letter writing. They may have taken the shape of their letters from the former and the underlying structural principle from the latter, thus arriving at a system where the cuneiform signs could stand for syllables in one context and for individual vowels or consonants in another.

𒀀	a, ā		ǧ, ǧa		b, ba		w, wi
	i, ī		ǧ, ǧi		f, fa		r, ra
	u, ū		t, ta		n, na		r, ru
	k, ka		t, tu		n, nŭ		l, la
	k, ku		d, da		m, ma		s, sa
	g, ga		d, di		m, mǐ		z, za
	g, gu		d, du		m, mŭ		š, ša
	ḫ, ḫa		ϑ, ϑa		y, ya		ϑr, ϑra
	č, ča		p, pa		w, wa		h, ha

5.4 Old Persian cuneiform

Ugaritic

Ugaritic is a Semitic language which was spoken in the city and region of Ugarit at the coast of northern Syria.[11] The discovery of Ugaritic cuneiform in 1929 was so astounding because it was used between the fifteenth and thirteenth centuries BC, at a time when all other cuneiform systems were still heavily pleremic. Ugaritic writing, however, is completely cenemic, using neither logograms nor determinatives.

Like the Old Persian script, Ugaritic combines the outer form of one tradition of writing with the inner form of another. As Segert (1984: 19) puts it, it is 'apparently a combination of the principle of consonantal alphabetic writing with the technique of cuneiform writing imported from Mesopotamia'. The Ugaritic system consists of 30 signs, corresponding by and large to the West Semitic linear alphabet. However, while the West Semitic alphabet consists of consonant signs only, Ugaritic has three vocalic signs indicating both short and long vowels (/a/, /i/ and /u/).

The traditional order of the cuneiform signs of Ugaritic is fundamentally the same as that of the West Semitic linear alphabet: 'a, b, g, ḫ, d, h,
w, z, ḥ, ṭ, j, k, š, l, m, ḏ, n, ẓ, s, ʿ, p, ṣ, q, r, i, ġ, t, 'i, 'u and ś. The last three
signs, the infrequently occurring ś and the signs denoting /i/ and /u/ in
combination with a glottal stop, are considered to be later additions to
the original consonantal alphabet consisting of 27 signs (Segert 1984: 23).

While Ugaritic texts are preserved on very few documents only, they
are extremely important because they testify once again to the
systematic changes following the transfer of scripts across languages and
the early understanding of the difference between the outer form of a
script and its underlying system. It is also noteworthy in this connection
that other Semitic languages, such as Akkadian and Hurrian, were also
written in Ugarit with the Ugaritic alphabet.

CONCLUSION

The spread of the cuneiform script throughout the ancient Near Eastern
world from Mesopotamia to Elam in the east, Persia in the south, the
Hittite empire in the north and Ugarit in the west, and its successive use
for a variety of unrelated languages, harbors a lot of insight about the
relationship between writing and language, both from a historical and
systematic point of view. Moreover, it is very telling as regards the interaction between, as it were, the software and the hardware of writing.
Clay, this most durable material thanks to which the oldest inscriptions
could survive in perfect shape for thousands of years, was responsible
for the development of the fundamental graphical building block, the
wedge-shaped impression. For more than twenty-five centuries the
wedge was the characteristic element of all cuneiform writing. By itself it
had no denotatum, but in combination conventionally-fixed configurations of wedges denoted linguistic units of various systemic levels. Once
the iconic quality of the earliest Sumerian signs was lost, the relation
between visual sign and linguistic denotatum was sense-discriminative
rather than sense-determinative; that is to say, parts of complex configurations of wedges did not correspond to parts of their linguistic
denotatum, no matter whether it was a word, morpheme, syllable or
phoneme. Thus the outer form of cuneiform is language independent.

The inner form of cuneiform is, however, intimately related to
linguistic structure. As demonstrated in this chapter, the spread of
cuneiform concurs with a development from pleremic to cenemic writ-

ing. The story of cuneiform is to be read, therefore, as the story of one script and several writing systems. All that Akkadian and Ugaritic texts share in common is the same script, but the underlying writing systems are as different as any two systems can be.

The most significant changes in the systematic make-up occurred whenever the cuneiform script was adapted to a new language. Akkadian cuneiform, consisting of an extensive inventory of three functionally different kinds of sign, remained stable for two millennia, but attempts at using the script for other languages – Elamite, Old Persian, Hittite – resulted in drastic changes that went far beyond filling some systemic gaps.

It is a matter of speculation as to whether or to what extent the difficulties of applying the system that had evolved in the context of one language to another were due to the fact that the former already existed as a written language, possibly far removed from its spoken counterpart, while the latter was yet to be reduced to writing and turned into a written language. It is obvious, however, that writing systems are adapted to structural peculiarities of the languages for which they are used. To the extent that writing systems are language sensitive, their transfer to new languages is bound to meet with difficulties. In order to cope with them, certain adaptations are necessary which can be implemented without much trouble, because the conservatism inspired by a literary tradition is no factor inhibiting sweeping changes.

It is clear, then, that languages exercise great influence on the development of writing systems; but the reverse is also true. Lexical borrowing mediated through writing or the adaptation of a writing system is one example. Sumerograms are found in most languages that were written with the cuneiform script. To what extent the corresponding Sumerian or Akkadian lexemes also entered the respective spoken languages is hard to tell, because our view on these languages is restricted given that all cuneiform writing came to an end some 2,000 years ago. Nevertheless, it can be argued that the spread of a script to other languages can affect these languages thoroughly. The following two chapters on the Chinese writing system and its derivatives substantiate this claim.

NOTES

1 It has been argued occasionally that the imperfect fit between Sumerian writing and Sumerian language indicates that there must have been another

language for which Sumerian writing was used prior to Sumerian (cf., for example, Reiner 1966). However, it seems to me that other reasons could be given for the imperfect fit. After all it is the earliest writing system that is at issue here. Its imperfect fit with the phonological form of the language could be due to the fact that there was no model for a better solution, or that it was standardized at an early stage before a satisfactory fit was achieved, or that there had been drastic phonological changes between the time when writing conventions became stabilized and the time of the earliest documents that allow for phonological reconstruction with any degree of certainty.

2 Several attempts have been made to link Sumerian with other languages such as Basque or Tibetan (Bouda 1938). A relation with the Caucasian languages has also been suggested (Bork 1924). The evidence for any of these claims is hardly compelling, however (Falkenstein 1964).

3 The first epic poem of world literature recorded by a Babylonian writer during the final period of Sumerian splendor in the third dynasty of Ur (about 2000); see Pritchard 1958.

4 The precursors of writing that Schmandt-Besserat has described also testify to the economic origin of writing in Mesopotamia. The title of her 1979 article, interestingly, reads like a pedagogical directive for present-day literacy programs: 'Reckoning before Writing'.

5 Roughly 3300–2900. Dating is conventionally made by referring to excavation sites. A chronology of the ancient Near East is to be found in appendix I.

6 The question of when and why the rotation occurred is not yet fully understood. For an overview of the literature and a fresh view on the problem cf. Powell (1981).

7 Capital letters represent cuneiform characters with sound values assumed to be close to the standard values of these alphabetic letters.

8 Cf. chapter 3 for a discussion of the dependency of the notion *sentence* on written language.

9 Chiera (1938: 65), for instance, speculated that 'it is not that they did not know how to carry the development further but that they refused to make further changes in their system of writing.'

10 Hittite was also written with another system known as 'Hittite hieroglyphic' between 1400 and 1200 BC. Hittite hieroglyphic was deciphered by Gelb (cf. Gelb 1931; 1963: 81ff).

11 The ruins of the city of Ugarit were discovered in 1929 at the excavation site known as Ras Shamra (cf. Herdner 1963).

6

An Alternative to the Alphabet: The Chinese Writing System

The Chinese writing system serves the longest uninterrupted literary tradition of all living languages and forms an essential part of one of the incontestably greatest and most original cultures of humankind.[1] It has been used continuously for more than 3,000 years, connecting the present with the past as no other writing system does. It has been admired for its beauty and its unifying power for the Chinese empire by some, while being criticized as cumbersome, imperfect, even primitive, by others who keep predicting its replacement by the more efficient alphabet. Yet the triumph of the alphabet came to a halt at the Chinese wall where it met its most important and successful rival. Therefore, and because in East Asia Chinese writing has created a cultural universe of its own, this system is deserving of special attention.

HISTORICAL BACKGROUND

Like Sumerian and Egyptian, Chinese was first used in writing by a people that settled in a river valley. Chinese writing appeared no later than the Shang dynasty which is traditionally said to have begun in 1766 BC[2] when the Yin people established the first complex political organization in China; but archeologists are still searching for evidence of the evolutionary stages of Chinese writing. At the end of the nineteenth century, excavations in the area of modern Anyang in the bed of the Yellow River brought to light the remains of the first city culture in China, and with it the earliest Chinese graphs generally acknowledged to be true writing (Chang 1963). They were found on bits of tortoiseshell and on ox and sheep scapulas; but the characters of these 'oracle bones' had already moved far from a purely naturalistic representation of objects. Judging by the extent to which these signs were conventionalized (Tsuen-hsuin 1962), it is reasonable to assume that in China writing was present considerably earlier.

The shell and bone inscriptions were used almost exclusively in divinatory texts of Shang rulers. Questions were inscribed on bones and on

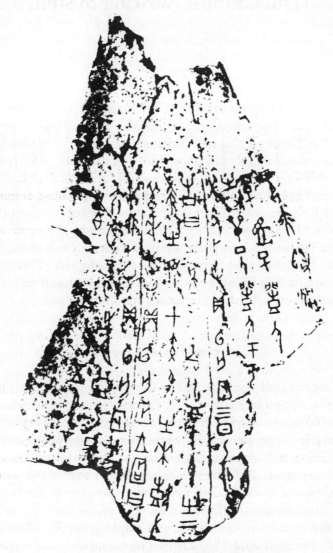

6.1 An early Chinese inscription on a scapula

the tortoiseshells which were then exposed to intensive heat. The resulting cracks in the surface supplied the oracular answers whose significance court diviners then interpreted. Figure 6.1 displays a typical oracle bone inscription.

Many of the characters of the earliest inscriptions closely resemble their modern equivalents. So far, out of a total of more than 2,500, some 1,400 could be identified as the models of standard Chinese characters and hence be interpreted unequivocally (Wen-Pu Yao 1981: 25). The first line of figure 6.2 lists some Shang characters; the modern equivalent of each of these characters is displayed immediately below.

	ox	sheep	tree	moon	earth	water	tripod
Shang	￥	￥	✖	ⅅ	⚲	⟩⟩⟩	𝍶
modern	牛	羊	木	月	土	水	鼎

6.2 Ancient Chinese characters of the Shang period and their modern equivalents

Bone and shell are very durable materials, and it cannot be ruled out that writing was practised earlier for purposes other than divination on different materials that did not survive.[3] Interesting indirect evidence for this assumption can be seen in the presence in the earliest documents of a character for 'book'; it consists of a picture of bamboo strips held together by two lines of cord (Needham 1978: 29). This suggests that surfaces other than bone and shell were also used for writing. Recent excavations at Banpo have, moreover, uncovered pottery with etchings on them which have been interpreted as predecessors of Chinese characters (Ho 1976). This may necessitate a revision of the view that the earliest writing in China dates from the middle of the second millennium. According to Wang (1980) it may reach back as many as 60 centuries.

Earlier scholars have sought connections between the Chinese script and that of Mesopotamia, and some of them (such as Ball 1913; Ungnad 1927) postulated the direct derivation of the former from the latter. But these assumptions have never been corroborated by hard archeological evidence. The only thing that can be said with confidence is that both systems had their origins in drawings of natural objects, but there is no such resemblance between early Chinese and pre-cuneiform Sumerian signs which would make it necessary to assume any historical relation between the two systems. Rather, while the question of its earliest emergence remains to be answered, it is clear that Chinese writing has to be considered a genuine independent development.

THE OUTER FORM

There is no doubt that pictures of concrete objects stood at the beginning of Chinese writing. These pictures never seem to have been as minute as the Egyptian glyphs. Instead, as with the Sumerian signs, linearization, reduction and conventionalization of the imagery set in early. This was essential because in the Shang period characters already numbered in the thousands. Hard surfaces like bone and shell favored an angular rather than rounded appearance of the characters, a design feature that was preserved in brush writing.[4]

Many of the characters on the oracle bones are pictographic, but they usually single out the conspicuous features of the object depicted while reducing the unimportant parts. For example, the character for 'cow', Ψ, highlights the U-shaped horns, and that for 'sheep', ⌄, the curved horns. In writing 'baby', ⸮, the early scribes focused on the large head. When they wanted to represent the verb 'to see', ⸔, they drew a single eye on a rump, a man looking.

Since the early system operated on the pleremic level, even more characters came into use, and there was little conformity in their creation. According to Barnard (1978), an expert in Chinese paleography, there was a great deal of unsystematic variation in the forms of the Chinese characters as they evolved in the Shang dynasty. First attempts at stylistic simplification were made during the Zhou period, but the characters of the 'great seal script' that evolved then still exhibit many variants. Standardization was impeded by the political and administrative disunity of that period.

The writing reform of Qin in 221 BC, when the empire was once again unified under a central government, was more successful and significant. Karlgren (1923) considers it the most important break in the history of the Chinese script, a history which he divides into two epochs: (1) the period from the beginnings to the Qin dynasty, and (2) the period from the fixing of the 'small seal script' by Li Su (about 200 BC) to modern times. Two changes of relative importance can be noted within the latter epoch. In the Han dynasty from which Chinese characters derived their name *Hanzi*, the small seal script gave way to the 'scribal script' first and then to the 'regular script' which is still used today in many publications. In a recent reform many characters were simplified, however (see Coulmas 1983). Figure 6.3 illustrates the metamorphosis of two characters from the Shang dynasty to the present.

	Shang	Great seal	Small seal	Scribal	Regular	Simplified
lái	來	來	來	來	來	来
mǎ	馬	馬	馬	馬	馬	马

6.3 Historical metamorphosis of the characters for lái *('to come') and* ma *('horse') from the Shang dynasty to the present day*

The regular script incorporates the fundamental graphical principles of Chinese characters. They are taught and memorized in this canonical form, and nowadays other writing styles are accessible only through the regular script. Calligraphy was cultivated early in China and has always been held in high esteem. In addition to the archaic small seal and the scribal scripts, three styles are used for calligraphy: the regular, the running and the cursive script styles. All of these were already extant during the Han dynasty and are still practised today. As illustrated in figure 6.4, the cursive style is much harder to read than the regular style.

For writing Chinese characters it is important to observe the principles of their graphic composition. In the simplified script of modern Chinese, each character consists of between one and twenty-five strokes. Formerly, the maximum number of strokes was even higher. This high complexity makes it immediately apparent why careful writing has always been very important. In order to determine the number of strokes of a given character, it is essential to know what counts as one stroke. The eight basic strokes[5] of which all characters are composed are listed in figure 6.5. Figure 6.6 indicates the directions of writing for the basic strokes.

6.4 *The sentence* Jīn shēng lí shuǐ *('Gold can be found in Lishui') is often used for practising calligraphy, because it contains both very simple and complex characters. The five columns illustrate five styles of writing in order of increasing cursivity (from left to right): small seal, scribal, regular, running and cursive*

Stroke		Name	
点	diǎn	dot
横	héng	horizontal
竖	shù	vertical
撇	piě	left-falling
捺	nà	right-falling
提	tí	rising
钩	gōu	hook
折	zhé	turning

6.5 *The eight basic strokes of Chinese characters*

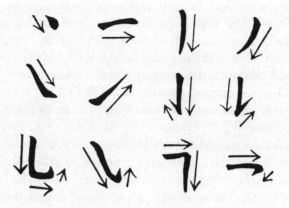

6.6   The directions of the basic strokes

In writing, it is also important to observe the order of strokes for each character because otherwise cursive writing is not legible. The general rules are from top to bottom, from left to right and from the outside to the inside. Some examples in figure 6.7 illustrate.

Example	Stroke order						Rule
十	一					十	First horizontal, then vertical
人	ノ					人	First left-falling, then right-falling
三	一		二			三	From top to bottom
州	ヽ	リ	州	州	州	州	From left to right
月	ノ	刀	月			月	First outside, then inside
四	丨	冂	冈	四		四	Finish inside, then close
小	亅	刂				小	Middle, then the two sides

6.7   The order of strokes of some simple characters

Chinese characters can be analyzed as configurations of individual strokes. Many of these configurations recur as the building blocks of more complex characters; that is to say, some characters can be parts of other characters. Thus, like the Sumerian signs, Chinese characters form a system based on double articulation where a number of signs serve a double function. For example, the character 語 ('word') is composed of the three parts 言, 五 and 口, all of which occur independently as characters in their own right. When occurring by themselves, they serve the sense-determinative function of designating a word; but when occurring as parts of other characters, they serve the sense-discriminative function of differentiating the composite character from others that are similar (cf. Coulmas 1984a). The economic advantage of double articulation is obvious: a limited number of elements provide the stock for forming a much larger, potentially infinite number of signs on a higher structural level. These elements are variously called 'keys', 'classifiers', 'determinatives' or 'radicals'. While the last term is the most common one, it is not used in this book because it suggests, wrongly, that this element is in some sense basic as a root is in Semitic languages. 'Classifier' describes the nature of the semantic elements more appropriately. They provide the basic principle for the organization of dictionaries, 540 in Xu Shen's etymological dictionary *Shuo wen jiezi* of some 10,000 characters compiled about 120 AD, and 214 in the great *Kang Xi* dictionary of 1716 which comprises more than 40,000 characters.[6] These 214 classifiers are still in use today. What role the classifiers fulfil in determining the linguistic value of a character is a question concerning the inner form of the characters which is discussed in the next section.

THE INNER FORM: THE PRINCIPLES OF CHARACTER FORMATION

The traditional classification of Chinese characters established 2,000 years ago in the *Shuo wen jiezi* distinguishes six classes of characters called *liù shu*, 六書 'the six writings'. They represent six different principles of formation or use.

1 The *pictographic* principle is presumably the oldest. It yielded characters which in their ancient form were simple pictures of concrete objects such as the characters for 'tree' and 'moon' in figure 6.2 above.

2 The *simple ideographic* principle underlies characters designating abstract notions such as numbers or the notions of above and below: 一 '1', 二 '2', 三 '3', 上 'above', 下 'below'.

3 The *compound ideographic* principle is next. The meaning of the characters in this group is a function of the meanings of its parts. For example, 信 (*xìn*) 'honest' consists of 亻 (*rén*) 'man', and 言 (*yán*) 'word'.

4 The *phonetic loan* principle is what is otherwise known as the 'rebus principle'. The characters in this group resulted from being used, by error or convention, for their phonetic value. They have been borrowed from writing the word for which they were originally created to another, homophonous one. A stock example of this type is the Shang pictograph 來 for a kind of wheat at the time called *lǝg*, which came to stand for the homo-phonous word *lǝg*, 'to come'.

5 The *semantic-phonetic compound* principle is an extension of the previous principle. In this class each character consists of a classifier and a phonetic: that is, an element indicating meaning and another indicating sound. For example, the character 糖 (*táng*) 'sugar', consists of the classifier 米, 'cereal', and the phonetic 唐 *táng*, which as a character is used as a proper name.

6 The sixth principle, called *chuan chù* or 'mutually interpretive symbols' in the *Shuo wen jiezi*, is a matter of dispute.[7] Rather than being a formation principle, it is a principle of use which can be described as semantic extension: one character is used to represent a word of the same or similar meaning, but different pronunciation, thus acquiring an additional pronunciation, for instance, 樂 (*yuè*) 'music', which was also used for *lè*, 'pleasure'.

Of these six classes those of the fifth type – that is, characters consist-ing of a classifier hinting at its meaning and a phonetic hinting at its pronunciation – is by far the most numerous. According to Karlgren (1923) some 90 per cent of all Chinese characters belong to this class.[8] It is, therefore, worthwhile taking a closer look at it.

The formation of the characters of the fifth type clearly relies on sound, yet Chinese writing is not cenemic because these characters also refer to meaning. Rather, Chinese writing is a complex fusion of cenemic and pleremic principles. It is interesting to compare the early develop-ment of cuneiform and character writing. Both systems started with

pictographs which were interpreted as logograms. With the need to refer
to words rather than objects, the pictographic principle was soon
relegated to a position of insignificance. The number of word signs
nevertheless increased as other formation principles took over, the
general tendency being to shift from pleremic to cenemic writing. Sound
became ever more important as a reference plane. So far the developments in Mesopotamia and in China are comparable; but as regards the
specific realization of this general tendency, both systems took a different course.

The total number of cuneiform signs is estimated to have been a little
more than 2,000 (Friedrich 1966: 44). When phonetization began to be
applied systematically in the ancient period, this number was reduced
quickly to between 800 and 900 signs and further to about 400 in the
common cuneiform of later periods. In China, by contrast, the number
of characters increased from about 2,500 on the Shang oracle bones to
almost 10,000[9] in the Han dynasty. By the twelfth century AD it had
soared to 23,000 and to as many as 49,000[10] in the eighteenth century.
Although this last figure includes many variants and obsolete characters,
and although only a limited subset have been in common use at any one
time,[11] it follows from these purely numerical observations that the
development of cuneiform signs and Chinese characters proceeded
along fundamentally different lines.

In the context of cuneiform (or Egyptian hieroglyphs, for that
matter), phonetization meant that signs were stripped of their meaning
and reduced to the representation of sound. The ensuing problem of
ambiguity was countered, so to speak, in a pleremic digression by the
introduction of a new kind of sign. Determinatives were employed to
ensure unequivocal indication of the meanings of syllabically written
words. As pointed out in chapter 5, determinatives indicated broad
semantic categories and were quite limited in number. The obvious
counterpart to cuneiform determinatives in the Chinese system are
semantic classifiers. For instance, the word *táng* can have various different meanings. By phonetization 唐 had come to stand for the syllable
táng. A semantic element 米, 'cereal', was added to single out the word
táng meaning 'sugar'. However, while in cuneiform this semantic
element would stand by itself, in the case of Chinese it became an
integral part of the character. This had two important consequences for
the character inventory and the structural make-up of its elements. First,
the modification of extant characters by additional elements led to an

enormous increase of their number. Second, rather than being reduced
to the representation of a syllable, each character continued to stand for
a word or morpheme.

As the economic advantage of sound writing was not fully exploited,
it was necessary in principle to have a character for every word or
morpheme. Thus the introduction of character inherent determinatives
– or, putting it differently, the expanding of the 'semantic–phonetic
compound principle' – was the most consequential step in the evolution
of the Chinese system. By applying the principle of determination differently, leaving the semantic element separate instead of making it part of
the character, the Chinese system might have become cenemic.[12] The
actual course of development, however, resulted in a heavily pleremic
system.

The relative importance of the cenemic and the pleremic aspects of
Chinese writing is a matter of considerable dispute. Why this should be
so can be appreciated if we inspect the respective roles of the semantic
and of the phonetic components of characters. Consider once again *táng*
as an example. As pointed out previously (p. 100), there are several
homophonous words *táng* as listed in figure 6.8.

If all characters for words with the phonetic shape *táng* incorporated
the phonetic 唐, the mapping relation between sound and graph would
be straightforward and simple. This is, however, not the case. The character 堂 is also used, independently and as a phonetic, to write homophonous words: for instance, *táng*, 螳 'mantis'. Here the classifier 虫
denotes an insect. In combination the phonetic for *táng* and the classifier

Phonetic		Meaning	Classifier*	
	糖	'sugar'	米	(cereal)
唐	塘	'embankment'	土	(earth)
táng	搪	'to block'	手	(hand)
	溏	'pond'	水 = 氵	(water)

* The shape of characters varies slightly depending on whether they occur
independently or as a part of another character.

6.8 The phonetic táng

for 'insect' make it clear what insect is referred to. It would be more economical to have just one phonetic for *táng* – that is, a one-to-one syllable/graph ratio – but these sound indicating elements can still be useful unless the same syllable is indicated by too many different such elements.

With respect to some syllables the syllable/graph ratio is very disadvantageous. For example, in current usage there are more than 10 different phonetics each indicating the syllables *ji*, *xi* and *shi*; and it would be difficult to find a syllable that is represented by one phonetic only. Mandarin Chinese has 1,277 tonal syllables. Karlgren (1923) has identified 1,260 phonetics under which he has classified some 6,000 of the most common characters. These two figures suggest a neat correspondence of an average one-to-one syllable/graph ratio; but a simple comparison is misleading, because both sides of the equation are multivalued with respect to each other. The second phonetic for *táng*,堂, for example, also stands for *cheng*. In 瞠 (*cheng*) 'to stare', it is the phonetic, while目, 'eye', is the classifier.

Another difficulty is the absence of any graphical or positional specialization corresponding to the functions of the elements combined into semantic–phonetic compounds. A simple character may thus serve as a phonetic in some complex characters and as a classifier in others. The character 刀, 'knife', for instance, is the classifier of more than eighty compounds and the phonetic *dao* in more than a dozen (Alleton 1970: 38). The resulting difficulty of determining the classifier and phonetic in a given compound character is further aggravated by the fact that there is no general rule for positioning the phonetic (or classifier) in the compound. The various possibilities are illustrated in figure 6.9.

6.9 *The position of phonetics (solid) and classifiers (traced) in compound characters (adapted from Alleton 1970: 38)*

The functional load and efficiency of phonetics in compound characters varies. Optimal efficiency could be defined as the property of a phonetic to designate unambiguously the same syllable in all characters of which it is a part. Even this criterion furnishes only a relative measure, however, because of the variable frequency of different phonetics: some occur in scores of characters, others only in a few. Keeping this in mind, three kinds of phonetics can be distinguished: (1) those that indicate the same syllable (including tone) wherever they occur; (2) those that indicate the same syllable except for tone wherever they occur; and (3) those that indicate critical features of a syllable, but not always the same. For example, 皇 occurs in at least six characters as the phonetic *huáng*, always indicating the same tonal syllable; the character 馬 is used as a phonetic in several characters indicating the syllabic value *ma*, irrespective of tone; and 堯 can best be described as indicating a syllabic value *Cao*, where 'C' can be a number of different consonants such as *y, j, x, q, n* or *r*, and where the tone is indeterminate. In a sense, therefore, 皇 is more efficient as a phonetic than 堯, for it is more accurate. This is not to say, however, that the latter is useless because, while it is less accurate, it provides a hint for the pronunciation of a great many characters.

The function of classifiers in semantic–phonetic compound characters can be described in a similar way. Some carry a high information load as regards meaning whereas others only give a vague hint. The general question is this: as every character has a meaning attached to it, how much does the classifier contribute to the identification of this meaning? Assuming that every classifier has a fixed meaning, it is necessary to distinguish between different kinds of classifiers as well as different kinds of occurrences of any given classifier. In some characters a given classifier indicates an essential semantic component of the morpheme represented; in others it provides only a dim clue; and in a third group it has no apparent relation whatsoever to the meanings of the morphemes for which they stand. In the third case the classifier only serves to differentiate the character from others that are similar, while in the first two cases it actively helps, in varying degrees, to identify the meaning. Similarly, some classifiers are semantically informative in all or most characters of which they are a part, whereas others are indicative only in some but not in others.

To measure the semantic information value of the classifiers objectively and compare them with respect to this is difficult because their distribution among characters varies greatly. In modern dictionaries with about 12,000 characters some classifiers, such as 9^{13} ('man'), 30 ('mouth'), 120 ('thread') or 140 ('grass'), head as many as 500 characters, but others serve only a handful or fewer characters as classifiers. Classifiers 204 ('to embroider') and 213 ('turtle') even seem to be listed as such only because the lexicographers did not know how to decompose and thus assign them to other classifiers (Alleton 1970: 44). Given that there are only 214 classifiers, some of which are practically useless as regards determining the meanings of characters, it is clear that the classifiers play only a limited role in semantic decoding. While their contribution to this process is hard to measure, it is possible to compare it with that of the phonetics. As the latter outnumber the former by a rate of between 5:1 and 8:1, depending on what count of the phonetics one takes as the basis,[14] the overall contribution of the phonetics to the decoding of characters must be greater than that of the classifiers. DeFrancis (1984: 128ff) reports on a study comparing the relative values of phonetics and classifiers of compound characters. He concludes that 'the phonetic element is far superior in predicting pronunciation than is the semantic element in predicting meaning.' If this is so, what then is a suitable term for describing the structural properties of Chinese characters appropriately?

LOGOGRAMS, IDEOGRAMS OR WHAT?

Most commonly Chinese characters are referred to as ideograms. Among those who make use of this term are (1) some who use it out of tradition or for lack of a better one, and (2) some who use it with meaningful intent. We need not deal with the former group here, but the latter cannot be ignored because this notion is, indeed, too full of meaning and speaks of a preconception.

One of the reasons why Western intellectuals have long been intrigued by Chinese writing is that it has been conceived, mistakenly, as many would argue today, as a system that speaks almost directly to the mind by means of visual images without mediation by the sound shapes of linguistic units; a system of ideograms similar to Arabic numbers or the ampersand &. Inaccurate reports by Christian missionaries have fostered this belief. Leibniz, for instance, in his quest for an alphabet of human thought – a topic which haunted him throughout his whole life – was led to think that an analysis of the system underlying the Chinese characters would prove to be fruitful for a better understanding of human thought.[15] In spite of his failure to construe a universal language and his eventual disillusionment regarding written Chinese as a potential model, these expectations did much to establish the common view that Chinese characters are ideographs, each one of which 'represents an idea' (Russell 1922: 35).

The most prominent defender of the notion that Chinese writing is ideographic in modern times is Creel who, in the 1930s and 1940s, engaged in a famous controversy with his colleague Boodberg. He was convinced that in the development of writing the Chinese preferred 'to continue along the pictographic, symbolic and ideographic path rather than to specialize on phonetics' (Creel 1936: 91). Although they knew the phonetic principle and used it to some extent in their ancient writing, they rejected it (Creel 1936: 94) because they found it insufficient (Creel 1936: 160). The Chinese developed ideographic writing, however, not only out of preference, but also driven by necessity (Creel 1938: 266). Even if their preference had been to develop a fully phonetic method of writing, they could not have done it because of the phonological poverty of their language and its predominantly monosyllabic words. The many homophonous words were bound to lead to ambiguities. 'The meaning could be made clear only with the help of ideographs' (Creel 1938: 267).

Creel's position, which is based largely on etymological considerations, has been challenged by Boodberg (1940) and Kennedy (1951) and, more recently, by DeFrancis. In his 1984 book DeFrancis synthesizes the arguments of his predecessors and the results of his own research in a forceful attack on what he calls 'the monosyllabic myth' and 'the ideographic myth'.

The 'monosyllabic myth' is a pillar on which the 'ideographic myth' stands. It says, briefly, that words in classical Chinese were monosyllabic and, because there were so few distinct syllables, therefore naturally favored an ideographic script.[16] It can be argued, however, as DeFrancis does, that 'monosyllabism' is really an artefact, a product of Chinese writing and lexicography, rather than a determining factor of the development of the characters. In modern Chinese the majority of words consist of two or more syllables. DeFrancis argues that, in speech, this tendency was already present in ancient times. Only in the terse and extremely compact style of Chinese writing did words occur in the truncated form of a single character denoting a single syllable. The

Western idea of a close relationship between written and spoken language may also have contributed to the monosyllabic myth. A favorite argument of its adherents is that Classical Chinese poetry, when read aloud, very often does not make much sense, while being quite intelligible in writing. This does not, however, prove that what was not comprehensible in speech had to be made so in writing by introducing distinctions on the graphical level which had no counterpart on the phonetic level; rather it suggests that poetry was composed on paper and that writing was considered as a form of communication with functions different from those of speech. Different things can be done with language when writing and when speaking. This is especially true under the conditions of a writing system whose units are more than mere visual substitutes of sounds, denoting as they do both sounds and meanings.

Chinese dictionary making is yet another factor contributing to the belief in monosyllabic words, because traditionally dictionaries list individual characters as entries. DeFrancis (1984: 181) cites Kennedy's observation that, of the 373 characters listed in a standard dictionary under the *insect* classifier, '186 are given dictionary meanings, while 187 are listed as undefinable except in association with other graphs.' In other words, half of the entries are bound morphemes rather than independent lexemes. This shows how misleading it is to look at characters as representing words. For DeFrancis (1984: 124) Chinese writing is, however inadequately, primarily syllabic but, since most characters also contain a semantic classifier, he cannot call it a syllabic system.

An argument often cited in support of the ideography notion has to do with Chinese dialects. It is noted with wonderment by many Westerners that what is written in Chinese characters can be read throughout China, in spite of the pronounced differences between the dialects which in speech are mutually unintelligible. For two reasons this argument is not very pertinent. First, until recently, mastery of the Chinese script was the prerogative of a very small elite, and this mastery was invariably acquired in conjunction with learning Mandarin. Second, to find mutually unintelligible dialects sharing a common written norm one does not have to restrict one's attention to non-alphabetically written languages; English is a perfect example. A speaker of Indian English from Bombay will be hard put to understand the broad drawl of a southern Texan, and the latter will find the dialect of Glasgow quite difficult to comprehend. Yet neither of them has any problems reading standard British or American English and relating it in some way to their own dialect. From this observation, no one would want to draw the conclusion that English orthography is ideographic. The fact that Chinese characters can be used across dialect boundaries cannot be taken to imply that either. Rather what it implies is that the representation of sound by the characters is not very accurate and that dialectal sound change is systematic.

Where do these observations leave us? We cannot avoid the conclusion that Chinese characters are inadequately described as either ideograms, logograms[17] or syllabograms. How then can they best be described? What is it that Chinese characters represent?

Jensen's (1925: 33) term *Formlautzeichen*, 'form-sound signs', and Friedrich's (1966: 19) notion of 'picture-idea writing' lack clarity. In recognition of the twofold nature of the great majority of all characters Cohen (1958: 49) describes the Chinese system as *une écriture idéophonographique*, which is preferable to Benvéniste's (1966: 24) *morphématique* because the latter could also be taken as referring to meaning only. Chao's (1968: 102) term 'morpheme–syllable writing' is much more to the point. Every Chinese character stands for a morpheme and for the syllable into which it is clad (cf. also Sampson 1985: 39).

In principle, there is a one-to-one mapping relation between characters and morphemes, while that between characters and syllables is a set of many-to-one relations since there are more characters than syllables. In most native Chinese individuals' mental dictionary there are probably also more morphemes than characters. To the extent that this is so and these individuals engage actively in writing, the syllabic aspect of writing is bound to become more dominant. But even though most present-day publications are supposed to represent 90 per cent of their content with the 1,000 most frequent characters, the system is far from being purely syllabic. While the phonetics are not nearly as vague in indicating the sound shape as the classifiers are in indicating meaning, there is still considerable vagueness on the level of sound signification. As distinguishing elements the classifiers are indispensable. Thus the Chinese system is best described as a 'morpheme–syllable writing system' in which classifiers and phonetics serve mutually diacritical functions: each determines the exact nature of the other which is only hinted at by the respective element itself.

From this description it appears that Chinese writing is intolerably vague and cumbersome, yet the ease and efficiency with which the system is used by those who have mastered it speaks against such a judgement. After all, the principle on which most Chinese characters are based, that of presenting cues simultaneously to both the sound and the meaning of a morpheme, may turn out to be a very practical foundation for an orthography.

CONCLUSION

The Chinese writing system has often been criticized as cumbersome and uneconomical, yet it has survived from antiquity to the present day, serving as it does the greatest literary tradition that has ever existed. As the only original development of writing in the region it had a more lasting effect on the cultural identity of East Asia than any other culture trait (cf. chapter 7). The significance of the Chinese system for the development and functioning of writing can be summarized in three points.

1   Historically the evolution of the system since the incorporation of semantic classifiers into the individual characters demonstrates that, contrary to what has often been suggested, there is no finality, nothing absolutely necessary, in the development of writing. More particularly, the alphabet or phonetic writing in general cannot simply be considered the evolutionary, let alone teleological, peak of the development of writing. Rather, it must be noted that the Chinese system, by an accident of history or by deliberate choice on the part of its users, retraced the course toward cenemic writing on which it was set early in its history and continued to unfold along pleremic lines. Phonetic writing was known in China for many centuries. It existed in India, from where other culture traits had been adopted. That it was not accepted by the Chinese literati testifies to the conservatism of the Chinese civilization and to the fact that, once established, writing systems are extremely persistent.

2   The Chinese writing system is suitable for Chinese, or if this is saying too much, it is at least more suitable for Chinese than it is for other languages, for Chinese is an isolating language, and the need for cenemic signs is felt less in writing such a language than one which has an intricate morphology with many grammatical morphemes. Like all original creations, the Chinese writing system thus reflects certain features of the language for which it evolved. This structural fit may be considered another reason why the Chinese system never changed its

type during the past 2½ millennia. A change of type – from pleremic to cenemic – was brought about only when it was applied to an unrelated language, Japanese (to be discussed in the following chapter).

3   Systematically, Chinese writing is a peculiar mixture of pleremic and cenemic principles. Although it is undoubtedly hard to learn, its proficient users emphasize its efficiency and speed as well as the fact that it adds a dimension to the visual manifestation of language which has no counterpart in purely phonetic writing. Appealing simultaneously to the reader's abilities of phonetic and semantic decoding, it operates in a way that only alphabetic systems with a long history such as the English approximate; simple phonologically defined phoneme–grapheme relations have been superseded by a great deal of etymological writing whose units map onto the morphemic and lexemic levels.

NOTES

1   Creel (1943: 15) estimates that until the middle of the eighteenth century more books had been published in Chinese than in all other languages of the world put together.

2   This date reflects traditional chronology rather than accurate historical record (cf. Levenson and Schurmann 1969). See appendix II for a Far Eastern chronology.

3   Wood and bamboo plates with inscriptions in black ink are known from the Qin dynasty. They contain legal texts and other official documents.

4   The Chinese writing brush was also introduced during Shang times (cf. Needham 1978: 29).

5   Traditionally, eight basic kinds of strokes are distinguished, but some specialists of the art of brushmanship list as many as 64 (Alleton 1970: 26). Counting strokes for the purpose of finding characters in reference works, however, is based on the eight strokes listed in figure 6.5.

6   In character dictionaries characters are arranged by classifier and number of strokes. Looking up a character thus involves at least two steps: (1) identifying the classifier and locating it in the dictionary, and (2) finding the character in question among those with the same classifier and consisting of the same number of strokes. The modern classificatory system of character dictionaries which is based on 214 classifiers is rather cumbersome. As more than half of all characters belong to one of the twenty most frequent classifiers (Chao 1948: 63), the entries for these classifiers are exceedingly long.

7   Wieger (1932: 10) explains the principle as 'acception du caractère dans un sens plus étendu, dérivé, généralisé, métaphorique, approprié, figuré, etc.'.

Creel (1936: 95) translates it as the *mutually explaining* principle and raises doubts whether this was a clearly defined category for the author of the *Shuo wen jiezi* himself. Chao (1968: 103) likewise calls it 'obscure', and DeFrancis (1984: 79) simply omits it from his discussion.

8 Saeki (1966: 56) gives the following percentage breakdown for the six categories: 1: 3%, 2: 0.4%, 3: 6%, 4: 0.5%, 5: 90%, 6: 0.05%.

9 As recorded in the *Shuo wen jiezi* of 120 AD.

10 In the *Kang xi* dictionary of 1716.

11 The total number of all the characters that have ever existed is impossible to ascertain, but it is said that it would reach 80,000 (DuPonceau 1838: 7; Alleton 1970: 47).

12 As a matter of fact, it has been argued that Chinese writing once was cenemic. Kennedy, aprovingly quoted in DeFrancis (1984: 84), suggests that 'at some period shortly after or coincident with the oracle bone period Chinese writing became an organized system of syllabic writing.' If that were indeed to have been the case, the history of Chinese writing would be an interesting example of abandoning a simple structural principle for the sake of a more complicated one.

13 There is a standard order of classifiers in Chinese and Western character dictionaries. The 214 classifiers are ordered for ascending number of strokes from one to seventeen. Within the 17 groups the order is arbitrary but standardized.

14 As pointed out above, Karlgren (1923) lists 1,260 phonetics, whereas Soothill (1942) only counts some 900.

15 'Cette recherche [des caractères Chinois] me paroit d'autant plus importante que je m'imagine, que si nous pouvions découvrir la clef des caractères Chinois, nous trouverions quelque chose qui serviroit à l'analyse des pensées' (Leibniz 1768, vol. 5: 484).

16 Bertrand Russell, one of the most learned men of his day, though not a specialist on matters of Chinese language, gave succinct expression to the myth: 'What is peculiar in China is the preservation of the ideographic system throughout thousands of years of advanced civilization – a preservation probably due, at least in part, to the fact that the spoken language is monosyllabic, uninflected and full of homonyms' (1922: 36).

17 DuPonceau (1838) seems to have been the first to promote the term 'logographic' as a better choice than 'ideographic'. But for the reasons just stated this is not satisfactory.

7

From Word to Syllable II:
Chinese Characters for other Languages

In view of the pre-eminence of Chinese culture, it is not surprising that, like other cultural achievements, the Chinese writing system was borrowed by neighboring peoples in the Far East, either living under Chinese sway or in independent countries. Like Sumer, China was a center from which writing radiated to other lands (Liu 1969). The possession of writing was both the result and an expression of China's cultural superiority, and Chinese writing was probably the most important single factor for exporting China's culture and establishing a common cultural bond throughout East Asia. However, it was not only or even primarily the Chinese writing system as an instrument which secured China's cultural dominance in that part of the world; rather it was the content of what was written and the fact that the study of Chinese texts was the chief means of getting to know it. To the borrowers, Chinese writing and the Chinese language were originally inseparable. This is an important point to note at the outset of this chapter because, while the influence of Chinese writing on other Asian cultures is often acknowledged, its nature is also often misunderstood. Consider Russell's remark on the function of the Chinese script in Japan as a typical example of this misunderstanding: 'To us, it seems obvious that a written word must represent a sound, whereas to the Chinese it represents an idea ... Even a Japanese, without knowing a word of spoken Chinese, can read out Chinese script in Japanese, just as he could read a row of numerals written by an Englishman' (Russell 1922: 35ff).

Nothing could be further from the truth. If a Japanese can read Chinese, it is because he has studied it and not, as Russell suggests and as is assumed by many, because the Chinese writing system is ideographic – that is, language independent – and can therefore be read in any language. When Russell wrote, Classical Chinese was an essential part of the high-school curriculum in Japan, though the way of reading it differed from Chinese in a peculiar manner. Nowadays, most Japanese would be at a loss if confronted with a Chinese text because, in the meantime, writing conventions in both China and Japan have changed significantly.[1] The thorough influence of Chinese culture on other Asian nations is due primarily to the classical Chinese works' becoming the canon of higher education throughout the region. For almost a thousand years until the nineteenth century, these works were studied in Chinese. Translations came later when the Chinese script was adapted to various languages. But at that point the Chinese language already had secured a significant place in the respective countries for the conduct of matters of government, culture and scholarship.

China's cultural influence is witnessed by large amounts of loan words in all neighboring languages. The Chinese script, however, has extended only eastward, not westward. This is a noteworthy fact because some of the languages spoken to the south-west of China (such as the Tibeto-Burman languages) are members of the same language family as Chinese, yet they came to be written with scripts related to the Devanagari system of Sanskrit rather than with the Chinese script. This shows that cultural diffusion is (1) independent of linguistic or ethnic relatedness and (2) not necessarily guided by efficiency and practicality. Linguistic affiliations do not coincide with the spread of culture traits. On linguistic grounds, one would expect that the Chinese writing system could be transferred with greatest ease to the languages most closely related to Chinese. Yet Tibetan, an isolating tone language like Chinese, came to be written with a system unrelated to the Chinese. Even some Chinese dialects in the extreme west adopted Indian-derived systems. On the other hand, the Chinese script spread to the east where it was adapted for languages not genetically related to Chinese: Korean and Japanese (members of the Altaic family) in the north, and Annamese (or Vietnamese), a language that belongs to the Mon-Khmer group of the Austro-Asiatic family, in the south. Thus, on linguistic grounds, the borrowing of Chinese characters for other languages was not the ideal solution, but linguistic criteria for adopting or abandoning a script (or orthography) are more often than not overruled by more powerful sociopolitical factors.

The structural differences between Chinese and these languages made adjustments necessary and led to drastic changes in the way Chinese characters were employed to represent units of language. Korean and Japanese in particular are so different from Chinese that supplementary native writing systems were developed for both languages. Annamese is closer and more similar to Chinese and hence posed fewer difficulties regarding the adaptation of the Chinese writing system. Annamese writing is therefore treated first.

ANNAMESE WRITING

The classification of Annamese has been a matter of debate. According to the majority view, it is a Mon-Khmer language, but some scholars assign it to the Tibeto-Burman group. Typologically, it is a tone language; and as in most tone languages its morphemes are monosyllabic. Every lexical or grammatical morpheme is realized as one syllable. Morpheme boundaries are most important and are clearly marked suprasegmental junctures. These structural features are almost parallel to Chinese, and therefore the adaptation of *Hanzi* created no particular structural difficulties. Yet many centuries passed between the time Chinese writing was first known in Annam and the employment of *Hanzi* for Annamese.

Annam has been part of the Chinese cultural universe since antiquity. For more than 1,000 years North and Central Vietnam was under Chinese suzerainty. The very name of the country is Chinese. It came into existence when, in the third century BC, the Chinese pushed south of Guangdong into the maritime plain which they named *Annam*, or 'Pacification of the South' (Crofts and Buchanan 1958). It was only in 968 AD that the Chinese rulers were replaced by an indigenous dynasty, the Dinh. By that time, Confucianism, Chinese writing and other Chinese achievements had become fixed in Annamese culture. Since administration was under Chinese control, it was natural that China's classical literary language *wényán* became the written language of Annam. From about the beginning of the present era, therefore, Vietnamese literature has been in Chinese and modeled on Chinese style. At the same time an orally transmitted folk-literature evolved. Thus, for a long time, written language and spoken language were not merely stylistically distinct, but were altogether different languages: Classical Chinese and Annamese.

Chũ nôm

Chinese characters were finally adopted for writing Annamese in the fourteenth century; that is to say, *Hanzi* were used as the building blocks for a Vietnamese script, called *chũ nôm*. This script is first attested in a literary document from 1343 AD and continued to be used until the present century. Even though Vietnamese began to be written with Roman letters in the seventeenth century under the influence of Portuguese, French and Italian missionaries, *chũ nôm* was a significant symbol of Vietnamese identity and nationality until this century.

The adaptation of *Hanzi* for writing Annamese followed three strategies, as outlined below.

1 A character is used by virtue of the sound it represents in Chinese, irrespective of its meaning, for a homophonous or phonetically similar Annamese word. For example, the character 行 represented the verb 'to go' which in Southern Chinese was pronounced *hàng*. It was thus adopted for writing the Annamese word *hàng* meaning 'line, order'.

2 A character is used by virtue of the meaning of the word it represents in Chinese, but given an Annamese reading. For example, 打 stands for the Chinese *tǎ*, 'to hit'. The Annamese word for 'to hit' is *dánh* which thus became the new reading of this character.

3 The third principle was the composition of new complex characters non-existent in Chinese. This was done by making use of standard formation procedures which had, however, not been exploited in Chinese. For example, in order to write the word *an*, 'to eat', the Annamese formed the character 咹 consisting of 安, which in Southern Chinese pronunciation is read *an*, and 口, the character for 'mouth'.

The three strategies of using Chinese characters for writing Annamese are summarized in figure 7.1.

Chũ nôm was gradually superseded by an alphabetic orthography which, however, was declared the official Vietnamese script only in 1910. Owing to the tonal features of the language, the Vietnamese alphabet makes use of many diacritics (cf. chapter 3, pp. 44f).

		Chinese		Annamese	
1	sound	*hàng*	行	*hàng*	
	meaning	'to go'		'line, order'	
2	meaning	'to hit'	打	'to hit'	
	sound	*tǎ*		*dánh*	
3	sound	*an*		classifier	phonetic
		安		口	安
	new character			唉	
	meaning			'to eat'	

7.1 Three strategies of employing Hanzi *for writing Annamese*

KOREAN WRITING

Like the Annamese the Koreans learned to write from the Chinese, and like them they used *wényán* as the written language for many centuries before they began to write their own language. The language of Silla, from which modern Korean descends, differs much more drastically from Chinese than Annamese, and therefore the adaptation of Chinese characters was more difficult. Old Korean (that is, the language that was spoken on the Korean peninsula in the first millennium AD) is not well attested. Scholars are thus uncertain and cannot agree about the pre-history of the Korean language (Martin 1975). Many believe it belongs to the Altaic languages, whereas others assume a common origin for Korean and Japanese. Grammatically Korean and Japanese are very similar, but these similarities do not allow a definitive judgement on their genetic relationship.

In the present context it is more important to note that certain grammatical features of Korean make the Chinese writing system extremely ill suited for it. It is (1) an agglutinative language where grammatical information is expressed by postpositions and postposed particles, which means that (2) words are usually polysyllabic, consisting of a content morpheme and one or more grammatical morphemes. As Chinese characters usually have lexical meanings, the grammatical morphemes of Korean were difficult to represent with Chinese characters, a problem not unlike that of writing Akkadian with Sumerian logograms. In Chinese, every character is associated with a meaning and a syllable. This tripartite structural unit had to be dissociated in order to write linguistic units without lexical meaning.

When in the seventh century AD the Koreans began to compile historical records, they wrote in Chinese, but they wanted to write about Korean things, people and places. Once again proper names thus played a crucial role for the development of writing, since they led to the first attempts of writing Korean with *Hanzi*, or *Hanja*, as Chinese characters are called in Korean. The Koreans used two adaptation strategies for writing their language with Chinese characters which are basically the same as the sound-based and meaning-based strategies described above for Annamese.

1 A character was used to represent a syllable irrespective of its meaning in Chinese. For example, Chinese 古 (*kŭ*), 'old', was used to write the Korean syllable, *ku*. This strategy is the same as the Chinese method of writing foreign proper names.
2 A character is used to represent a Korean word which corresponds to the Chinese word for which the character was used in the first place. For example, 水 stands for 'water' in Chinese. In Korean this *Hanja* was thus given the reading *mər*, 'water', while the Chinese word is *shŭi*. This strategy is a genuine Korean invention which was replicated later on a much larger scale by the Japanese.

Ido

The next step in using Chinese characters for Korean was to write *Hanja* in Korean word order. This resulted in Chinese being transformed into the language of Silla. Only one character was used in a special way: 之 became a grammatical indicator for verb endings. Gradually the use of *Hanja* in Korean word order developed into a written language of its own right known as 吏道, *Ido*, or 吏文, *Imun*, which became the official script of the chanceries. *Ido* was systematized at the end of the seventh century by Solch'ong, a scholar in the service of King Sin-mun. It was a mixed system with both pleremic and cenemic elements. A special set of characters was selected for their syllabic values and used for grammatical morphemes. Lexical morphemes, many of which were of Chinese origin, were written with *Hanja* in the usual manner. Since the characters used for writing grammatical morphemes were not graphically distinct from the others, a rather cumbersome system resulted whose complexity was further aggravated as the number of characters used as syllabic signs increased. It was only much later, probably in the thirteenth and fourteenth centuries, that some of the grammatical morpheme characters were simplified and thus became graphically recognizable. Some of the simplifications were as follows:

$$\text{压} \rightarrow \text{厂} ; \text{ 伊} \rightarrow \text{亻}; \text{ 尼} \rightarrow \text{匕} ; \text{ 羅} \rightarrow \text{丿}$$

These characters were called *Kugyol*. Exact dating of their origin is not possible, but it seems that they were first developed as an auxiliary system for indicating readings in Classical Chinese scripts: that is, as a means enabling the Koreans to read Confucian and other classical texts in their own language.

A further method of using *Hanja* is distinguished by some scholars, while others treat it as a variety of *Ido* used during the ninth and tenth centuries. Known as *Hangch'al*, this method is based on the proper name writing of *Ido* and makes use of two principles: (1) lexical stems are written with *Hanja* to be read in Korean (in accordance with the meaning-based adaptation strategy); and (2) suffixes and all other grammatical morphemes are written with *Hanja* to be read in Sino-Korean (in accordance with the sound-based adaptation strategy). A proper understanding of the text was necessary for determining the correct reading of characters.

Another problem with this system was that the syllable structure of Korean is much more complex than that of Chinese. The grammatical morphemes could not, therefore, be represented very well with *Hanja* adapted in accordance with the sound-based strategy. In sum, it can be said that writing Korean with Chinese characters was a rather laborious exercise resulting in a highly artificial written language which, as long as it existed, never really rivalled classical Chinese, let alone replaced it.

Han'gul

Eventually the Koreans came to express their dissatisfaction with this state of affairs:

While there is a great difference between the Korean language and the Chinese, there are no proper letters that the Korean people can use in writing their language and expressing their thoughts. From the time of the Silla Dynasty a system of writing known as I-du has been used in the daily life of ordinary people as well as in Government business. But it is too complicated, imperfect, and inconvenient a system for the Koreans to use freely in expressing their own ideas and thinking, because too many Chinese characters are involved in it. Koreans are in great need of their own letters with which they can write the Korean language. (Lee 1970)

This pronouncement was made by King Sejong who is credited with providing his people with what is probably the most remarkable writing system ever invented. It is a unique alphabet called *Han'gul*, which was promulgated in a Royal Rescript under the title *Hun Min Jong Um* (訓民正音), 'the correct sounds for instructing the people', issued in 1446 out of 'pity with the common people' who were unable to express themselves properly in *Ido*. In this document the new script is explained and philosophically justified, which makes *Han'gul* a very special case because, rather than being developed in a piecemeal way, it is the product of deliberate, linguistically informed planning (Ledyard 1966). A philosophical justification of the new script was necessary because the members of the educated elite were naturally opposed to change. Although it was hard to disagree with the assessment that 'Chinese characters fit the Korean language like an angular handle fits a round hole' (Lee 1970), a practical justification for departing from established practice was not enough, as nothing could command respect in Korea at that time unless it was dignified by Chinese origin. Thus in the Royal Rescript the elements of the new script were shown to be structurally isomorphic with basic metaphysical categories of Chinese philosophy which came in sets of five, such as 'North', 'South', 'East', 'West' and 'Center', or 'Water', 'Fire', 'Wood', 'Metal' and 'Clay'. The basic vowels were shown to be also five: ㅗ /o/, ㅜ /u/, ㅏ /a/, ㅓ /ə/ and ㅣ /i/. As matter was composed from the basic elements, it was argued, all other vowels were representable in terms of the five basic vowels.[2]

In the present context, more interesting than the philosophical justification of *Han'gul* is the sophistication of its linguistic motivation. One of the extraordinary features of this system is the systematic relationship that holds between the outer form and the inner form of its basic elements. *Han'gul* characters were designed to depict the actual places of articulation of the phonemes they represented. For example, the symbol ㅋ for /k/ pictures the tongue touching the palate. Systematic relationships between elements of the phonological system are thus mapped by graphical relationships between the respective signs. The system consists of 28 basic signs; 24 of them are used today. The 28 original characters and the 24 in contemporary use are given in figures 7.2 and 7.3, respectively.

The basic signs do not suffice to write all phonemes of the Korean language; however, the linguists who devised the system realized that

Consonants	ㄱ	ㅋ	ㆁ	ㄷ	ㅌ	ㄴ	ㄹ	ㅂ ㅍ
	k·g	k	ŋ	t·d	t	n	r.l	p,b p
	ㅁ	ㅈ	ㅊ	ㅅ	ㅿ	ㆆ	ㆁ	ㅇ
	m	dʒ	tʃ	s ʜs	z, ʒ	ʔ	h	

Vowels	·	—	ㅣ	ㅗ	ㅏ	ㅜ	ㅓ	ㅛ
	ʌ	ɯ	i	o	a	u	ʌ	jo
	ㅑ	ㅠ	ㅕ					
	ja	ju	jʌ					

7.2 *The original* Han'gul *letters*

Consonants (14)	name	ㄱ kijʌk'	ㄴ niɯn	ㄷ tigɯt'	ㄹ riɯl	ㅁ miɯm	ㅂ piɯp'	ㅅ shiot'
	sound	k·g	n,ɲ	t·d	l,r	m	p·b	s,ʜs
	name	ㅇ iɯŋ	ㅈ dʒiɯt'	ㅊ ʧiɯt'	ㅋ kiɯk	ㅌ tiɯk	ㅍ piɯp	ㅎ hiɯt'
	sound		dʒ	ʧ	k	t	p	h

Vowels (10)	name sound	ㅏ a	ㅑ ja	ㅓ ə	ㅕ jə	ㅗ o	ㅛ jo
	name sound	ㅜ u	ㅠ ju	ㅡ ɯ	ㅣ i		

7.3 *The 24* Han'gul *characters presently in use*

certain phonemes are phonetically related to others. They also considered some phonemes more basic than others and therefore created signs for the latter by adding diacritics to the ones used for the former. Moreover, these diacritics were applied in a highly systematic way. For instance, all aspirated consonants are represented by adding a bar to the sign of the respective non-aspirated consonants. Palatalization is likewise indicated by an additional stroke. Diphthongs, too, are represented by adding the same element in all cases to basic vowel signs. The relationship between simple and complex signs that characterizes the *Han'gul* system can best be described as the relation of diacritics to a base. Of all systems that were actually invented as writing systems, the Korean script comes closest to treating distinctive features as the basic units of representation. It is quite understandable and justified, therefore, that the Royal Rescript of 1446 emphasizes the system's minuteness and flexibility in representing sounds: 'Hangul is able to make a clear distinction between surd and sonant, and to record music and song. It is good for any practical use, and even the sound of the wind, the chirp of birds, the crowing of cocks, and the barking of dogs can be exactly described with it' (Lee 1970).

As a result of the depth of its underlying phonological analysis, *Han'gul* has been called 'the most rational of all writing systems' (Watanabe and Suzuki 1981: 137), and while the system does not represent a phonological feature analysis of present-day Korean, the depth of the analysis is there (cf. Sampson 1985: 143). In principle, it is possible to write *Han'gul* in linear order, but the system's designers must have been aware that breaking down the continuum of linguistic sounds into phonetic features, while being useful for its accurate written representation, is inconvenient for reading. They also recognized the syllable as an important unit of speech. Instead of writing the basic signs in linear succession, as is commonly done in alphabetic scripts, they are stacked together to form units that can be perceived as representing syllables. These syllabic units were designed to conform with the square frame of Chinese characters (Kôno 1969). Although the composite parts of the syllabic frames are easily distinguishable, it is the syllable that is given greatest prominence as a written unit. Figure 7.4 illustrates how vowel and consonant signs are combined to form syllable blocks.

Every syllabic frame is constructed in a different way according to the shapes of the *Han'gul* letters. In every frame consonant and vowel elements are united to form a syllable. Theoretically, vowels could stand

Vowels → Consonants ↓		ㅏ	ㅑ	ㅓ	ㅕ	ㅗ	ㅛ	ㅜ	ㅠ	ㅡ	ㅣ
		a	ya	eo	yeo	o	yo	u	yu	eu	i
ㄱ	g(k)	가	갸	거	겨	고	교	구	규	그	기
ㄴ	n	나	냐	너	녀	노	뇨	누	뉴	느	니
ㄷ	d	다	댜	더	뎌	도	됴	두	듀	드	디
ㄹ	r(l)	라	랴	러	려	로	료	루	류	르	리
ㅁ	m	마	먀	머	며	모	묘	무	뮤	므	미
ㅂ	b	바	뱌	버	벼	보	뵤	부	뷰	브	비
ㅅ	s	사	샤	서	셔	소	쇼	수	슈	스	시
ㅇ	※	아	야	어	여	오	요	우	유	으	이
ㅈ	j	자	쟈	저	져	조	죠	주	쥬	즈	지
ㅊ	ch	차	챠	처	쳐	초	쵸	추	츄	츠	치
ㅋ	k	카	캬	커	켜	코	쿄	쿠	큐	크	키
ㅌ	t	타	탸	터	텨	토	툐	투	튜	트	티
ㅍ	p	파	퍄	퍼	펴	포	표	푸	퓨	프	피
ㅎ	h	하	햐	허	혀	호	효	후	휴	흐	히

7.4 The basic combinations of vowels and consonants in the Korean alphabet (adapted from Ministry of Education 1983, Education in Korea)

by themselves, but that would create a rather uneven and irregular outer appearance. For the sake of uniformity the consonant sign for /j/, namely ㅇ, is therefore used in conjunction with vowel signs to represent syllables without consonants. In syllable final position, this sign stands for a velar nasal.

As for the facility of learning *Han'gul*, its makers knew that they had succeeded in creating a truly demotic script which 'an intelligent person can understand before the morning is over. And even the thick-headed can master it in ten days' (Lee 1970). This is an obvious advantage over Chinese. *Han'gul* is, indeed, so consistent and systematically beautiful with respect to outer and inner form that its superiority over the cumbersome *Ido* system must have been evident to everyone. Yet the Koreans continued to use Chinese, both in the form of the written language *wényán* and in their new script. In *Han'gul* texts Chinese loan words are written with Chinese characters to be read in Sino-Korean. Since Chinese loan words form a substantial part of the Korean vocabulary, Korean texts are interspersed with Chinese characters. Native Korean words are usually written with *Han'gul*, however. Hence there are almost no native readings of Chinese characters, a feature characteristic of the use of *Hanzi* in Japan. The Democratic People's Republic of Korea (DPRK) has abolished the use of Chinese characters after the division of the country, while they continue to be used in South Korea. Like Latin- or Greek-based loan words in Western languages, Chinese loan words, or rather the ability to write Chinese loan words with *Hanzi*, are felt to be indicative of a writer's erudition and refinement. This is still so in the Republic of Korea, as it is in Japan. However, thanks to the availability of *Han'gul*, Chinese characters no longer function as a filter making the written language the prerogative of the educated elite.

JAPANESE WRITING

Like the Koreans, and with their assistance, the Japanese first acquired writing in the guise of Chinese; and like Korean, Japanese is as different from Chinese as any language could be. Hence the development of Japanese writing and written language exhibits obvious parallels with that of Korean yet, under the hands of the Japanese, Chinese characters were transformed to become what is often said to be the most intricate and complicated writing system ever used by a sizeable population. Sansom's description can be quoted here as a representative assessment: 'One hesitates for an epithet to describe a system of writing which is so complex that it needs the aid of another system to explain it. There is no doubt that it provides for some fascinating field of study, but as a practical instrument it is surely without inferiors' (Sansom 1928: 4).

The Chinese system itself pales in comparison with the Japanese when it comes to complexity and seeming impracticality. Indeed, *Kanji*, as Chinese characters are called, are used in a way so different from their models that only tradition justifies their name.

According to traditional Japanese accounts, Chinese writing was brought to Japan by a Korean scholar named Wani. As early Japanese chronicles blend legend and record, no exact dating of this event is possible. Reliable written evidence of Japan's literary history is available from the seventh century AD, at which time the practice of writing Chinese was, however, already firmly established.

The Japanese started out much like the Koreans; that is, they first used the Chinese written language and then gradually began to introduce certain syntactic changes which made possible a Japanese interpretation of the Chinese writing. This style became known as *Kanbun*, literally '*Han* writing' or '*Han* literature' in reference to the Han dynasty. A distinction is made between *Jun-Kanbun*, or genuine Chinese, and *Hentai-Kanbun*, or 'abnormal *Kanbun*', abnormal namely with respect to standard Chinese grammar. Actually, *Hentai-Kanbun* became the normal way of reading and writing Classical Chinese in Japan. It can be described as the Japanese version of Classical Chinese, or as a standard method of reading Classical Chinese in translation.[3] *Kanbun* is a written language which played a crucial role in the formation of Japanese culture, comparable to the position Latin enjoyed until the eighteenth century in Europe as the language of scholarship, religion and certain literary genres. It is thanks to this 'nativization' of Classical Chinese that Chinese characters could function as a means of communication across languages. However, *Kanbun* is a language quite unlike Japanese, and few writers could actually speak it (Sato Habein 1984: 8).

Kanji

The initial steps of adapting *Hanzi* to writing Japanese were similar to the Korean adaptation process, but the eventual result was very different. The Japanese, too, applied the two adaptation strategies described for Annamese and Korean.

1   A Chinese character was used to write a Japanese word whose meaning was the same as that of the Chinese word for which the character was used in Chinese. The character 人, for instance, which in Chinese stands for the word *jen*, 'man', was used to write the Old Japanese word for 'man', *Fitö*. This meaning-based way of using Chinese characters is called *kun* in Japanese philology, which means 'gloss' or 'meaning'. *Kun* itself is one of the many Chinese loan words which were channeled into Japanese through the medium of writing. It was applied in *Kanbun*, the writing style associated with it.

2   The other method of using Chinese characters resulted from the need to write Japanese grammatical elements not present in Chinese.

Like Korean, Japanese is a language of the agglutinative type. Grammatical relations are expressed by suffixes. For these the Japanese chose characters on the basis of the pronunciation of the Chinese morphemes associated with them. For instance, the Old Japanese topic particle *Fa*, modern *wa*, was written with the character for Middle Chinese *puâ*, disregarding the meaning of the Chinese word, 'wave'. This sound-based method of using Chinese characters is conventionally called *Manyôgana* after the earliest literary monument where it was used, the poetic anthology *Manyôshû*, compiled in 759 AD. The poems in this collection are phrased in Japanese syntax. *Manyôgana* can be described as Chinese characters stripped of the meanings with which they are associated in Chinese; thus basically a cenemic system. To illustrate its application beyond grammatical morphemes, in *Manyôgana* the Japanese word *kumo*, 'cloud', was written with the two characters久母, which in Chinese are associated with morphemes meaning 'long time' and 'mother', respectively. The characters were chosen only for their syllabic values, *ku* and *mo*. Using *Hanzi* to write syllables rather than other units of sound suggested itself because they designate syllables in Chinese. As a syllabic script, however, *Manyôgana* is cumbersome and highly redundant, since the average relation between characters and syllables is more than ten to one. In the language of the eighth century there were some 88 syllable types in Japanese, but over 970 Chinese characters were used to write them.

The two adaptation strategies led to the development of two writing styles and, eventually, two written languages, a modified Chinese-style writing called *Kanbun*, 'Chinese writing', and a genuine Japanese style called *Wabun*, 'Japanese writing'. However, as in Korean *Ido*, both uses of Chinese characters also occurred in combination. In particular, the more than 4,500 poems of the *Manyôshû* combine the two methods of writing, a practice which can be regarded as the earliest model of present-day writing conventions (see below).

On *and* kun

As pointed out above, the importation of the art of writing from China, the intense cultural contact with the more highly developed neighbor and the peculiar intertwining of the two languages, Chinese and Japanese, in *Hentai-Kanbun*[4] led to a massive influx of Chinese loan words into Japanese. These words were naturally written as they were in

Chinese and the respective characters were pronounced in Chinese through the filter of Japanese phonology: that is, Sino-Japanese. However, nothing prevented characters used for Chinese loan words from being used in accordance with the meaning-based adaptation strategy too; that is, providing them with a native Japanese pronunciation. Apparently nobody foresaw the consequences of this practice, or, if they did, they could not stop it, because writing developed in an unplanned way. Many characters were indeed adapted in accordance with both strategies, and thus acquired both a Sino-Japanese and a native Japanese reading. These two readings are called *on yomi* and *kun yomi*, respectively, where *on* means 'sound' – that is, the original Chinese sound – and *kun* 'meaning', as explained above. *Yomi* means 'reading'. For example,水, 'water', is read *sui* as the Sino-Japanese loan morpheme (from Chinese *shŭi*) and *mizu* where it stands for the native Japanese word.

As if this were not difficult enough, the Japanese continued to borrow and adapt Chinese characters as time went by. As a result, a single character may have two or three possible *on* readings reflecting the Chinese pronunciations of different periods or regions. The earliest phonetic use of Chinese characters is based on the phonology of northern Chinese until roughly the sixth century and is called *go on*, 'the *go* (= Chinese Wu) pronunciation' (R. A. Miller 1967: 102). Later this pronunciation was superseded by that of the dialect of Ch'ang-an, the capital of the great Tang dynasty (618–907), which is called *kan on*. Finally, there is *tô on*, a somewhat misleading name as it seems to refer to the Tang dynasty, but actually reflects Chinese pronunciation varieties of later periods, including those of Sung (960–1271), Yuan (1271–1368) and Ming (1368–1644). When *kan on* first came into use, there was an effort to make it the official pronunciation of *Kanji*, but *go on*[5] readings were never abolished, chiefly because they were firmly associated with Buddhist usage. Thus, rather than replacing earlier pronunciations, the later ones were added, yielding multiple syllabic values for many characters. An illustration is provided in figure 7.5, which lists three *on* readings and one *kun* reading for some sample characters.

There are not too many characters which have *tô on* readings in addition to *go on* and *kan on*, but quite a number have the latter two. The resulting complexity of a system making use of these multivalued elements is reminiscent of multivalued cuneiform signs of Akkadian writing, in which both the Sumerian superstratum and the Akkadian

	go on	*kan on*	*tô on*	*kun*
京	kyô	kei	kin	miyako
外	gyô	gai	ui	soto
行	gyô	kô	an	kudari
明	myô	mei	min	akashi
和	wa	ka	o	nagi

7.5 On and kun *readings of* Kanji

translation of Sumerian words furnished readings for the signs. Actually, the picture that emerges from figure 7.5 is somewhat simplistic. It should not be taken to suggest that a *Kanji* can only have three *on* readings or that all *Kanji* have only one *kun* reading. Consider for instance 頭, a character with four *on* readings and six *kun* readings.

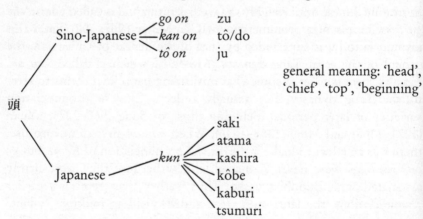

general meaning: 'head', 'chief', 'top', 'beginning'

The obvious question that poses itself in view of this situation is that of how to decide on the correct reading of a given *Kanji*. The answer is that in many cases this is very difficult and to a large extent dependent on the context. Present writing is regulated by convention and greatly facilitated by the combined use of *Kanji* and *Kana* (see below), but old texts are almost impossible to read without a great deal of contextual knowledge and familiarity with usage. While there are certain rules of thumb, they are just that; and hence often violated. For instance, in compounds *Kanji* tend to have Sino-Japanese readings (that is, *on* readings), but compounds consisting of two characters with *kun* readings are also common. Moreover, compounds may combine characters with both kinds of readings.[6] Coyaud (1985) lists seventy-two *on-kun* compounds and ninety-nine *kun-on* compounds. *Kanji* used in combination to form compounds do not unequivocally determine each other's readings: that is, compounding does not disambiguate multiple readings. Coyaud (1985) has counted several hundred bi-*Kanji* compounds with two or more possible readings usually associated with different meanings.

The reverse phenomenon is also rampant: there are scores of homonymous words in Japanese, since several *Kanji* compounds have the same pronunciation (Kindaichi 1957: 83ff). For example, there are more than ten words, *seika*, with unrelated meanings, such as 'result', 'midsummer', 'net price', 'hymn', 'vegetables and fruits', 'confectioner', 'sanctification', 'reputation', 'sacred flame', '(regular) curriculum' and 'essence'. The homophony of these words is not reproduced in writing since there are as many different *Kanji* compounds as there are meanings. Two factors are responsible for the enormous number of homophones in the Chinese loan word layer of the Japanese vocabulary: (1) the loss of phonetic distinctions of Chinese syllables through their adaptation to Japanese phonology, and (2) the tendency to treat *Kanji* rather than syllables as the material of word formation. Table 7.1 shows some examples of the phonological distinctions which were neutralized in Japanese.

TABLE 7.1   *Neutralization of phonetic distinctions in Japanese*

Character	Middle Chinese	Eighteenth-century Sino-Japanese	Japanese meaning
口	/kʼəu/	/ko:/	mouth
広	/kua/	/ko:/	wide
甲	/kap/	/ko:/	armor
交	/kau/	/ko:/	associate with
劫	/kïap/	/ko:/	threat

The problem of homonyms has often been said to be a characteristic feature of Chinese. As Coyaud (1985) has clearly demonstrated, it is a much more serious problem in Japanese. Notice, however, that in Japanese it is a Chinese heritage since it is restricted, by and large, to Sino-Japanese words (Hayashi 1982). For purposes of clarification, homophonous Sino-Japanese words can usually be paraphrased by Japanese (near) synonyms. From the point of view of the Chinese character this means that it is possible to fall back on the *kun* reading in order to explain the *on* reading. To illustrate the specific link that *Kanji* form between the two strata of the Japanese vocabulary, imagine that *sphygmomanometer* and *blood pressure meter* were both written with the same characters 血圧計 which could be pronounced in either way. Usually character compound words are read with Sino-Japanese pronunciation. However, someone who lacks sufficient knowledge of Sino-Japanese can still read them with the often more familiar Japanese pronunciation.

Given this kind of relationship between the spoken and the written language, it is hardly surprising that, to a greater extent even than in the West, the latter is commonly considered to be the primary form of language rather than a mere rendition of speech. The long-standing association of multiple readings with one written sign poses interesting questions about the status of spoken and written units in Japanese and their mutual relationships. Morioka (1968) has argued that *Kanji* represent morphemes in such a way that their Sino-Japanese and Japanese readings are to be regarded as allomorphs. This suggestion is hard to reconcile with the common notion of 'allomorph' because the Japanese and Sino-Japanese readings of any given *Kanji* lack phonetic similarity since they are of different origin. However, even if the terminological choice is not quite satisfactory, it cannot be denied that Chinese characters have acquired a unique and very peculiar function in Japanese in letting synonymous or semantically closely related words of two complementary strata of the lexicon appear as different realizations of an underlying graphic form.[7]

Ateji

Two special uses of *Kanji* remain to be mentioned: (1) the so-called *Ateji* or deviant characters, and (2) their use for writing non-Chinese loan words. *Ateji* are characters that are assigned irregular readings and meanings, often in a playful, rebus-like fashion. For example, the word *hiniku*, 'sarcasm', is written with the characters of 'skin' (皮) *hi* and 'meat' (肉) *niku*. The practice of writing western loan words with *Kanji* is particularly common in literary works. Examples are *seminario* (神学校) 'seminary' and *daiyamondo* (金剛石) 'diamond' which were borrowed from Portuguese and English, respectively.

Kokuji

Finally, it should not be left unnoted that, like the Annamese and the Koreans, the Japanese have created quite a few *Kanji* of their own. Alexander (1951) provides a list of almost 250 of these *Kokuji* 'domestic signs'. Although one should expect that they have only *kun-*, or Japanese, readings but no *on-*, or Sino-Japanese, readings, some *Kokuji* do have *on-*readings. Some of the 'made-in-Japan' characters have been borrowed in Chinese and Korean, which once again demonstrates that in the world of *Hanzi* literacy both word formation and lexical borrowing are heavily dependent on, and mediated by, the written language unit.

Kana

The complexities of writing Japanese with Chinese characters are amazing; that much should have become obvious from what has already been said. That they have survived until the present is all the more astonishing – for those, at least, who believe in efficiency and simplicity – as the Japanese for the past thousand years have had at their disposal a simple and efficient syllabic writing system. Actually, two isomorphic syllabaries came into existence, now called *Katakana* and *Hiragana*. They consist of 48 syllable signs each which, together with a few diacritic devices, provide a complete and workable cenemic notation for the Japanese language.

Katakana evolved in the ninth century from auxiliary marks used, as it were, as *matres lectionis* (cf. chapter 8, pp. 146–9) or 'reading aids' by Buddhist monks studying Chinese texts. All of these marks were derived from *Manyôgana*: that is, Chinese characters adapted to Japanese in accordance with the sound-based strategy (figure 7.6). Thus from their inception *Katakana* were used in conjunction with, and as auxiliary signs for, Chinese characters.

so se su si sa ko ke ku ki ka o e u i a

ho he hu hi ha no ne nu ni na to te tu ti ta

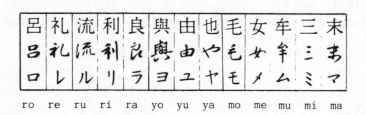

ro re ru ri ra yo yu ya mo me mu mi ma

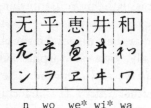

n wo we* wi* wa

* no longer in use

7.6 Katakana *and the Chinese characters from which they are derived*

Hiragana differ from *Katakana* only with respect to the shape of the signs. This system was first called *onnade*, 'women's hand', because it was used by women. Like *Katakana*, it is based on *Manyôgana*; but unlike the former they were drawn from the simplified and stylized

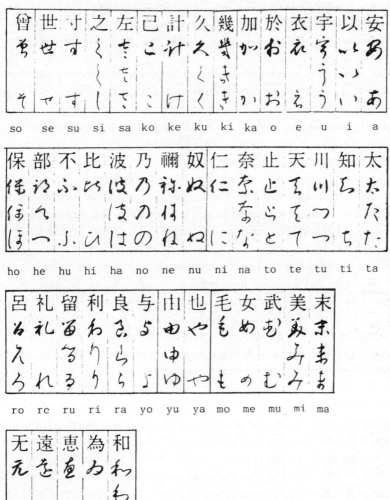

7.7 Hiragana *and the Chinese characters from which they are derived*

Sôgana, the cursive forms of *Manyôgana* (figure 7.7). The creation of *Hiragana* was perhaps more important for the development of writing in Japan than that of *Katakana*, because they came to be used without Chinese characters and were thus instrumental for establishing the

Japanese written language *Wabun*. Many of the greatest poetic works of the Heian period were written in *Hiragana* by women. Men, however, continued to cultivate Chinese characters and *Kanbun* as status symbols.

The *Kana* syllabaries are usually arranged in five horizontal vowel rows and ten vertical consonant columns. The order of the consonants, *k*, *s*, *t*, *n*, *h*, *m*, *y*, *r* and *w*, bears witness to the influence of an Indic-inspired phonological analysis, as it is by and large the same as that of all Indic scripts (R. A. Miller 1967: 128). The Indic influence was, of course, mediated through the study of Buddhism.

The orthographic conventions for using the syllabaries have changed over the centuries since the Heian period, and have become really standardized only in modern times. They concern two different aspects of usage: (1) the representation of sounds, and (2) the combination of *Kana* with *Kanji*.

Sound changes have led to the erosion of some phonetic distinctions. For example, [w] became lost before vowels except [a] and [o], [d] changed to [dž] before [i] and [u]. Therefore sign–sound correspondences had to be adjusted periodically. Other areas of *Kana* orthography that called for explicit rules are the representation of long syllables and palatalized syllables. Each *Kana* sign stands for a mora: that is, a short syllable. Syllables with long vowels count as two moras and are represented by two *Kana*. Thus conventions had to be established for what *Kana* signs to use for indicating vowel length; again, phonological convergences made this an important issue. As for palatalized syllables, no separate *Kana* signs exist, so the signs for *ki*, *si*, *ni*, *hi*, *mi* and *ri* are used in conjunction with those of the *y*-column. What would have to be transcribed bisyllabically, for example, as [ni-ya] according to the usual values of the *Kana* signs thus actually stands for the single syllable [nja] or [ña].

As regards the use of *Kana* and *Kanji* in combination, the auxiliary use of *Katakana* led to the practice of writing content morphemes with Chinese characters, and grammatical morphemes and function words with *Kana*. Until the second half of the nineteenth century mostly *Katakana* were used in this function, but in contemporary usage they have been replaced by *Hiragana*. Nowadays *Katakana* are used chiefly to write non-Chinese loan words, onomatopoeic words and for emphasis. The functional specification of *Kanji* for lexical stems and *Hiragana* for function words and grammatical endings and particles is a simple and reasonable principle, but it is not applied consistently. There are both vowel-stem verbs and consonant-stem verbs in Japanese. Assuming that lexical stems are written with *Kanji*, the representation of the former follows this principle, but the latter do not because the consonant that actually belongs to the stem is also represented in the first *Kana* sign representing the ending. For example, *kaku*, 'to write', is a consonant-stem verb. The ending here is *-u* rather than *-ku*, yet the syllabic sign used for the ending is that for the syllable *ku*.

The combination of *Kana* and *Kanji* in running text characteristic of contemporary usage provides the reader with some grammatical structure, as lexical and grammatical morphemes are graphically distinguished, and hence facilitates the reading process. It also helps to disambiguate multivalued *Kanji*. Enough difficulties remain, however, to make present Japanese writing extravagant and a formidable task to learn and master. Maybe the clearest indication of this can be seen in yet another way of using *Kana*: they are printed in smaller type alongside or above unfamiliar Chinese characters that are not among the 2,000 *Jôyô Kanji* officially designated for current use or characters that are given non-standard readings.

Summing up the use of Chinese characters for writing Japanese, it is no exaggeration to say that without them the Japanese language would not be what it is. Japanese is undoubtedly one of the prime examples of a language having been thoroughly influenced by the way it came to be written. For centuries language contact with Chinese was intense, but in the absence of a common land border this contact was largely mediated through writing. Its sediment are the many Sino-Japanese loan words, now constituting (according to some estimates) more than 50 per cent of the Japanese vocabulary, which came into existence primarily in the written language. Through the adoption of *Hanzi* the Japanese language entered into a relation of mutual borrowing with Chinese that is unique in the history of language and can best be described as a written *Sprachbund*.

SOME PRACTICAL ISSUES

Chinese characters are the building blocks of the only non-alphabetic writing systems about whose use, storage and functioning under both normal and pathological conditions a sizeable body of research has been carried out, allowing comparisons with alphabetic scripts. Is is therefore worthwhile discussing, briefly, some of the prominent issues of this research.

The most important general question is that of whether the structural peculiarities that distinguish *Hanzi* from linearized phonemic representations of language have any implications for differences with respect to memory and processing mechanisms. For example, Park and Arbuckle (1977) examined the memory of Korean subjects for words written in Chinese characters and *Han'gul*, finding that words presented in the former were remembered better than words presented in the latter. These findings suggest that there is indeed an intrinsic difference with respect to the processing mode of the two scripts in question.

Another avenue of approach has been pursued by Tzeng and his collaborators (Tzeng et al. 1977, 1979) who have investigated the question whether and to what extent the reading of Chinese characters involves phonological mediation through speech recoding. They found that while lexical access is possible directly from visual input, phonetic recoding is needed for the working memory stage, which led them to the conclusion that there are systematic differences between the processing of Chinese characters and alphabetically written words, but that a dichotomy between the presence and the absence of phonetic recoding may be too simplistic to explain these differences.

Makita (1968) was among the first to report on the rarity of reading disabilities in Japanese children as compared with their alphabetized Western peers, again suggesting that the structural differences between alphabetic writing systems on the one hand, and syllabic and morphographic systems on the other, have functional correlates in differing processing mechanisms. Since the early 1970s many experiments have been carried out to investigate the hypothesis that different writing systems rely on different functions of the brain and/or are localized in different parts of the brain. Most remarkable in this regard is Sasanuma's work on Japanese aphasic and alexic patients (see Sasanuma 1975).

A conspicuous symptom of Japanese alexic patients is the dissociation of *Kanji* and *Kana*. This important discovery is the most interesting evidence to date of neurological differences associated with different writing systems; however, its explanation has proved to be a great challenge because there are various and different patterns of dissociation. Some patients lose *Kana* while retaining *Kanji*; for others it is the reverse. Loss and preservation of both *Kanji* and *Kana* can be unevenly distributed among productive, receptive, and mnemonic skills. Recovery can proceed at an uneven rate for the two kinds of characters; both *Kanji* and *Kana* can be read with and without understanding. Obviously, therefore, the dissociation of *Kanji* and *Kana* is in itself a complex symptom which does not offer itself readily to explanation.

Many experiments have been carried out by presenting sets of words written in *Kanji* or *Kana* to patients with different types and locations of brain damage in order to find out whether preferences for *Kanji* or *Kana* can be localized.[8] As yet it is not at all clear how the results of such experiments are to be interpreted; but it is clear that the differences between morpheme-based writing systems and sound-based writing systems are not just superficial differences of coding, but relate to neuropsychological differences concerning the storage and processing of written language units. Research in this general area opens up new and promising perspectives for a better understanding that, for literate speech communities and literate individuals, scripts are a part of the overall system of the language for which they are used rather than being mere mapping devices, and have a powerful effect on the formation of language units and on the linguistic consciousness of their users.

NOTES

1 See below and, for the recent Chinese writing reform, chapter 13.
2 Ong (1977) has pointed out that a writing system deeply affects what he calls the noetic process, the shaping, storage, retrieving and communication of knowledge. The philosophical justification of *Han'gul* exemplifies the pertinence of this observation, illustrating as it does that a writing system can be linked with the rest of a culture, its philosophical outlook and cosmological orientation. Similarly Becker (1983), in reporting on his experience of learning the Burmese script, remarks that a writing system is a powerful mode of analysis, a basic mnemonic framework, a pattern that connects the root metaphors of a culture; and that going from one literacy to another, like going from orality to literacy, is not merely a technological step, but a major break in the pattern of learning and cognition.
3 The reading of *Hentai-Kanbun* texts is aided by auxiliary marks providing the Japanese reader with clues which show how to rearrange the Chinese word order to correspond to Japanese. Signs used for this purpose include number signs, characters for 'upper', 'middle' and 'lower', and characters for 'heaven', 'earth' and 'man'. They are written on the left side of the columns of

running text indicating sequential transpositions on successive levels of embedding. In short sentences only the linear order needs to be changed, while complex sentences may require transpositions on several levels.

4 The extent of the language contact triggered by writing can be appreciated if we consider R. A. Miller's (1967: 131) remark that 'it can accurately be said of the Heian and later periods that people often did not really know what language they were writing in, Chinese or Japanese; and we are often in no better position to make a judgment on the question when we study some of the documents they produced.'

5 There are a number of systematic relationships between *go on* and *kan on* readings. For instance, initial /m/ in *go on* became /b/ in *kan on*; *go on* initial /n/ became /d/ or /j/ in *kan on*; final /ki/ in *go on* became /ku/ in many *kan on* words. For a detailed description of the phonological changes underlying the shift from *go on* to *kan on* in Chinese and their reflections in Japanese see R. A. Miller (1967: 105ff).

6 The words so written are, obviously, hybrids consisting of Sino-Japanese and Japanese morphemes. In present-day Japanese such hybrids constitute a substantial part of the lexicon ranging for different kinds of texts between 5 and 18 per cent (Miyajima 1977).

7 Suzuki (1977: 416) may be going a little bit far when he informs his Western reader that 'in their speech the Japanese are heavily dependent on the graphic image of the word that is stored in their mind. This means that unless the Japanese know how the word is written it is often difficult for them to understand what is said.' However, given that most homophones are Sino-Japanese and that Sino-Japanese words form the high or bookish stratum of the vocabulary, his argument is not quite as strange as it would seem.

8 Paradis et al. (1985) provide an excellent overview which makes the experimental and clinical research on differences between *Kanji* and *Kana*, most of which is published in Japanese, available to the Western reader.

8

Semitic Writing: Syllables or Consonants?

Semitic languages are spoken in western Asia. The group of languages so classified comprises the great literary languages: Akkadian, Aramaic, Hebrew, Syriac, Arabic and Ethiopic, as well as several other languages of the Middle East. They are characterized by many similarities and common elements in their phonology, morphology, lexicon and syntax. The grouping of the Semitic languages and their scripts is usually based on their geographic distribution: the eastern group (sometimes also referred to as north-eastern) in Mesopotamia, the northern (or north-western) group in Syria and Palestine, and the southern group in Arabia and Ethiopia. These last two groups are often collectively referred to as West Semitic (Driver 1976).

The writing of the languages of the eastern group, of which Akkadian is the most important member, is at the heart of the cuneiform tradition discussed in chapter 5. It always remained a very involved system, making use of both cenemic syllable signs and pleremic word signs and determinatives. Similarly the Egyptian system, despite decisive advances in the direction of a cenemic system, never discarded word signs or determinatives. Both cuneiform and the Egyptian hieroglyphics came to the threshold of a purely cenemic system. However, the final step was taken neither in Egypt nor in Mesopotamia, but in the region between these ancient centers of writing which extends from the Sinai peninsula to northern Syria. In this chapter, the term Semitic writing is used to refer to systems that were developed in this western region rather than to the cuneiform writing of eastern Semitic languages.[1]

It is now generally agreed that the first writing system free of determinatives and logographic signs which could easily be transferred from one
language to another was used by the Phoenicians in northern Syria
where it was created in the second half of the second millennium. However, the transitory steps leading from logographic and syllabic writing
to phonemic writing are not so well understood. This is due to the confusing diversity of scripts that came into existence then in the eastern
Mediterranean and to the fact that certain archeological findings have
defied unequivocal interpretation.

As Diringer (1968: 146) has pointed out, already the literati of classical
Greece and Rome adhered to conflicting theories about the origin of
alphabetic writing, attributing it variously to each of the most ancient
literary cultures: Egypt and Assur; the Hebrews or the Phoenicians (that
is, western Semitic peoples living in between these centers); and also to
Mycenae or Crete. The fact that all of these various hypotheses were
seriously discussed highlights an important aspect of the region in-
habited by the western Semitic peoples: it was at the international cross-
roads of influences from powerful and flourishing adjacent cultures. The
trading ports at the eastern Mediterranean coast were in contact with
Egypt, Crete, the Aegean islands, Anatolia and also with peoples further
east. The ensuing cultural multiplicity, the many languages that came
into contact with each other, as well as the knowledge of the existence of
different writing systems such as Egyptian, Assyrian and Hittite must
have created the ideal conditions for experimenting with new possibilities and simplifications.[2] The many new forms of writing that evolved in
Syria, Palestine and Sinai bear witness to the prolific cultural development of this region in the second millennium. Two places of special
interest are Byblos on the Syrian coast and Ugarit further to the north.
Both cities attracted a great deal of attention because after their
discovery they were considered for some time to be possible birth places
of Old Semitic writing, the former being the excavation site of inscriptions testifying to Egyptian influence, and the latter the place where the
cuneiform alphabet was discovered. Both finds date from the middle of
the second millennium. While constituting important steps in the
development of Semitic writing, the scripts of Byblos and Ugarit both
present problems which are still waiting for a solution.

The Ugaritic script was deciphered shortly after its discovery in 1929 (Segert 1983),[3] making available a host of excavated documents of various kinds. None of these, however, provided any clues as to how the Ugaritic system came into existence. Diringer (1968: 150ff) gives expression to the now commonly accepted view that its creators borrowed the idea for consonant writing from an already existing West Semitic alphabet,[4] while they devised letters consisting of wedge-shaped elements as they were used to writing on clay. Thus the Ugaritic alphabet, which consists of twenty-seven consonant letters and three alephs for the glottal stop preceding /a/, /i/ and /u/, offers little by way of an explanation for the origin of Old Semitic consonant writing.

Byblos was one of the most ancient cultural centers of the Phoenicians. Intensive contacts with Egypt were attested in the third millennium. On historical grounds it is, therefore, a plausible assumption that the script of the Byblos inscriptions originated under Egyptian influence. The system consists of at least 114 signs and is hence thought to be a syllabary.[5] Graphical similarities suggest that more than twenty signs have been borrowed from the Egyptian hieroglyphic script, but the readability of the Byblos script is still a matter of dispute. Dhorme (1948), one of the decipherers of Ugaritic, claims to have deciphered the script which he regards as a 'plethoric' syllabary: that is, a system whereby different signs have the same syllabic value (Diringer 1968: 115). The language of the Byblos inscriptions, according to Dhorme, is Phoenician. However, Dhorme's purported decipherment is not universally accepted among Semitic scholars. Instead, his claims have met with reactions ranging from outright rejection (Sobelman 1961) to cautious optimism (Friedrich 1966) at best.

Another important, but no less problematic, potential key to understanding the origin of Old Semitic consonant writing is the Proto-Sinaitic script which was discovered on the Sinai peninsula in 1904. On the basis of archeological evidence, the inscriptions were dated to the fifteenth century. The question that the discovery of this script raised was whether it could possibly be the missing link between the beginning of consonant phoneme representation in Egyptian hieroglyphic writing and its systematic completion in Semitic writing. The close geographic proximity of the Sinai to Egypt made such a solution historically plausible and hence very attractive.

As early as 1916, the British Egyptologist Gardiner identified a recurrent group of signs as the name of the Canaanite goddess Ba'alat and thus provided support for the assumption that the language of the Sinaitic inscriptions is Semitic. Gardiner's approach was quite ingenious. On the basis of graphical similarities, he paired Proto-Sinaitic signs with Egyptian hieroglyphs, but rather than assuming that the former had the same sound value as their presumptive Egyptian models, he suggested that their sound value was derived by means of the acrophonic principle[6] from the Semitic translations of the Egyptian word signs. This means that the initial consonant of the Semitic translation equivalent of a given hieroglyph would determine the sound value of the Sinaitic sign. For example, Gardiner assumed that the hieroglyph ⊂⊃ *p-r* 'house' was the model of the Sinaitic sign ▭ or ▢. As the Semitic word for 'house' is *bait* or *bet*, its sound value would thus be *b*. The important point here is the semantic correspondence between the meaning of the Egyptian glyph and the meaning of the name of the Semitic letter: *bet*, the second letter of the Semitic alphabet, means 'house'. Further, the Egyptian glyph ⬭ *j-r-t* 'eye' was matched with the Sinaitic sign ⊃. Since the Semitic word for 'eye' is *'ain*, this sign was assigned the sound value '. This approach led Gardiner to the hypothesis that the group of signs represented in figure 8.1 was to be interpreted as the consonant skeleton *b-'-l-t* of the above mentioned name of the goddess Ba'alat.

Gardiner's suggestion was welcomed enthusiastically by other scholars (cf. Friedrich 1966: 60), and some are still optimistic that a solution along the lines of his reasoning will eventually be found (W. F. Albright 1966). However, little progress has been made since Gardiner's first success and, unless future excavations yield more data, the prospects for the decipherment of the Proto-Sinaitic script are slim. Given the scarcity of the available documents and the present state of our knowledge about them, Diringer's assessment seems realistic. He writes: 'The early Sinaitic writing cannot be regarded as the great mother-alphabet of all the alphabetic scripts, and does not represent "the

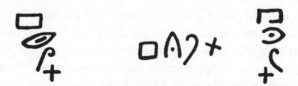

8.1 *Proto-Sinaitic inscription assumed to represent the name of the Canaanite goddess* Ba'alat *(adapted from Friedrich 1954: figure 63)*

missing link" between the Egyptian hieroglyphic writing and the ... Semitic alphabet' (Diringer 1968: 150).

Other attempts to link Old Semitic writing to a foreign source which have been discussed seriously include the assumption that a forerunner of the Phoenician alphabet was consciously invented by an individual who, however, borrowed the principle of consonant writing from Egypt while creating the signs with arbitrary sound assignments (Bauer 1937). Similarities between Old Semitic letter forms and individual signs of the syllabaries of Crete and Cyprus have attracted the attention of several scholars (such as Evans 1909; Praetorius 1906), and others suggested a connection with Hittite hieroglyphic (Sayce 1910). The various theories about the origin of the Old Semitic alphabet are reviewed at length in Jensen (1969: 246ff) and Diringer (1968: 145ff). None of them has succeeded in convincing the scientific community. Jensen's position, therefore, seems the most reasonable one. He envisages a number of parallel developments of competing writing systems in Palestine and Syria which may or may not have influenced each other to various degrees (Jensen 1969: 271). Eventually the Phoenician script which was the simplest of all prevailed, and it seems that its phenomenal success started out from the port town of Byblos. However, in the absence of compelling evidence documenting the origin of the Phoenician script, Diringer's warning is still as true as it was when he wrote it more than forty years ago: 'A single new discovery may compel us to alter completely an opinion considered hitherto beyond doubt' (Diringer 1943: 90).

To sum up this section, at the present state of our knowledge about the origin of Semitic consonant writing, we have to rest content with registering the fact that West Semitic writing was fully developed around the turn of the second millennium, and subsequently split up into a variety of scripts built on the same structural principle.

WEST SEMITIC WRITING PROPER

The oldest comprehensible text in West Semitic writing is the so-called 'Ahiram epitaph', an inscription on the sarcophagus of King Ahiram.[7] The language of this document is Phoenician. The Phoenician script is of great significance because it is the parent script of all Western alphabets,[8] but it was not the only script to develop out of the oldest West Semitic system. As of the tenth century, two other forms can be distinguished: namely, Canaanite and Aramaic. The latter is of no less importance than the Phoenician because it gave rise to the most widely used modern Near Eastern scripts, Hebrew and Arabic.

South Semitic writing is much younger than the North Semitic systems, but structural reasons speak against looking at it as a mere off-shoot of North Semitic writing. In terms of modern scripts it is less important, although this branch, too, split up into a number of different scripts. Figure 8.2 gives an overview of the most important scripts that were derived from the northern and southern branches of West Semitic writing.

This diagram is not an exhaustive listing of West Semitic scripts, but it does indicate the major junctures. Within the northern branch, the Phoenician and Aramaic were historically the most significant scripts. The former was used for about a thousand years, developing gradually into the so-called Punic script of the Phoenician colonies in the western Mediterranean. Figure 8.3 presents a sample dating from the fourth century BC. In later times, the Punic script became very cursive, and as some letters all but lost the features that distinguished them from others, it became increasingly hard to read. The Canaanite script developed in close proximity to the Phoenician script. Its unique feature is that it marks word boundaries with dots and sentence boundaries with strokes.

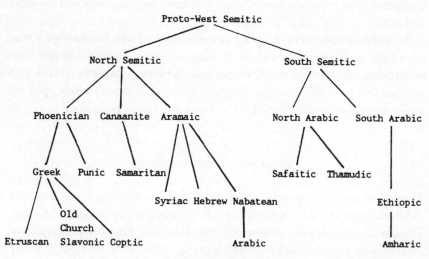

8.2 West Semitic derived scripts

1 bšnt	2 'rb'	3 lmlk	4 mlkytn
the year	four	of King	Milkiaton

8.3 Phoenician inscription of a fourth century Phoenician-Greek bilinguis from Edalion, Cyprus

The most important derivative of the Phoenician script is, of course, the Greek alphabet and its offshoots which are discussed in the next chapter.

The third main derivative of North Semitic is the Aramaic script whose oldest documents date from the ninth century BC and were found in North Syria. It became very important because, in the late Assyrian period (roughly from 1000 to 600 BC), the Aramaic language became the international lingua franca throughout the Near East, Asia Minor and the Middle East, including the Persian empire where it was used as the administrative language. As a consequence, the Aramaic script gradually replaced Assyrian cuneiform.

Owing to its political importance the Aramaic script was uniform and quite stable for many generations, but at the end of the third century it split up into several new scripts such as the Syriac, Palmyran and Nabatean scripts, among others. The most important was the Hebrew script, the medium of all Jewish writing, religious as well as secular. The Jews had been using the Aramaic script since the fifth century and then gradually standardized its form until they arrived at the conspicuous square form whereby each letter is put into a square frame. It is still difficult to pinpoint the date of the emergence of the Hebrew square script (kĕtāb merubbāʿ). On the scrolls of the Dead Sea dating from the first century BC it is already fully standardized.[9] In later times, two varieties of this script developed: the Sephardic (that is, Oriental-Spanish) type which is characterized by rounded lines, and the Ashkenasic type which is angular. Figure 8.4 gives the complete alphabet of the latter type.

Some of the Aramaic derived scripts such as the Palmyran script were used by Aramean people who had migrated to other places. On the other hand, the Aramaic script was also adopted by peoples living outside Palestine in other parts of the Near East. The Nabateans, for

צ ṣādhē	ם final mēm	ח ḥēth	א 'āleph
ץ final ṣādhē	נ nūn	ט ṭēth	ב bēth
ק qōph	ן final nūn	י jōdh	ג gímel
ר rēš	ס sāmekh	ב kaph	ד dāleth
ש šín	ע ajin	ך final kaph	ה hē
ת tāw	פ pē	ל lāmedh	ו wāw
	ף final pē	מ mēm	ז zajin

8.4 The letters of the Hebrew alphabet with their Romanized names

example, were Arabs who used Aramaic as a cultivated language. Their script, which is attested in many inscriptions between the first century BC and the third century AD, is important as the immediate forebear of the Arabic script (see below p. 150).

The Aramaic script also gave rise to some other alphabets not mentioned here, but the Hebrew square script and the classical Arabic alphabet were its most important derivatives. Like the Phoenician, the Canaanite and all other North Semitic scripts, they are consonantal alphabetic scripts generally consisting of less than thirty letters. A brief discussion is in order of the inner form of this system.

THE INNER FORM OF NORTH SEMITIC ALPHABETS

The outstanding characteristic of all North Semitic scripts is that they indicate consonants only but no vowels. s ths sntnc ndcts, ths prctc ds nt rlly crt ny dffclts fr th rdr wh knws th lngg. Context helps to decide on the correct reading of a group of consonant letters which might allow for several different possibilities. Conspicuous though it is, the absence of vowel signs has yet to be explained in a universally accepted manner.

The view most commonly held is that the Semites deliberately did not mark the vowels because the consonants are so obviously more important for the lexical content of Semitic words. Another theory, first proposed by Schmitt (1938) and also adhered to by Gelb (1963), assumes that Semitic writing was first syllabic and that the syllable signs were only gradually reduced to pure consonant letters.[10] This is not the place to resolve this dispute, which is better left to historians and students of ancient Semitic texts. However, the outcome will not affect the general assessment of consonants occupying a position of special significance in the system of Semitic languages.

It is a peculiar feature of the Semitic languages that the majority of all Proto-Semitic lexemes have roots consisting of three or two consonants. The entire morphology operates on the basis of these roots producing different lexical items by altering the vocalic environment. It is not only morphological derivatives that can be recognized by virtue of their common consonant root but also lexical equivalents across cognate languages as table 8.1 illustrates.

TABLE 8.1   *The Semitic root qbr, 'to carry'*

		Imperative				
		Hebrew	Syriac	Ugaritic	Arabic	Ethiopic
Singular 2 m.		qəbur	qəbor	qbr	'uqbur	qəbər
	f.	qibri	qəbor	qbr	'uqburi	qəb(ə)rī
Plural 2 m.		qibru	qəbor	qbr	'uqburu	qəb(ə)rū
	f.	qəborna	qəbor	qbr	'uqburna	qəb(ə)rā

Table 8.1 only lists the singular and plural masculine and feminine forms of the imperative of the verb 'to carry'. Many other inflected forms of the same root *qbr* could be added for each of the five languages. For present purposes, however, the forms listed in Table 8.1 are sufficient, and they illustrate three things.

1 The omission of vowels must have facilitated the adaptation of the Semitic alphabet to ever more languages. Abstraction from vowels made related words and the way they should be written readily recognizable.
2 While the consonantal root clearly constitutes the semantic core, the multiplicity of possible forms with the same root is also an imperfection, the extent of which the above sample sentence

of 'Consonant English' cannot really illustrate because there are
not nearly as many homographic words in English when their
vowels are not represented.

3 The absence of vowels in the script creates most difficulties for
the study of ancient Semitic languages. Ugaritic is included here
among the sample languages because the principle of consonant
writing was applied there very rigidly, and as a result considerable uncertainty remains as to the vowels of the forms in
question.

It is clear then, that Semitic scripts are based on, and reflect analytic
insight into, a vital structural feature of the Semitic languages. However,
the same structural feature that, on the one hand, makes the representation of consonants only seem like an appropriate way to write Semitic
must be seen, on the other hand, as a chief reason why the omission of
vowels was not a completely satisfactory solution, creating as it does
more ambiguity than it would for the representation of languages in
which consonantal roots do not play the role they play in Semitic
languages (namely, that of being the common element of scores of cognate words). Especially for the listing of words out of context the representation of consonants only was a serious problem. For example,
Phoenician *'b* could be interpreted as either /'ab/, 'father' or /'abiː/, 'my
father'. It is not surprising, therefore, that the principle of not denoting
vowels was eventually subjected to certain modifications.

Matres lectionis

One of these modifications was the by-product of early sound changes
in Phoenician and other North Semitic languages that resulted in the
loss of short vowels in the final position. The form /'abija/, 'of my
father', for instance, was reduced to /'abij/. Before the reduction it was
written as *'bj*. After the reduction its pronunciation converged with that
of /'abiː/ 'my father'. Now the *jodh* (here indicated as ⟨j⟩) could con-
veniently be taken to indicate the long final vowel of /'abiː/. In this way a
'weak' consonant sign was taken to represent a long vowel. This principle of expressing long vowels with consonant signs which had lost
their original function was gradually expanded. The male name
/panamuwa/, for instance, which was written *pnmw*, lost its final /a/ and
was reduced to /panamuː/. The *waw* ⟨w⟩ thus appeared as the written

representation of the long vowel /uː/. This kind of writing is known as *scriptio plena* 'full writing'.

Plene writing is first attested in word final position, but in later times was also used in medial position, as for instance in the name 'David', usually written *dwd*, which in *scriptio plena* appears as $d^a w^i j^i d^i$. Here the *jodh* ⟨jⁱ⟩ does not stand for an independent syllable. Its only purpose is to indicate that the preceding consonant, ⟨w⟩, is read with an /i/ rather than another vowel. Consonant signs that are used for this purpose of indicating the vowel quality of a syllable are called *matres lectionis* or 'mothers of reading'. Their existence is clear evidence that the omission of vowels was perceived as a weakness of Semitic writing, even though it was economical and sufficient for most purposes.

A major change was brought about by the Hellenization of the Near East in post-Alexandrian times. Greek became an important language which exercised an influence on the native languages of the region as the source of many loan words. Indicating vowels became a practical necessity in the case of the many Greek proper names and loan words because their correct pronunciation could not be inferred on the grounds of contextual information.[11] Greek writing was, of course, fully developed by this time and could be taken as a model for vowel indication. Independent vowel signs that had been won by the described method of using as *matres lectionis* the consonant letters of *jodh* and *waw*, and later *he* and *'aleph* for /iː/, /uː/, /oː/ and /aː/, respectively, could be inserted between consonant signs in a manner similar to Greek writing. In *Punic*, the Phoenician derivative that spread to the western Mediterranean and became subject to Latin influence, the use of *matres lectionis* was systematized in this way. The characteristic laryngeal sounds that are written with *'aleph*, *ajin*, *he* and *heth* fell out of the phonological system of Punic and could hence be used to indicate vowels after the Latin model between consonant letters. This innovation resulted in a considerable alteration of the outer appearance of the script which was a serious obstacle to the universal acceptance of *plene* writing in Semitic scripts. Also, the *plene* system was incomplete (providing no letter for the vowel /e/) and unsystematic (using the letters *waw* and *'aleph* both to represent more than one vowel). Moreover, the system was designed to represent only final vowels, although it was later extended to long vowels in internal position. Yet another problem with the *matres lectionis* was that these letters kept their consonant value, too, so that they became dual-function graphemes. In sum, *plene* writing was not felt to be the ultimate means of representing vowels but the indication of vowels was desirable, and therefore other means had to be devised.

Punctuation

As a supplement to *matres lectionis*, additional diacritical marks were introduced in some alphabets for the indication of vowels. This applies to Syriac and Hebrew, and also to the Arabic alphabet which does not, however, belong to the same epoch. The diacritics for vowel indication are essentially dots and dashes grouped in various ways around consonant letters. The first attested samples are found in Syrian inscriptions, where words with identical consonantal roots were distinguished in such a way as to mark a 'strong' vowel with a dot over the preceding consonant letter, and a 'weak' vowel with a dot under it. For example, /ka:tel/ 'killing' was distinguished from /kətal/ by marking the long /a:/ with a dot above the initial consonant and the schwa with a dot under it as illustrated in figure 8.5.

```
        /ka:tel/          /kətal/
        'killing'         'he killed'
```

8.5 First indication of vowels by punctuation

When the punctuation of Hebrew writing developed is not exactly clear, but a Syrian influence seems likely. Historically, there was more than one system of diacritical marks for the vocalization of Hebrew writing (Jensen 1969: 302ff). The one that is presently used for printing holy books, poetry and children's books was developed by the Masoretes at about 800 BC and is known as the 'Tiberian' system after the city of Tiberias in Palestine. Vocalization according to the Tiberian system, the vowel system of Biblical Hebrew, may be represented as follows:

$$\text{/i/ /e/ /ä/ /a/ /ɔ/ /o/ /u/}$$

In addition to these symbols the schwa symbol ⊤ must be mentioned; it originally indicated the absence of a vowel, but has come to stand for /ə/

בְּרֵאשִׁית· בָּרָא·אֱלֹהִים אֵת·הַשָּׁמַיִם·וְאֵת הָאָרֶץ: וְהָאָרֶץ
הָיְתָה תֹהוּ וָבֹהוּ וְחֹשֶׁךְ עַל־פְּנֵי תְהוֹם וְרוּחַ אֱלֹהִים מְרַחֶפֶת עַל־פְּנֵי
הַמָּיִם:

*bə-rē'šíp bārā' älōhim' ep ha-ššāmajim wə' ep hā-'äräṣ. wə
hā-'äräṣ hājəpā pōhū wā-βōhū wə hošäχ 'al-pənē pəhōm,
wə rūäḥ 'älōhim mərahäfäp 'al-pənē ha-mmājim.*

In the beginning God created the heavens and the earth. Now the earth was
unformed and void, and darkness was upon the face of the deep; and the spirit of
God hovered over the face of the waters.

8.6 Moses 1: 1,2

in syllable initial position. The schwa is also used in combination with
other diacritical marks to represent the vowels /a/, /e/ and /o/ with
pharyngeal quality. Figure 8.6 provides an example of punctuated
Hebrew writing with transcription and English translation.

Some features of Hebrew Orthography

Punctuation made the representation of vowels in Hebrew complete,
unambiguous and fully systematic. Together with the *matres lectionis*,
which remained part of Hebrew writing, the diacritical marks represent
the five basic vowels, /ä/, /i/, /o/, /u/ and /e/. As a matter of fact, there is
even some overdetermination for vowels in modern Hebrew because the
graphemic distinction between 'long' and 'short' vowels is still present in
the script, but has been neutralized in speech (Navon and Shimron 1984:
94). It is rather ironic, therefore, that this consonant script exhibits
certain redundancies with respect to vowel representation. For example,
the vowel /i/ may be represented either by the letter *jodh* (as a *mater
lectionis*) or by a dot under the preceding consonant, or by both.

Notice that the introduction of diacritical marks has not led to the
abandonment of consonant writing; rather, vowel punctuation is used
for certain purposes only. Thus two orthographies of modern Hebrew
coexist: the pointed system which specifies vowels unmistakably, if
somewhat redundantly, and the unpointed system which omits every
indication of vowels and relies heavily on context for their correct
identification.

In unvowelized texts those letters serving as *matres lectionis* may be ambiguous, because they are also used for the representation of consonants. In order to reduce the ambiguity of consonant/*mater lectionis*, letters are sometimes duplicated indicating consonantal rather than vocalic value. However, at present there is no uniform convention for the treatment of *matres lectionis*, a fact which again underscores the predominance of consonants in Hebrew writing. Skilled readers are practised in reading unvowelized texts in which some of the vowel phonemes of Hebrew are not represented.[12]

The Arabic alphabet

The other important consonant alphabet in contemporary use is that of Arabic which, like the Hebrew, is a religious script whose spread followed that of the faith of its users (Diringer 1968: 210). The Arabic script is the youngest of the North Semitic scripts and began in the fourth century AD. As the script of the Qur'ān it spread out from the Arabian peninsula throughout the Near East, western, central and south-eastern Asia, as well as to great parts of Africa and some peripheral regions of Europe. It was adapted to more languages belonging to more families than any other Semitic script. Some of them are Turkish, Farsi, Urdu, Kashmiri, Malay, Uighur, Kazakh, Somali, Swahili, Berber, Spanish and Slavonic.

Like all other Semitic scripts, it is a consonant alphabet typically applied to the writing of consonant roots. However, while the classical North Semitic alphabet consists of twenty-two letters only, Arabic has a richer inventory of consonants, and comprises twenty-eight basic letters. Some of the additional letters were created by adding diacritical marks to others. For instance, a dot was added to the letter for /ḥ/ to distinguish the tense voiceless velar /ḫ/. Similarly, new letters were created by adding diacritics for voiced and voiceless fricatives, emphatic /ḍ/ and emphatic /ẓ/, as well as for a special Arabic /s/ phoneme. In addition, a ligature was formed of *lam* and *'alif* which is often counted as the twenty-ninth letter.

Vowel indication in Arabic writing developed along the lines of other Semitic scripts: that is, with *matres lectionis* and diacritical marks. Vowels are consistently marked, however, only in the Qur'ān and in poetry. The long vowels /aː/, /iː/ and /uː/ are represented by the consonant letters *'alif*, *ja* and *waw*. The use of *ja* and *waw* as *matres lectionis* for /iː/ and /uː/ is natural in view of the Aramaic (or rather Nabatean) origin of the Arabic script. Only the use of *'alif* for /aː/ can be considered a specifically Arabic development. For the corresponding short vowels /a/, /i/ and /u/ three diacritics are used which are derived from some- what simplified forms of the *matres lectionis*: a horizontal bar over the consonant sign (*fat'ha*) for /a/; a horizontal bar under the consonant sign (*kasra*) for /i/; and a little hook over the consonant sign (*damna*) for /u/. In addition, a little circle above a consonant letter (*djasma*) indicates the absence of a vowel.

It is a characteristic feature of the outer form of the Arabic script that all letters except *'alif*, *dal*, *ḏal*, *ra*, *za* and *waw* occur in four different forms depending on their position in the word: independent, initial, medial or final. Figure 8.7 lists the independent forms of the twenty- eight letters and their sound values; figure 8.8 gives their names and variant forms.

Of the languages to which the Arabic alphabet was applied, some have a richer inventory of phonemes than Arabic. New or derived letter signs had to be invented for writing these languages.[13] The Persian alphabet, for example, has four additional letters for /p/, /č/, /z/ and /g/; and its extension to Urdu produced another four for /ṭ/, /ḍ/, /ṛ/ and /ǧ/. For Malay the *nun* was modified with a diacritic to represent the palatalized nasal /ŋ/.[14]

The great distribution of the Arabic script led to the formation of a variety of different national and language-specific types much like the peculiarities of the Roman alphabet in its many specific applications. The association with Islam imbued the Arabic script with great con- servatism: that is, an unwillingness on the part of the literati to change it – or rather, the conventions of using it – for the writing of Arabic. The religiously inspired establishment of a written standard for Arabic resulted in a strongly normative attitude toward the written language and a growing cleavage between spoken and written Arabic (Mahmoud 1979). Eventually only the peculiar social dynamics of 'diglossia'[15] could justify the recognition of spoken and written Arabic as varieties of one and the same language.

SOUTH SEMITIC SCRIPTS

The South Semitic scripts originated in the Arabian peninsula and extended up to Syria in the north and to Abyssinia in the south. The most important members of this group are the South Arabic script and the Ethiopic script. The former is very symmetrical and regular with an angular appearance of its outer form and no vowel indication in its inner form. Because of its similarities with North Semitic systems it is not discussed here in detail. The Ethiopic script, by contrast, exhibits some characteristic features not found in any North Semitic script.

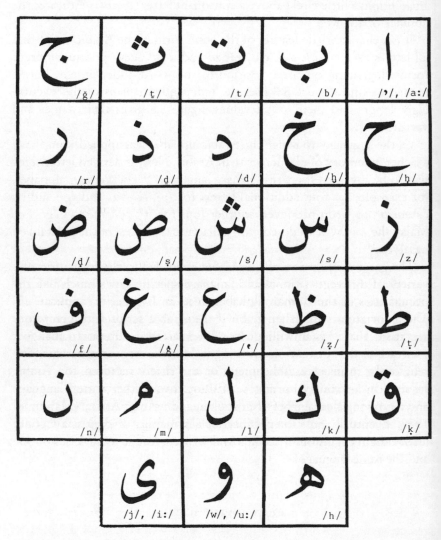

8.7 The Arabic alphabet: independent letter forms and sound values, to be read in Arabic fashion from right to left

Name	Initial	Medial	Final	In isolation	Sound value	Name	Initial	Medial	Final	In isolation	Sound value
'elif			l	١	'	ṭā	ط	ط	ط	ط	ṭ
bā	ب	ب	ب	ب	b	ẓā	ظ	ظ	ظ	ظ	ẓ
tā	ت	ت	ت	ت	t	'ain	ع	ع	ع	ع	'
ṭā	ث	ث	ث	ث	ṯ	ġain	غ	غ	غ	غ	ġ
ǧim	ج	ج	ج	ج	ǧ	fā	ف	ف	ف	ف	f
ḥā	ح	ح	ح	ح	ḥ	ḳāf	ق	ق	ق	ق	ḳ(q)
ḫā	خ	خ	خ	خ	ḫ	kāf	ك	ك	ك	ك	k
dāl			د	د	d	lām	ل	ل	ل	ل	l
ḏāl			ذ	ذ	ḏ	mīm	م	م	م	م	m
rā			ر	ر	r	nūn	ن	ن	ن	ن	n
ẓā			ز	ز	z	hā	ه	ه	ه	ه	h
sīn	س	س	س	س	s	wāw			و	و	w
šīn	ش	ش	ش	ش	š	jā	ي	ي	ي	ي	j
ṣād	ص	ص	ص	ص	ṣ	lām-elif			لا	لا	lā
ḍād	ض	ض	ض	ض	ḍ						

8.8 The Arabic alphabet: names and variant letter forms

Old Ethiopic was first written in the typical Semitic manner without vowel signs, but in the fourth century AD the writing of Ethiopic underwent drastic changes. The resulting script is interesting because of its unusual and quite un-Semitic vowel indication. It operates by means of systematic alterations in the form of consonant symbols which were thus turned into syllable signs. Vowel indication in Ethiopic may be described as a system of diacritical marks that have become integral parts of the basic consonant signs. The unit that is represented by any one sign of the Ethiopic script is a CV syllable, but the system has the analytic depth of an alphabet because the formal elements corresponding to consonant and vowel respectively are clearly recognizable. The system distinguishes seven vocalic values: /æ/, /u/, /i/, /a/, /e/, /ə/ and /o/. The syllable signs of C + schwa are also used for representing consonants without a following vowel. With this exception, the values of all signs are unambiguous. Figure 8.9 presents the complete list.

Whether the Ethiopic script came into existence as a gradual transformation of the South Semitic script or was the result of deliberate efforts is still an open question (Diringer 1968: 180). The Ethiopic vocalization is unique in the Semitic world. The only other place where this

	a	u:	i:	a:	e:	(ə)	o:
h	ሀ	ሁ	ሂ	ሃ	ሄ	ህ	ሆ
l	ለ	ሉ	ሊ	ላ	ሌ	ል	ሎ
ḥ	ሐ	ሑ	ሒ	ሓ	ሔ	ሕ	ሖ
m	መ	ሙ	ሚ	ማ	ሜ	ም	ሞ
s	ሠ	ሡ	ሢ	ሣ	ሤ	ሥ	ሦ
r	ረ	ሩ	ሪ	ራ	ሬ	ር	ሮ
š	ሰ	ሱ	ሲ	ሳ	ሴ	ስ	ሶ
q	ቀ	ቁ	ቂ	ቃ	ቄ	ቅ	ቆ
b	በ	ቡ	ቢ	ባ	ቤ	ብ	ቦ
t	ተ	ቱ	ቲ	ታ	ቴ	ት	ቶ
ḫ	ኀ	ኁ	ኂ	ኃ	ኄ	ኅ	ኆ
n	ነ	ኑ	ኒ	ና	ኔ	ን	ኖ
'	አ	ኡ	ኢ	ኣ	ኤ	እ	ኦ
k	ከ	ኩ	ኪ	ካ	ኬ	ክ	ኮ
w	ወ	ዉ	ዊ	ዋ	ዌ	ው	ዎ
'	ዐ	ዑ	ዒ	ዓ	ዔ	ዕ	ዖ
z	ዘ	ዙ	ዚ	ዛ	ዜ	ዝ	ዞ
j	የ	ዩ	ዪ	ያ	ዬ	ይ	ዮ
d	ደ	ዱ	ዲ	ዳ	ዴ	ድ	ዶ
g	ገ	ጉ	ጊ	ጋ	ጌ	ግ	ጎ
ṭ	ጠ	ጡ	ጢ	ጣ	ጤ	ጥ	ጦ
p	ጰ	ጱ	ጲ	ጳ	ጴ	ጵ	ጶ
ṣ	ጸ	ጹ	ጺ	ጻ	ጼ	ጽ	ጾ
ḍ	ፀ	ፁ	ፂ	ፃ	ፄ	ፅ	ፆ
f	ፈ	ፉ	ፊ	ፋ	ፌ	ፍ	ፎ
p	ፐ	ፑ	ፒ	ፓ	ፔ	ፕ	ፖ

8.9 *The Ethiopian alphabet*

peculiarly syllabic kind of vowel indication is found is India, where the same principle underlies practically all of the many scripts that evolved for Indic languages. Since the Kharosthi script (the earliest Indic script exhibiting the same structural principle) predates the Ethiopic script by several centuries, Friedrich's (1966: 93) suggestion of an Indian influence on the formation of the Ethiopic script has much to recommend it.

The Ethiopic script runs from left to right, another feature distinguishing it from all other Semitic scripts. It is the system of the Ge'ez language which, because of the conservatism attached to its written norm, has long been dead as a spoken language, but has been preserved as the language of the Ethiopian church. Since about the thirteenth century, Amharic has evolved as the official language of Ethiopia (Mulugeta 1987), and the Ethiopic script has been adapted to Amharic as well as Oromo, Tigr, Tigriña and other languages of Ethiopia.

CONCLUSION

The Semites cannot lay any claim to being the inventors of writing, but they have contributed more than any other ancient people to the perfection of the technique of reducing speech sounds to visible marks. By so doing, they have provided the foundation of a literary tradition in which it is possible, and usually found desirable, that there is a close correspondence between written language and spoken language. Even though the Arabic example in particular is a clear deviation from this general pattern, the Semitic alphabet in its various forms (including, of course, the Arabic alphabet) makes it possible to treat as the relevant units of writing the relevant units of speech, and thus represent the sounds of speech in a comparatively faithful manner.

Moreover, the simplicity of the system and the small number of its basic signs facilitates its acquisition. Thus, as a writing system that is simple and more flexible than any of its predecessors, the Semitic alphabet offered great potential for the spread and popularization of the art of writing. Yet any theory that attributes the spread of literacy to the alphabet or, more generally, to alphabetic writing, should be judged with great care and skepticism; but then, this is true of all monocausal explanations of historical processes.

The basic structural principle underlying the Semitic alphabet – namely, the representation of (consonantal) phonemes – greatly facilitated the transfer of a given script to other languages. In comparison with Sumerian–Akkadian cuneiform or Chinese, for example, the transfer to hitherto unwritten languages became infinitely easier. Nevertheless, Semitic alphabets are not equally suitable for all languages, and the predominant role that all Semitic scripts assign to consonants bears witness to their language-specific origin. Vowel phonemes are underrepresented in Semitic alphabets, and this is also true of all other alphabets derived from them. Like all writing systems, the prototype of the alphabet was developed in the context of particular languages and designed to suit their specific features. The structural make-up of Semitic consonant scripts testifies to this linguistic origin.

NOTES

1 As most historians of writing were trained as Semitists, Semitic writing is the most intensively researched area of the study of writing and scripts. This chapter is limited, therefore, to a brief overview of the most important systems. The reader is referred to the extensive work by Driver (1976), Diringer (1968), Friedrich (1966) and Jensen (1969) for more detailed documentation.

2 Childe (1982: 189) stresses the economic need for the merchants of this region to develop a simple script that would allow them to be their own bookkeepers and make them independent of professional clerks.

3 Actually, Ugaritic was deciphered more or less independently by three scholars: Hans Bauer, Paul Dhorme and Charles Virolleaud.

4 The excavations of Ras Shamra have brought to light lists revealing the order of the Ugaritic alphabet (cf. chapter 5, p. 88). The fact that it is basically the same as that of the West Semitic alphabets is often cited as evidence of the Ugaritic alphabet's being modeled on an extant West Semitic alphabet (cf. Diringer 1968: 151; Friedrich 1966: 75).

5 The term 'pseudo-hieroglyphic' has become current as a descriptive label for the Byblos script. Cf. Diringer (1968), also Sznycer (1973).

6 The assumption of the acrophonic principle (from ἄκρο or 'front' + φωνὴ or 'sound') is that the initial sound of a word sign becomes the sound value of that sign when transferred from pleremic to cenemic use.

7 The dating of this document is still not agreed upon. Friedrich (1966: 75) cites the year 1000 BC as the most likely approximate date, while Diringer (1968: 158) puts it in the eleventh or even twelfth century.

8 The Greeks themselves referred to their alphabet as *phoinikia grámmata*, Phoenician letters.

9 The Dead Sea Scrolls were discovered in 1947. They contain several fragments of the Bible, such as the book of Isaiah (cf. Burrows 1955, 1958).

10 Gelb (1963, 1980) even argued that Hebrew writing is a pre-alphabetic syllabary. The most forceful argument against this assumption is put forward in Jensen (1969, chapter XI). Basically, Jensen cites the fact that many syllables in Hebrew end with a consonant. In such CVC syllables, the final letter represents a consonant, a fact that Gelb does not deny. If it is agreed, then, that a letter may stand for a consonant at the end of a syllable, it might as well be admitted that a letter may stand for a consonant at the beginning of a syllable.

11 Notice that this is yet another instance where proper names played an important role for the development of writing. Cf. the development of Akkadian (chapter 5, pp. 80–4ff) and of Korean and Japanese (chapter 7, pp. 116, 124f); see also chapter 11.

12 For a more detailed treatment of Hebrew writing see Birnbaum (1971).

13 It is interesting to note that, in the process of adapting the Arabic alphabet to other languages, no letters were dropped, because the Arabic script served as a channel for the introduction of Arabic loan words which are usually spelled in the receiving languages in the same way they are spelled in Arabic.

14 One particular characteristic of the Arabic script facilitates the formation of new letters. It distinguishes some of its basic consonant letters by varying numbers of dots associated with a basic sign. This principle is easily extended to the creation of new letters fulfilling the needs of other languages. Sommer (1942) provides a list of the additional signs needed for Farsi, Urdu, Afghan, Sindi and Malay.

15 Diglossia as a consequence of writing and restricted literacy is discussed in chapter 10.

9

The Alphabet

HISTORICAL BACKGROUND

The dating of the origin of alphabetic writing in Greece is a matter of considerable historical dispute. The Greeks themselves have not kept any historical records, just as they have left no documents suggesting that they were aware of the fact that pre-alphabetic writing had been available in Mycenaean times. It is clear that the Greek alphabet was complete and firmly established in pre-classical times, but it is not so clear exactly when the alphabetic tradition began. There is something like a blind spot on the historical map of Greece between the time when Mycenaean writing disappeared and alphabetic writing became a part of Greek culture. By conservative accounts the period of post-Mycenaean illiteracy was as long as 300 years extending from the twelfth to the ninth century (Goody and Watt 1968: 39). These so-called dark ages of Greece – dark because we know little about them – came to an end at the latest around 800 BC at the time of the Phoenician ruler Pygmalion of Tyre. The beginning of fully developed alphabetic writing was certainly not later than that (McCarter 1975); but the prehistory of the Greek alphabet may have extended almost as far back as the collapse of the Mycenaean civilization. New archeological discoveries suggest that the spread of Phoenician writing throughout the Mediterranean occurred earlier than has been assumed previously.[1] Naveh (1973) made a very radical claim; he advanced the date of the Greek adoption of the Phoenician script to about 1100 BC.[2] His hypothesis is based on the paleographic similarity between the Greek script and certain Old Phoenician inscriptions of the late Bronze Age. With claims like this the discussion about the dating of the Greek alphabet has been reopened. The emerging consensus is that the gap between the Greek alphabet and its precursors is less wide than many have assumed so far. To set the time of adoption of the Phoenician alphabet by the Greeks at the tenth century at the latest does not seem too daring a supposition.

It is necessary to emphasize the continuity of the development in the eastern Mediterranean because, as will become clear presently, the Greek alphabet has sometimes been treated as if it had made its appearance on the stage of world history suddenly and unexpectedly. However, the tradition originating in Phoenician writing is just as remarkable as the Greek innovative contribution to it. The latter must be seen in the context of the former, and it must be recognized that the Phoenician script was almost as efficient as the Greek alphabet. The continuity of the Phoenician tradition is conspicuous and noticeable even in our time. Both the graphical form and the arbitrary ordering of letters have remained recognizably the same, if not completely unchanged, over a period of some 3,500 years from 1500 BC to the present. Nevertheless, in certain accounts alphabetic writing begins in Greece.

THE ALPHABETIC HYPOTHESIS

Rather than stressing the fact that the Greeks adopted an extant system from the Phoenicians which they then augmented and modified, or that the adoption of the alphabet was the return of writing to Greece after it had lapsed back into illiteracy, adherents of the 'alphabetic hypothesis' highlight the new quality of the Greek alphabet which they view as the necessary conclusion of a natural development that leads from logograms through syllabic signs to the decomposition of syllables into signs for consonants and vowels (Gelb 1963). According to this view, only the Greek alphabet is really worthy of that name. Semitic consonant writing that preceded it and from which it was derived cannot justly be called 'alphabetic'. One of the most outspoken proponents of this view was the late Marshall McLuhan, whose interpretation of all of Western civilization hinges on the uniqueness of the alphabet. To him alphabetic writing and civilization were all but identical as becomes apparent in the following remark: 'Diringer's observation that the alphabet is "now universally employed by civilized peoples" is a bit tautological since it is by alphabet alone that men have detribalized or individualized themselves into "civilization" ... Without the phonetic alphabet [cultures] remain tribal, as do the Chinese and the Japanese' (McLuhan 1962: 63).

This is the alphabetic hypothesis in its crudest form. It attempts to relate certain of the achievements of civilization to changes in the means and mode of communication, and especially to different forms of writing.[3] What is surprising about this approach is that it was ever taken seriously and discussed by serious scholars. For the explanation of history every monocausal approach is problematic anyway and, with respect to the case under discussion here, one cannot help being amused or puzzled. To describe one of the most advanced civilizations of the world as 'tribal' only because it makes use of a non-alphabetic writing system is capricious if not absurd. Non-alphabetic people are not even recognized as individuals. The decisive step towards acquiring individuality is not writing as such, but alphabetic writing; that is, writing according to the principle of representing the individual sounds which are systematically relevant in a language. Indeed, the principle of one letter for one sound is celebrated as the very foundation of Western culture and thinking: 'By the meaningless sign linked to the meaningless sound we have built the shape and meaning of Western man' (McLuhan 1962: 65).

The 'meaningless sign linked to the meaningless sound' in this understanding is, of course, the letter of the Greek alphabet, rather than a meaningless syllable sign linked to a meaningless syllable in cuneiform or any other writing system. The Greeks are thus credited with nothing less than uplifting humankind. By some scholars the Greek letters are even invested with magical powers. Havelock, for instance, who likes to philosophize about the 'literate revolution in Greece' (Havelock 1982), notes in a recent article that 'the Greek alphabet has created the literature we read, whether in Greek, Latin, English, or any contemporary European tongue, including Russian' (Havelock 1986: 411ff.).

Havelock, like McLuhan, attributes to the alphabet the power to create things and thus fails to make a proper distinction between an instrument, its inventors and users, and the way it is employed in a society. Greece was, no doubt, in many respects the cradle of Western civilization, and it is a fact that the full alphabet is first encountered on Greek soil in the pre-classical period. It must have been tempting to bring these two facts together and stipulate a causal link between them. It seems that historians and scholars of writing were so impressed by the flexibility and systemic simplicity of alphabetic writing that they perceived it as a great leap forward rather than a small, however important, step in the evolution of civilized humanity. The Phoenician connection could not be denied because the ancient Greeks themselves were aware of the source of their script, but the significance of the Semitic heritage was often played down rather than highlighted.

Gelb (1963) acknowledges the importance of the Oriental roots of the Greek alphabet, but in his theory there is a wide gap between it and its Semitic forerunners, which do not qualify as alphabets but are considered to be syllabaries consisting of signs for consonants 'plus any vowel' (cf. chapter 8 above). By stressing the structural innovation of representing both consonants and vowels with letters of the same kind, scholars such as Gelb and Diringer have helped to lay the foundation of the alphabetic hypothesis. Its substance was, however, provided by philosophers and anthropologists who regarded the Greek alphabet as decisive for the superiority of Western civilization. Hegel, for instance, apodictically called the alphabet 'in and by itself more intelligent'. Simple and abstract as it is, it gave rise to abstraction and logical reasoning (Goody and Watt 1968; Olson 1977). Only the Greek alphabet separated sight and sound, speculated McLuhan. By so doing it created the autonomy of the senses and thus elevated human consciousness to a new level. 'So long as any other meaning is vested in sight or sound, the divorce between the visual and the other senses remains incomplete, as is the case in all forms of writing save the phonetic alphabet' (McLuhan 1962: 61).

What McLuhan seems to assume is that (1) the phonetic alphabet is a completely cenemic writing system and (2) cenemic writing without any pleremic elements is the superior and therefore preferred form of representing language visually. Both assumptions invite serious criticism, provoking the question of whether McLuhan really understood the fundamental principles of alphabetic writing. 'Speech', he writes, 'is the "content" of phonetic writing' (McLuhan 1962: 61), the tacit implication being that while in Semitic consonant root writing there is a direct link between the written form and meaning which, in conjunction with that between graph and sound (consonant), determines the pronunciation of the written word, the full alphabet makes any reference to meaning unnecessary. Instead, access to meaning is mediated entirely through the representation of sound. Theoretically this assessment of alphabetic writing seems to be quite elegant and attractive, but it does not have very much to do with how the alphabet works once it is applied to writing a particular language. Almost all alphabetic scripts have betrayed the purely cenemic ideal, for alphabetic writing too makes use of direct relations between letter and meaning, and it is arguable that this is inevitable (see below, p. 169f). It is hard, therefore, to avoid the conclusion that the adherents of the alphabetic hypothesis, to some extent, see what fits their theory rather than the facts. On one hand, the alphabet is described as the logical and necessary outcome of a consistent development but, on the other hand, its uniqueness is stressed. Rather than saying that the alphabet would have been discovered, or invented, sooner or later in any event, it is said that it took the genius of the Greeks to create it.

THE ADAPTATION OF THE SEMITIC ALPHABET TO GREEK

What then is it that makes the Greek alphabet so special? The point that needs to be emphasized in answering this question is that the Greek alphabet is the result of an adaptation process across linguistic boundaries. Whenever a script was borrowed and adapted to a language belonging to a language type or language family other than that in whose context it was developed, important changes in the systematic make-up of that script resulted. The Semitic alphabet applied to a non-Semitic language could not be used to represent the sounds of that language without significant adaptations. The lack of signs for vowels was crucial here since, in contrast to the Semitic languages, vowels in Greek occupy a position on a par with consonants. By finding a solution for the problem of vowel indication the Greeks overcame this obstacle, thus making the alphabet more suitable for both their language and other non-Semitic languages. Systematic vowel indication by signs of the same type as the consonant letters was the real achievement of the Greeks. It made the alphabet more efficient not only for the representation of one language, but also for the transfer to other languages. Semitic alphabets could easily be transferred from one Semitic language to another, but their adaptation to languages of another family proved more difficult. In this regard the high evaluation of the Greek development is entirely justified. Transforming a consonant script into a full alphabet with letters for both consonants and vowels clearly is a significant step[4] because the script can more easily and more faithfully map the relevant sounds of language. Not being confined any more to consonants only,

Old Phoenician				Classical Greek	
Letter	Sound	Name	Meaning of Name	Letter	Name
⟜	'	'aleph	ox	A	alpha
⟍	b	beth	house	B	beta
⟍	g	gimel	camel	Γ	gamma
⊲	d	daleth	door	Δ	delta
⋺	h	hē		E	epsilon
⊥	z	zain	weapon	Z	zēta
⋈	ḥ	ḥeth		H	ēta
⊕	ṭ	ṭhet		θ	thēta
⩻	j	yodh	arm	I	iōta
⟋	k	kaph	palm of hand	K	kappa
↙	l	lamed	goad	Λ	la(m)bda
⋛	m	mem	water	M	mȳ
⋋	n	nun	fish	N	nȳ
‡	s	sāmekh	fish	Ξ	xī
O	'	'ain	eye	O	omikron
⟅	p	pe	mouth	Π	pī
⋏	ṣ	san			
Φ	q	qoppa			
⟁	r	resh	head	P	rhō
W	š	shin	tooth	Σ	sīgma
+	t	tau	cross mark	T	tau
Υ	w	waw		Υ	ypsīlon

9.1 The Old Phoenician models for some of the letters of the Classical Greek alphabet

the alphabet is no longer the script of a particular language or of the languages of a particular type. How was this achieved?

An important part of the continuity of the Phoenician tradition are the names of the Phoenician letters. The Greeks adopted them together with the letters. There is, however, an important difference between the

Old Phoenician letter names and the Greek; the former have a meaning. Sixteen of the twenty-two Old Phoenician letters are named after common objects (see figure 9.1), a clear indication of the effectiveness of the acrophonic principle underlying the selection, if not the creation, of Phoenician letters. Only the letters for /h, ḥ, ṭ, ṣ, q/ do not bear common object names in Phoenician. In Greek, of course, the Phoenician words have no meaning other than as designations of letters.

The Phoenician words were borrowed into Greek stripped of their original meanings, indicating to the Greeks nothing but their own initials. Whether the Greeks adopted the acrophonic principle together with the names of the Phoenician letters is not quite clear, but they employed it in any event, and by so doing arrived at the sound values of their letters. Certain phonological differences between Phoenician and Greek made it difficult, however, to apply the acrophonic principle in exactly the same way in Greek as it was applied in Phoenician. While all Phoenician words have initial consonants, many Greek words begin with vowels. Moreover, some Phoenician consonants are not phonemic in Greek and therefore not readily perceived by native speakers of Greek. The glottal stop is the most prominent example. As it is not an element of the phonemic system of Greek, the Greeks pronounced the name of the first letter of the Phoenician alphabet not with an initial glottal stop as the Phoenicians would, but with an initial vowel. The result was that they added the letter *alpha* as a genuine vowel sign to the Phoenician consonant script, thus introducing a feature that changed the type of the system.

Other consonant letters of the Phoenician inventory that assumed vocalic quality in Greek were *hē* (ᴈ) for Greek *epsilon* /e/; *waw* (Ɣ), used in older periods of Greek for the semivowel /w/ and later developed the vocalic value /u/ of *upsilon*; *yodh* (ⴏ) /j/ became Greek *iōta* /i/; and *'ain* (O) became /o/, *omicron*. In word final position, most of these letters had already been used in Semitic writing as the so-called *matres lectionis*. In Greek the application of this device was extended and systematized. In principle the Greek alphabet was suitable for representing all the phonemes of the Greek language. It was undoubtedly the simplest and most flexible writing system developed so far, since with it any word could be spelled out without recourse to the cumbersome device of classifiers, logograms or imperfectly fitted syllable signs. Systematic vowel indication is attested in the earliest Greek documents; no developmental state with defective vowel writing is known.

However, the vocalic system at which the Greeks had arrived by adapting the Phoenician alphabet to the needs of the Greek language underwent considerable changes from the earliest attested documents to the classical period. An important feature whose representation changed significantly was vowel quality. While in the early documents vowel length was not marked, in the classical system only *alpha* and *iōta* continued to be used for both short and long vowels. Short /e/ was differentiated from /e:/ when the consonant /h/ expressed by Phoenician *heth* was lost and its letter acquired the value /e:/ of *eta*, distinguishing it from /e/ of *epsilon*. The *omega* 'big o', Ω and ω, was introduced to distinguish /o:/ from *omikron* 'little o', /o/. Vowel length could thus be marked for /o/ and /e/, but the Greek alphabet took no note of and neither did it develop distinct symbols for long as opposed to short /i/, /a/ and /u/. The representation of /u/ which was first expressed by Old Phoenician *waw* also changed as this sound came to be realized as /ü/ in many contexts. The /u/ sound was therefore represented by combining *omikron* and *ypsilon*. Originally another sign had been derived from Phoenician *waw* for the representation of a labiodental /w/, later /f/, which soon fell out of use, however.

Further modifications of the archaic alphabet followed later as supplementary signs were introduced for the aspirated stops /ph/ and /kh/ – that is, φ and χ respectively, and for the double consonant /ps/, ψ.[5] After these supplementary letters no further additions were made, but in other respects the Greek script was not complete in the early documents. Word boundaries were not marked, and there was no punctuation. Neither was there a distinction between capital and small letters. Moreover, while the Greek alphabet was one unitary system, it was not used in a uniform way. There was, in other words, no standardized orthography. The principle of sound writing was so faithfully followed that dialect differences are clearly documented in the earliest records. There were several writing conventions which are commonly divided into three groups: (1) the archaic alphabets of the Dorian islands, (2) the Eastern alphabets of the Aegean, the west coast of Asia Minor and Attika, and (3) the Western alphabets of western Greece and the colonies of Sicily. The Classical Greek alphabet achieved its standardized form only late in the fifth century BC.

The Greek alphabet is the prototype of all fully vowelized alphabets which developed in the Greek colonies and from there spread to many parts of the world. To mention but a few of the ancient scripts, the Phrygian, Lykian and Lydian alphabets came into existence in Asia Minor. In Egypt the Coptic alphabet eventually replaced the hieroglyphs as well as the hieratic and demotic scripts. Extending to the north on the Balkan peninsula, the Greek alphabet became the model of the Old Church Slavonic, the Cyrillic, the Old Rumanian and the Albanian scripts which in turn are the sources of all further developments in eastern Europe. The Greek colonies in Sicily were the breeding grounds of the Old Italic and Etruscan scripts from which the Latin alphabet was derived. This most important alphabet replaced other scripts that evolved on the Italian peninsula to become the official script of the western half of the Roman empire. As the script of the major branch of Christianity, the Latin alphabet spread further and to more languages than any other script before or after.

The Romans gave up the acrophonic principle and, except for *ypsilon*, *zed* and *yodh*, did not borrow the Greek (Phoenician) letter names, but they kept the basic order of the letters. The Latin alphabet eventually became very important as the script of the Western world, but it did not constitute any structural progress over the Greek alphabet. The same is true of the Cyrillic alphabet with its additional letters and ligatures, as well as of every other alphabetic script derived from the Greek model. They all share the basic feature: that is, the type of vowel indication. While the Semitic scripts indicate vowels by means of optional diacritics to independent consonant letters, and the Brāhmī-derived Indic scripts (as well as the Ethiopian script) have vowel marks that are attached to, or integrated into, the basic consonant signs (see below, chapter 10), the Greek script and all its derivatives provide independent vowel signs. These basic commonalities of all alphabets should not be taken to imply that there are no significant differences between alphabetic scripts. Quite the opposite is true. The systemic choices that the scripts of specific languages make in putting the basic elements of the alphabet to use are many. Some of the principles which come to bear and with respect to which they differ are discussed in the following section.

To conclude this section, let us emphasize three points that should be kept in mind when considering *the* alphabet and alphabetic scripts.

1   The most significant developments in the history of writing were achieved whenever a script was borrowed and adapted to a new language across linguistic types. Systematic vowel indication in the Greek alphabet is no exception. It is the result of adapting a Semitic script to a non-Semitic language.

2   The often alleged universality of the alphabet is a potential rather than an actual feature of the Greek prototype. Just as the Phoenician alphabet was unsuitable for the representation of all of the phonemes of Greek, the Greek alphabet cannot be applied to other languages without modifications and additions. Like all writing systems, the Greek alphabet came into existence in the context and for the representation of a particular language. It was not designed as a universal transcription system. Its Semitic heritage is conspicuous and noticeable in the scripts of many languages. Most alphabetic scripts have a deficit with respect to the vowels of the language for which they are used, as the vocalic phonemes almost invariably outnumber the available vowel letters.

3   The purely cenemic character of the alphabet is a matter of systemic principle rather than a characteristic of alphabetic scripts of individual languages. The limitations of the inventory of the letters of the alphabet (which, even with additional diacritics, is smaller than the number of phonemes of most languages), on the one hand, and the continuous change of language which gradually leads to a shift in the fit between letters and phonemes on the other, make it seem inevitable that the ideal of a simple cenemic system will be compromised in the course of time by the encroachment of pleremic elements.

SOME PRINCIPLES OF ALPHABETIC WRITING

That the alphabet is a cenemic writing system consisting of meaningless letters for the representation of meaningless sounds is a general and highly abstract statement which does not say very much about how the alphabet is used for particular languages (cf. Abercrombie 1949). Clearly, reading and writing alphabetically does not consist only in relating strings of meaningless signs with strings of meaningless speech sounds, and neither is the alphabetic representation of a language based on a simple phoneme-letter relation as depicted in figure 9.2.

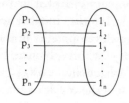

9.2 The ideal of phoneme writing: a bi-unique relation between phonemes and letters

A simple example is sufficient to show that the relations between phonemes and letters in alphabetic scripts are much more complex and do not conform to this ideal. The phoneme /ə/ of English, for instance, can be represented by every one of the five available vowel letters ⟨a⟩, ⟨e⟩, ⟨i⟩, ⟨o⟩ and ⟨u⟩, and conversely the letter ⟨a⟩ can represent a number of different phonemes such as /ə/, /a/, /ɑ/, /ɛ/ and /æ/ (figure 9.3). Moreover, the letter ⟨a⟩ in English fulfils other functions in environments such as *beat*, *breakfast* or *aunt*, which cannot be described adequately by referring to the phonemic structure of English alone.

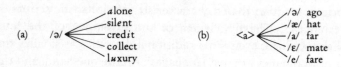

9.3 Multivalued relations between phoneme and alphabetic symbols (a) and between an alphabetic symbol and phonemes (b)

The alphabet is based on, and incorporates, a phonemic analysis, but it is noteworthy that this analysis is hardly ever consistently applied in alphabetic writing. This is so because there is a fundamental difference between the alphabet as a systematic principle and an alphabetic orthography of a given language. Of the alphabet it can be said that each letter stands for a speech sound, but although there are good reasons to assume systematic relations between the phonological structure of a language and its orthography, it cannot be taken for granted that the latter can be derived from the former.[6] Ὀρθογραφία, after all, means 'correct spelling': that is, spelling according to an accepted standard. Orthographies are subject to historical contingencies and conscious interventions, while the alphabet is an abstract principle. Therefore the alphabet is put to use in many different ways which do not allow for a uniform description of the relation between phonemes and letters.

The longer an alphabetic orthography is in use without readjustment, the more complicated the grapheme–phoneme correspondences become. The written norm of the language takes on a life of its own, becomes partly independent of speech and eventually exercises a certain influence on speech (W. Haas 1970). The relative independence of spoken and written norms,[7] or pronunciation and spelling, that thus emerges makes an orthography something much more complex than a faithful mapping of phonology.

Since alphabetic orthographies relate – in however complicated a fashion – to the phonological structures of language, and since they are subject to historical contingencies, there are necessarily considerable differences between these language-specific systems. They differ first of all with respect to the inventory of letters reflecting, to some extent, differences in the phonemic inventory of the languages, and second with respect to the systemic levels on which they operate. That is to say, they differ as regards the relations between letters and speech sounds. Alphabetic orthographies have access to a variety of systemic levels or subsystems of language assigning variable prominence to one level or another. With Scheerer (1986) three kinds of alphabetic orthographies can be distinguished.

1 Shallow orthographies operate on a level close to the phonetic surface structure reflecting the phonemic distinctions of the language. The Spanish and Serbo-Croatian orthographies belong to this type approximating, as they do, phonemic representations of these languages (Gibson and Levin 1975).

2 Intermediate orthographies, by and large, operate on the phonemic level, but also incorporate morphophonemic information. The Dutch spelling system is an example of this type (de Rooij and Verhoeven 1988).

3 Deep orthographies map on to a deep level of morphophonology and contain a significant amount of morphemic and lexical information. The orthography of English is the most widely discussed example of this kind (Venezky 1970; Sampson 1985: 207–13).

For orthographies of all three kinds it is necessary to distinguish the units of the inherent analysis from the units of representation. In alphabetic orthographies the units of analysis are phonemes; non-phonemic phonetic distinctions are generally disregarded. The basic signs of the system – that is, the letters – stand for phonemes, and all phonemes of the respective language are represented although some phonemes may be represented by more than one letter, and some letters may be used to represent more than one phoneme. Furthermore, some phonemes may be represented by combinations of letters, and certain letters may fulfil functions other than representing phonemes. Still, the unit of analysis underlying the elements of alphabetic orthographies is the phoneme. This does not, of course, imply that the phoneme is the only unit of representation of alphabetic orthographies. Rather, the basic signs are typically combined in such a way as to mark units of other structural levels as well, such as morphemes, words, sometimes parts of speech, and, with the help of additional signs, also clauses, sentences and paragraphs.

Orthographies of the third type (that is, deep orthographies) deviate most drastically from a purely phonemic representation. In an often quoted passage Chomsky and Halle (1968: 49) refer to English orthography as 'a near optimal system for the lexical representation of English words'.[8] This is hardly what one would expect as a major virtue of an alphabetic orthography, but it is what is bound to happen if a spelling system is used unchanged for a long time. For the past 400 years English spelling has experienced few significant changes, whereas the spoken language changed extensively (Venezky 1972). As a result, most regularities of English spelling become apparent only on the level of morphophonemic representation. To the extent that this is the case, English orthography as well as other orthographies of this type can be said to reintroduce pleremic elements into a cenemic system. Some of the principles that are operative in this regard are discussed in what follows.

Etymological spelling

In many orthographies purely phonemic representations of words are corrupted for the sake of graphically preserving their etymologies. For example, *breakfast* continues to be spelled with ⟨ea⟩ although the first vowel of the word is [e], because it is etymologically related to the verb *to break*. The ⟨w⟩ in *acknowledge* points to its etymological relation with *to know*. 'Silent' letters such as ⟨l⟩ in *folk*, ⟨k⟩ in *knife*, or ⟨w⟩ in *wrestle* are etymological remnants rather than representations of phonological units. Silent ⟨e⟩ in English occurs in many affixes of Latin and French origin such as, for instance, *-able*, *-age*, *-ance*, *-ate* and *-ative*, and is therefore statistically associated with words originating from these languages (P. T. Smith 1980: 35).

Etymological spelling is common in learned words, especially words of Latin origin. *Sign-* in *signal* and *paradigm* in *paradigmatic* are spelled phonemically, but as isolated words they contain a letter, ⟨g⟩, which has no counterpart in the phonemic representation. *Medicine–medical* and *righteous–right* are similar pairs where the rationale for the spelling of the first lies in the relation with the second. In this way, the spelling of a word often relates to that of other words belonging to the same paradigm, or to its own history. The *h-muet* in many French words such as *honeur*, *humeur*, *hôpital*, *humide*, *hiver*, etc., is etymological, testifying to their Latin origin. In English, too, the spelling of the corresponding words can be regarded as etymological with the additional peculiarity that they also exemplify the mechanism of spelling pronunciation, because they were borrowed for English from French rather than from Latin at a time when the ⟨h⟩ was no longer pronounced in French.

The observation that certain etymological spellings are quite regular has motivated some scholars (such as Albrow 1972) to propose different subsystems of English spelling. Etymological spelling paradigms would form one such subsystem in this view. In general, etymological spelling is a deviation from phonemic spelling which is evidence of the speech community's linguistic awareness and its readiness to acknowledge the independent existence of the written norm of its language.

Paradigmatic similarity

Another deviation from phonemic representation which is found in many alphabetic orthographies is based on the principle of making the graphemic representation of different units of a given paradigm as similar as possible. Vowel and consonant alternations which can be predicted from general morphophonological rules are neglected in writing in order to preserve the graphic identity of a morpheme or word. The shift from /ks/ to /gz/ in *anxious–anxiety* is an example of such a consonant alternation in English. Devoicing of final consonants in German and their orthographic representation can be interpreted similarly. For example, in the German *Tag*, *Tage* ([tak], [tagə]), the principle of paradigmatic similarity motivates the letter ⟨g⟩ for both the voiced and the voiceless form. The representation of vowel length in German is another instance where the principle of paradigmatic similarity can be seen at work. The letter ⟨h⟩ is sometimes attached to a vowel to indicate length. Whenever this is the case, the ⟨h⟩ is used in all forms of the paradigm, such as *stehlen*, *stahl*, *gestohlen* (to steal). In other cases, vowel length is not marked in writing, as in *gebären*, *gebar*, *geboren* (to give birth). Here too all forms of the paradigm are treated equally. This kind of distribution of ⟨h⟩ in German is very regular, apparently without exception (cf. Eisenberg 1983).

Like etymological spelling, the preservation of morphemic invariance in writing historically implies a growing influence of the written language on the native speaker's knowledge about his or her own language. It should be noted, however, that this principle operates selectively within particular orthographies, and that its salience varies greatly across languages.

Word representation

While in early Greek no spaces were left between the letters of the alphabet to indicate word division, modern orthographies using the Greek, Latin or Russian alphabet represent the word as an independent unit. Perhaps a better way of saying this is that alphabetic orthographies usually group letters in clusters with some space intervening between the clusters. Readers of the respective language then come to recognize such clusters as 'words'. To some extent, at least, the orthographic word is an artefact and a structural unit which is superimposed on the representation of the speech continuum. In the spoken language breath pauses do not consistently co-occur with word boundaries; yet words are intuitively obvious units of speech because of their contextual distribution.

That word separation in writing interferes with the faithful mapping of speech is particularly conspicuous where phonetic groups reach across word boundaries. The so-called *liaison* in French is a prominent example. Phonetically the French equivalent of 'the friends' is to be represented as [le za · mi], but the orthographic segmentation is quite different: *les amis*. In other orthographies this phenomenon, which can be described as external sandhi,[9] is represented at the expense of marking word boundaries, as for example in the Devanagari script for Sanskrit (cf. chapter 10, below).

Representing external word structure is one instance where writing exhibits analyticity. In most alphabetic orthographies external word structure is marked, while the internal word structure or morphemic structure is ignored, or only occasionally marked to facilitate pronunciation, as in *re-elect* where the hyphen serves to prevent the reading /riːl/ of the first four letters, or to disambiguate two forms, as in *hopped* where the second ⟨p⟩ distinguishes the preterite of *hop* from that of *hope*. In Chinese, by contrast, word boundaries are left unmarked, while morphemes are consistently represented as individual units. Of course, both words and morphemes are pleremic rather than cenemic units of language.

Homograph avoidance

Many alphabetic orthographies violate the strictly phonemic representation of words for the sake of incorporating semantic information in yet another way: they differentiate homophone words. *Bear* v. *bare*, *blue* v. *blew*, *eye* v. *aye*, *hare* v. *hair*, *mail* v. *male*, *not* v. *knot*, *no* v. *know*, *rain* v. *reign*, *vain* v. *vane*, are only some examples. Some such pairs, such as *phrase–frays*, are not easily recognized because the differentiation on the orthographic level tends to supersede the identity on the phonetic level. Homograph avoidance is an orthographic feature which is exploited widely in the interest of direct lexical access.

Capitalization of words of certain form classes is an additional means of differentiation serving the same purpose. The German orthography, for instance, makes extensive use of capital letters to differentiate homonyms which would be homographs without them. *Wagen*, 'car' (noun) v. *wagen*, 'dare' (verb), *Arm*, 'arm' (noun) v. *arm*, 'poor' (adjective), *Wand*, 'wall' (noun) v. *wand*, 'wound' (past participle), *Warte*, 'look-out' (noun) v. *warte*, 'wait!' (verb) are some examples that illustrate the point.

Differentiating homonyms on the graphemic level has obvious advantages for the decoding process, but it is an additional burden for the acquisition of an orthography making extensive use of this principle.

Loan word identification

Another characteristic principle of many alphabetic systems is that words of different origins are spelled according to different grapheme–

phoneme correspondence rules. The phoneme /f/, for instance, is typically represented with the letter ⟨f⟩, but in a certain subset of words such as *philistine*, *philosopher* and *phenotype*, it is expressed by ⟨ph⟩ in several European orthographies. These words are of Greek origin, and since the ⟨ph⟩-for-/f/ spelling is used in Greek loan words or Greek derived words only, this spelling can be considered a marker of this subset of words in English and other European languages. Similarly, the phoneme /k/ is spelled /ch/ in words of Greek origin in English: for example, *chlorine*, *chronology*, *cholesterol* and *psychology*. Marking words as foreign is not the only function of these and similar spelling conventions. They also serve the function of preserving the identity of many loan words across languages in which they may be pronounced differently. This is not a marginal point because many of these learned words belong to scientific or technical terminologies, and their graphic identity facilitates international communication in certain specialized fields.

By adopting loan words in their original spelling orthographies tend to become heterogeneous, incorporating different sets of rules that apply to different parts of the lexicon. In German, ⟨ou⟩ can be used to represent /u/ in French loan words such as *Coupon*, *Courage* and *Coupe*, but not in Germanic words such as *kurz*/**kourz*, 'short', *Kugel*/**Kougel*, 'ball' or *Kummer*/**Koummer*, 'grief' (asterisks signal deviant forms). That the notion of loan word is a graded one finds expression in the fact that the spelling of loan words is sometimes brought into agreement with native conventions as they become progressively nativized. For example, the French loan word *Cousine* is nowadays frequently spelled *Kusine* in German.

The principle of spelling loan words in English is to preserve the source language orthography but then pronounce the orthographic word as if it were English. Loan words are hence not readily recognized in speech. The principle of Spanish orthography, by contrast, is to preserve the 'sound' of the foreign word in so far as Spanish phonology permits this. The spelling of loan words is therefore adapted to the Spanish orthography which makes them sometimes difficult to recognize in writing.

It should be noted once again that, like the other principles discussed above, the application of the principle of identifying loan words by a special set of spelling rules varies greatly across alphabetic orthographies. Dutch, for example, hardly uses it, while in English and German it singles out large parts of the lexicon and thereby systematically distinguishes different lexical strata. The ⟨ph⟩ spelling for /f/ in German and English is an example. It is applied only in Greek derived words. Some comparisons illustrate this point.

English	German	Dutch
phoneme	Phonem	foneem
photographer	Photograph/Fotograph	fotograaf
physical	physisch	fysisch
phantom	Phantom	fantoom
pharmacology	Pharmakologie	farmacologie

CONCLUSION

The alphabet is simple, but many alphabetic orthographies are not. The alphabet is a system of cenemic signs, each of which represents a speech sound. However, typically alphabetic orthographies do not consist of simple rules mapping letters on to phonemes because most orthographies have fewer symbols than their languages have phonemes. Therefore alphabetic writing is, on the one hand, often underdetermined with respect to the phonological features to be represented in writing a given language and, on the other hand, relies on principles that deviate from phonological representation. Some of these principles which operate on, and refer to, levels of linguistic structure other than phonemic or phonetic representation were discussed above: etymology, paradigmatic similarity, word representation, homograph avoidance and loan word identification. All these principles conflict with, and reduce the generality of, those rules that operate on the phonemic level: that is, the proper level of alphabetic writing.

In some very shallow orthographies, especially those of recent origin, the relations between phonemes and letters are regular and relatively simple. However, this cannot be considered as typical of alphabetic writing. It is much more likely that a reader of an alphabetic script must consider linguistic information of different kinds in order to handle the system proficiently. Knowledge of etymology, form class, morphemic segmentation, abstract lexical representation, morphophonological rules and derivations and the interrelations between all of these is necessary to various degrees in order to grasp the totality of the regularities that make up an alphabetic orthography. To average readers, some of these regularities do not appear regular at all because, not being professional linguists, they lack the necessary analytic insight.

It should also be noted that, in spite of the often praised universality of the alphabet, an alphabetic orthography is not equally suitable for all languages. Furthermore, existing alphabetic orthographies differ in large measure in quality. Alphabetic writing is generally both underdetermined with respect to some linguistic features, and ambiguous with respect to the representation of others. To some extent, underdetermination and ambiguity are counterbalanced by redundancy, but for many languages the Roman, Greek or Cyrillic alphabets are too restricted and require substantial augmentation with special characters and diacritics. Vowels, vowel quality, tones and suprasegmental features such as stress and intonation especially are poorly represented by alphabetic scripts and, therefore, languages in which these features are numerous and phonemic usually pose problems for the creation of a suitable orthography.

It is well known that, under the differing conditions which govern their use in various languages, the letters of the Roman alphabet are pronounced quite differently. This is so because even though phonemes are what the isolated letters of the alphabet in principle represent, most orthographies are not phonemic notations of the respective languages. Trivial as it may seem, it is important to keep in mind that alphabetic orthographies are both alphabetic *and* orthographies, which is to say that they are by their very nature designed to fulfil two disparate functions. On the one hand, their systematic make-up allows for a more faithful and flexible representation of speech sounds than any other writing system; on the other, they are an effective means of regulating and not just mapping pronunciation and are, therefore, not intended by their users just to faithfully represent the sounds of their speech but to fulfil other functions as well.

The perennial tension between these two functions is a necessary rather than an accidental and avoidable characteristic of alphabetic writing because, like a language, an orthography is a social and hence historical fact. The simplicity of the underlying system is bound to be corrupted once it is put to use. For the Roman maxim *verba volant, scripta manent*, 'the words are gone but what has been written remains', is true of all writing irrespective of the system that is being used. Writing is not a phonetic or phonemic transcription, and neither is a text simply speech written down. In languages with an alphabetic written tradition the mutual relations between writing and pronunciation are highly complex, for the twofold function of written signs tends to be to represent and prescribe sounds. Since language changes continuously, while orthography does not, but is adjusted deliberately from time to time according to different and sometimes irreconcilable principles, the written representation of a language necessarily gains a certain autonomy which in turn implies that every alphabetic orthography that is used for some time develops an increasingly complex relationship between letters and phonemes.

NOTES

1 Isaac Taylor (1899: 44) was convinced that the seventh century BC afforded the first firm standing ground for the study of Greek epigraphy. Half a century later, Gelb in 1952 (here quoted from the revised second edition of 1963) adopted the ninth century as the most likely time of introduction of Phoenician writing to Greece.

2 A similar suggestion was made much earlier by Larfeld (1907: 304ff) who also estimated the time of borrowing as the eleventh century.

3 McLuhan was, of course, not the first to emphasize the uniqueness and superiority of alphabetic writing. Isaac Taylor (1899: 3) wrote that 'every system of non-alphabetic writing will, however, either be so limited in its power of expression as to be of small practical value, or, on the other hand, it will be so difficult and complicated as to be unsuited for general use.' He did not go as far as McLuhan (1962) who called the users of other writing systems, notably the Chinese and the Japanese, 'tribal', but he also remarked that 'without the alphabet any complete system for the graphic representation of speech is an acquirement so arduous as to demand the labour of a lifetime' (Isaac Taylor 1899: 3).

4 Voegelin and Voegelin (1961) have called this 'a change of types', viz. a change from the 'independent consonant (IC) type' to the 'independent consonant + independent vowel (IC + IV) type'.

5 The literature on the question of the origin of the supplementary letters is quite extensive. The two basic hypotheses, (1) the differentiation of existing Greek letters, and (2) borrowing from non-Greek sources, are discussed at length in Jensen (1969: 462ff).

6 Diachronically viewed, the phonology of any language precedes its orthography, and the relationship between both should therefore be described in terms of deriving the orthography from the phonology. Synchronically this

may not be the most reasonable approach, however. Householder (1972), for example, has convincingly argued that, in the case of English, it is more economical and theoretically elegant to derive the phonology from the orthography. It must be noted, furthermore, that despite the historical priority of speech over writing, an orthography may exercise considerable influence on the phonology of a language in the course of time (cf. Levitt 1978).

7 I am using the notions of spoken and written norm in the sense developed in Vachek (1973).

8 Much earlier Bolinger (1946) introduced the notion of 'visual morphemes' demonstrating with many examples that the morpheme is a relevant unit in written English.

    Cf. Insup Taylor (1981: 35ff) for a discussion of Chomsky and Halle's contention that English orthography represents English words (also Henderson 1982: 95ff).

9 Herslund (1986) treats French *liaison* as a case of external sandhi.

10

Writing in India

India is a literate culture of great eminence where the art of writing has been held in great esteem since antiquity; but the most revered literature was composed before the advent of writing in India, and it continued to be transmitted orally for many centuries thereafter. The Brahmins have always regarded written transmission of knowledge as less valuable than oral. India is the home of several of the most highly cultivated written languages ever known in history; but it is also the home of a much greater number of languages for which a writing system has never been developed. Simple cenemic scripts were available in India twenty-three centuries ago, but literacy remained severely restricted, and until recently was not necessarily regarded as a condition of social recognition or dignity.

It is apparent contradictions of this kind that make the study of writing in India so intriguing. They are evidence of the coexistence and intertwining of a literate and an oral tradition unique to Indian culture and history.

HISTORICAL BACKGROUND

The study of writing in India is mainly concerned with two periods separated from each other by about 2,000 years. Despite persistent efforts, no convincing connection has been established as yet between the two. The first period involves the early Indus valley civilization of the third millennium BC, and the second period involves what is generally considered the beginning of Indic writing proper in the fifth century BC.

The Indus valley script

Since the 1920s, excavations of the ruins of Harappa in the Punjab and Mohenjo-daro in Sindh have brought to light some 2,500 steatite seals which are engraved with concrete images and an as yet undeciphered script (figure 10.1). The discovery of the remains of a pre-Aryan civilization in India which flourished between 3500 and 2000 BC has proved to be of considerable interest to scholars of various backgrounds. Without discrediting attempts to arrive at an historical assessment of the archeological findings that can link the Harappan civilization to Indian history, it may be noted that scholars belonging to certain ethnic groups in India have a keen interest in claiming these earliest instances of writing as part of their own cultural heritage. For example, in his book on the Austric civilization of India, Hembram cites Austric peoples such as the Santals as the true descendants of the pre-Aryan civilization in the Indus valley and concludes 'that the entire Indian civilization is just an off-shoot of the great Harappan civilization' (Hembram 1982: 4). Nowadays, the Austric peoples of India are among the most backward. They enjoy special constitutional protection but very little social prestige. But if Hembram's claim could be substantiated, they would all of a sudden become the true forebears of Indian civilization. Similarly, some Tamil scholars have tried to incorporate the Harappan civilization into their cultural heritage and have suggested Dravidian interpretations for the inscriptions on the Harappan seals (cf., for example, Mahadevan 1970, 1986; Dani 1983).[1] Always in competition with the Aryan Hindus in the north, Tamil nationalists would certainly like to see evidence that their contributions to Indian civilization predate those of the Aryans. However, so far the Harappan seals have not yielded any evidence to allow such a conclusion.

Owing to the fragmentary evidence, assured knowledge about the Indus valley script is extremely limited. Not even the number of different signs is agreed upon, some scholars counting as many as 400, while others reckon only 150. The inscriptions that have been found are very short, and the language is unknown (Allchin and Allchin 1982: 212). Thus very little can be said about the system, and even the assumption that the inscriptions were used for labeling merchandise rests on speculation. The available evidence suggests that Harappa, like Crete, was a civilization with very restricted literacy which did not survive the destruction of the urban centres where it existed. At present, there is no

10.1 Steatite seals with Indus valley script

reason to believe that the Indus valley inscriptions will reveal anything about the origin of Indic writing proper.[2]

INDIC WRITING PROPER

The beginning of comprehensible writing in India dates from the fifth century BC but the earliest long documents, the Asoka inscriptions, belong to the middle of the third century BC. As of that time, writing in India grew into one of the richest and most varied literary traditions ever, although – with the possible exception of the Indus valley script – no genuine script creation took place on the Indian subcontinent. India boasts well over 200 different scripts which are, however, all derived from one source, the Brāhmī script. Although the early history of writing in India is still poorly understood, it is now generally agreed that it can be traced back eventually to a Semitic source. Opinions vary, however, as to where to look in the Semitic world for the model of the earliest Indic script, some favoring a North Semitic origin, while others consider a South Semitic connection more likely. Jensen (1969: 355) assumes that the idea of alphabetic writing was borrowed from the Phoenicians and then modified to suit the needs of the Indo-Aryan languages. Gelb (1963: 187) and Diringer (1968: 262), on the other hand, regard a South Semitic model as the more likely parent script because the principle of vowel indication in the Ethiopian script is the same as in all Indic scripts. For present purposes it is enough to note that the Indic writing systems are derived from a foreign, most probably Semitic, source.

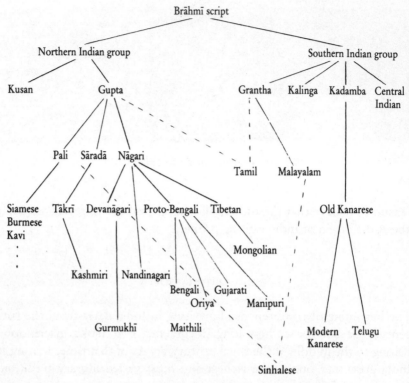

10.2 *The most important Brāhmī derived scripts*

The Asoka edicts of 251 BC were redacted in two different scripts: the Kharosthi script, which is also known as 'Indo-bactric', and the Brāhmī script. The left running direction of the Kharosthi script points to a Semitic connection. As Aramaic was in the third century BC the most important administrative language in the Middle East (extending from Syria to Persia and Afghanistan), it seems likely that the northern Indian empire borrowed the Aramaic script which was also left running. For some time the Kharosthi script and the Brāhmī script were both used in India, but eventually the latter prevailed, and it is the Brāhmī script from which all other Indic scripts originated. Figure 10.2 provides an overview of the most important Brāhmī derived scripts.

THE SYSTEM OF INDIC SCRIPTS

As discussed in chapter 8, all Semitic scripts are consonant scripts. The Kharosthi script, however, is not. Rather, every letter sign has as its value a consonant plus what is called an 'inherent vowel' /a/: that is, unless otherwise specified, every letter is to be read as a syllable C + *a*. Yet the Kharosthi script is not syllabic because the other vowels are indicated by systematically modifying the basic consonant sign with additional diacritical marks. For example, a vertical stroke is added to indicate /e/ and thus transform the values of the basic signs for /ka/, /ga/, /gha/, etc., into /ke/, /ge/, /ghe/, etc. Consonant clusters are represented by ligatures where two or more basic consonant signs are joined together and where the inherent vowels of each of them except the last are muted. The principle of vowel indication of the Kharosthi script is illustrated in figure 10.3. It is fundamentally the same as that of the Brāhmī script which is much more important than the Kharosthi script since it is the source of all other Indic scripts including those that have survived until the present time.

Like the Kharosthi script, the Brāhmī script is a Semitic derivative, and again it is first attested in left running inscriptions. However, as of the Asoka edicts, its direction is from left to right. The principles of vowel indication resemble those of the Kharosthi script (see figure 10.4).

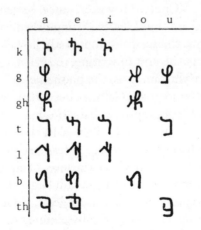

10.3 Vowel indication in the Kharosthi script

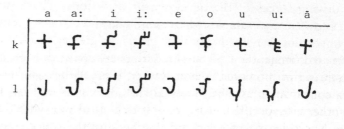

10.4　Vowel indication in the Brāhmī script

They can be summarized as follows.

1　The Brāhmī script has signs for syllabic – that is, initial – vowels:
　Ⱶ /a/, ⁚ /i/, L /u/ and ◁ /e/.
2　Every basic sign has a consonant and the inherent vowel /a/ as
　its value.
3　Other vowels are represented by modifying the respective C +
　a sign in a like manner for all basic consonant signs.
4　Consonant clusters are represented by ligatures, all but the last
　consonant elements of which lose their inherent vowel.
5　The inherent /a/ vowel can be muted by a special diacritic.

As can be inferred from these principles, the basic unit of writing in
the Brāhmī script is the syllable. The structural principles of the script
enable the representation of syllables of various different kinds: V, CV,
CCV, CCCV, CVC, VC, etc. However, since vowels are indicated by
diacritical marks and are thus clearly distinguished from the consonant
part of the basic signs, the script cannot justly be called 'syllabic'. As in
the old Ethiopic script the unit of writing, the syllable, is not the same as
the unit of the underlying analysis, the phoneme.

For theoreticians who, like Gelb, believe that 'writing must pass
through the stages of logography, syllabography, and alphabetography
in this, and no other, order' (Gelb 1963: 201), the structure of the Old
Indic system is very disturbing, because in terms of this teleological view
it appears to be a retrogression. Once the level of alphabetic writing has
been reached, there can be no return to a unit larger than the phoneme as
the unit of written representation; this, at least, is Gelb's theory of the
development of writing. However, rigidly clinging to such a principle is
the result of overestimating the significance of economy and simplicity

as the driving forces of the development of writing. The history of writing knows many examples where simplicity and economy proved to be less important than unequivocality, precision, greater differentiation, resistance to change, the desire to be different or other factors that are hard to accord with rational assessments of the possibilities and needs of optimizing a system. Thus it should not be assumed, for the sake of a developmental theory, that it is necessary either to part with the idea that, on the one hand, Indic writing is derived from a Semitic source or, on the other, to regard Semitic writing as syllabic rather than consonantal. Theories can be consistent, but there is little reason to believe that people who struggle with the adaptation of a given writing system to a language for which it was not created usually go about this business in a very consistent manner. The hypothesis that the syllabic–phonemic Brāhmī script was derived from, or inspired in its development by, a Semitic consonant script should thus not be discarded for theoretical reasons alone. The Indic way of indicating vowels as obligatory diacritics of basic consonant signs may have originated from the Semitic practice of optional vowel indication by means of diacritics. Yet, until corroborated by hard archeological evidence, this explanation of the origin of Indic writing, too, can be regarded only as a plausible hypothesis.

One thing, however, is clear: whatever form of Semitic writing was introduced into the north-west of India in the eighth or seventh century BC was thoroughly nativized and recreated – that is, consciously redesigned along segmental phonemic lines – by the ancient Indians. The order in which the letters of Indic scripts are arranged is clear evidence of this, since it follows purely phonological principles (Kannaiyan 1960). As is well known, the Indians cultivated grammatical scholarship to an extent unparalleled by any nation of antiquity.[3] The phonological principles underlying the arrangement of the Indic scripts testifies to thorough scientific analysis. The letters are classified in accordance with places of articulation: vowels and diphthongs first, then consonants – that is, consonants with an inherent /a/ or schwa – gutturals, palatals, cerebrals [palatals], dentals, labials, semivowels and spirants, in this order. It is interesting to note that their phonological insight did not induce the Indians to discard the syllable as the unit of written representation. On the contrary, its significance is recognized implicitly by the structural make-up of all Indic writing systems, and explicitly by the Indian phoneticians.

Around the beginning of the present era, two main types of Brāhmī derived scripts evolved: the northern group and the southern group. Each encompassed a large number of scripts. Although they were all built on the same principle of diacritical vowel indication, and although some were almost isomorphic, they were by no means so similar that having learned one enabled one to read others. There was considerable variation, especially as regards the outer form of the various systems.

The northern group

The Brāhmī-derived scripts of the northern group cover a vast territory extending from north-western India to Nepal and Tibet in the north, across the subcontinent to Bengal and what is now Bangladesh, and further east to south-east Asia. The Gupta script, which evolved in the fourth century AD, was the first Brāhmī derivative of more than regional importance. Directly and indirectly it gave rise to many other important scripts, notably the Pali and Nagari scripts. As of the eleventh century, the latter is known as *Devanagari* (from the Sanskrit *deva*, 'heavenly'). As the script of Sanskrit literature[4] it became the most widely used script in India. In addition to Sanskrit, other Indo-Aryan languages are written with Devanagari, such as Hindi, Nepali, Marwari and Kumaoni, as well as many languages of other affiliations such as Mundari-Ho and Gondi. Nowadays Devanagari is often used for the reduction to writing of hitherto unwritten languages. Because of its importance, the Devanagari system is here described in some detail.

The Devanagari alphabet consists of forty-eight letters, thirteen vowels and thirty-five consonants, which supposedly represent every sound of the Sanskrit language. Sanskrit (from *saṃ-skṛta* 'elaborated') is that phase of the literary language of ancient India which is described in the grammar of Panini (see figure 10.5).[5]

The order of the alphabet in figure 10.5 is that devised by the ancient Indian grammarians. Sanskrit dictionaries are arranged in this order. The vowel letters at the beginning of the list are shown in two forms, initial and medial, the initial form being the canonical form, while the medial form is to be considered as an abbreviation. There is no medial form for the short /a/[6] because this vowel does not occur in the post-vocalic position and, at the same time, is the inherent vowel of the unmodified consonant letters. Its long counterpart /a:/ does have a medial as well as an initial letter sign, however. Nasalization is expressed by a dot placed above the letter which is thus modified, for example, तं /taṃ/. This

Vowels		Consonants				
*	+					
श्र अ	– a	क k	} gutturals	प p	} labials	
श्रा आ	ा ā	ख k-h		फ p-h		
		ग g̱		ब b		
		घ g̱-h		भ b-h		
		ङ ṅ		म m		
इ	f i	च c	} palatals	य y	} semivowels	
ई	ी ī	छ c-h		र r		
उ	० u	ज j		ल l		
ऊ	० ū	भ्र झ or j-h		व v		
		ञ ñ				
ऋ	८ r (or ṛi)	ट ṭ	} cerebrals	श ś (or ç)	} spirants	
ॠ	८ ṝ (or ṛī)	ठ ṭ-h		ष ṣ		
ऌ	८ ḷ (or ḷi)	ड ḍ		स s		
		ढ ḍ-h		ह h		
		ण ṇ				
ए	े e	त t	} dentals	: ḥ (visarga)		
ऐ	ै ai	थ t-h		ं ṃ or ṁ (anusvāra)		
ओ	ो o	द d				
औ	ौ au	ध d-h				
		न n				

* initial form of letters   + medial form of letters

10.5 The Devanagari alphabet for Sanskrit

device is known as *anusvāra*, 'after-sound'.[7] Similarly, weak aspiration is indicated by the *visarga*, a colon after the preceding letter, as in सः/saḥ/. Medial vowel signs neutralize the inherent /a/ of the consonant letter to which they are attached.

Two additional conventions are applied for the muting of the inherent /a/ in other environments.

1 In word final position, an oblique stroke, called *virama*, is added to the consonant letter, for instance प /pa/, but प् /p/. A VC-syllable is thus written with an independent vowel letter first and then a consonant letter muted by means of a *virama*.

2 Consonant clusters are represented by ligatures: that is, the conjoining of two or more consonant letters. Every consonant letter which is followed directly by another thus loses its inherent vowel.

The ligatures have to be learned separately because in many cases their sound value is hard to infer on the basis of the graphical composition of the complex letter sign. As all of the basic letters have a vertical stroke and the characteristic horizontal line on top,[8] ligatures are often formed by adding a distinctive stroke only to the letter which keeps its inherent vowel. For example, the consonant cluster /nt/ is represented by conjoining the letters for /n(+ a)/ न and /t(+ a)/ त to form the ligature न्त /nta/. Some very common ligatures are listed below.

क्क /kka/	क्ख /kkha/	क्त /kta/	क्त्य /ktya/
क्त्र /ktra/	क्त्व /ktva/	क्थ /ktha/	क्न /kna/
क्म /kma/	क्य /kya/	क्र /kra/	क्ल /kla/
क्व /kva/			

While in Hindi and other modern Indian languages efforts are made to avoid ligatures, the ligatures of Sanskrit are complex and very numerous. Their great number as well as the indication of vowels by separate letters (except for the weak inherent /a/) suggest that the primary value of the letters is consonantal rather than syllabic. The inherent vowel is probably a remnant of the Semitic derivation of this script.

The medial vowel signs are to be understood as diacritics to the consonant signs, since they are graphically defined with respect to a consonant sign as the pivot. This non-linear vowel marking has resulted in certain inconsistencies: for example, both /i/ and /i:/ were originally written as curves above the consonant sign, the former to the left and the latter to the right. In hand writing they were not well distinguished as both marks often appeared as an arch on top of the horizontal line of the consonant letter. For the sake of clear distinction, the curves were later prolonged with a vertical downward stroke, one to the left, the other to the right. As a result, medial or final /i/ is now written before the consonant after which it is pronounced: for example, चि /ci/, नि /ti/ and ग्नि /yi/, where ि stands for /i/.

Like all Indian scripts, Devanagari is written from left to right. Word boundaries are not marked, except at certain junctures, as the horizontal bars forming the upper part of all consonant letters are usually linked to form an unbroken line. The line is only broken between words ending on a vowel, diphthong, nasal (*anusvāra*) or weak spirant (*visarga*) and words with an initial consonant. In all other cases words are linked to each other as they are in speech, requiring the observation of euphonic rules called sandhi, now a household term of modern phonetics (Allen

1962). The marking of sandhi is important in Sanskrit orthography, which can be interpreted as evidence of the priority the ancient Indian linguists assigned to the sentence over the word. Rather than writing successions of isolated words, Sanskrit orthography is sensitive to breath groups representing connected discourse. Isolated words were considered by the Indian grammarians primarily as pedagogical devices. Since in natural discourse they are not usually articulated in isolation, but rather part of a modulated sound continuum, the Indian grammarians distinguished the boundaries of such words in writing only where they coincided with breath pauses. Sentences, on the other hand, are marked regularly by a perpendicular stroke (I). Two such strokes (II) are used at the end of a text. Figure 10.6 illustrates this.

व्यवहारान्नृपः पश्येद्विद्वद्भिर्ब्राह्मणैः सह ।
धर्मशास्त्रानुसारेण क्रोधलोभविवर्जितः ॥ १ ॥

*vyavahārān nṛpaḥ paśyed vidvadbhir brāhmanaiḥ
saha dharmaśāstrānusāreṇa krodhalobhavivarjitaḥ*

The ruler shall examine the trials together with learned Brahmins in accordance with the law, free of ire and passion.

10.6 Sanskrit text in Devanagari script (adapted from Jensen 1925)

In spite of its importance, the Devanagari alphabet has never acquired the pan-Indian status which, for economic or chauvinistic reasons, some wish it had (Ray 1960; Pattanayak 1979). It was used as a model for several other scripts, notably Gurmukhi which in the sixteenth century was devised for writing Punjabi, the language of the Sikhs. Today, it coexists in India with at least ten other major scripts and scores of others of lesser importance. Some of the major ones are derived from it; others share with it the common Brāhmī origin, and still others are unrelated (such as Roman and Perso-Arabic).

Another important member of the northern group of Brāhmī derived scripts is the Bengali script which has been used for more than half a millennium for Bengali, Assamese (with four additional letters) and Manipuri, as well as for some Tibeto-Burmese languages and for

Santhali, an Austric language spoken in West Bengal, Bihar and Orissa. Oriya, the dominant regional language of the state of Orissa, has its own script which is derived from the Bengali script. Structurally it is very similar, but its outer form is markedly distinct since, instead of the horizontal bar characteristic of both Devanagari and Bengali, it has a kind of arch which may be a result of writing on palm leaves with an iron stylus. Also closely related to the Bengali script are the Gujarati and Kaithi scripts which were developed for writing the Gujarati and Bihari languages, respectively. Bihari is now written with Devanagari.

The northern group of Brāhmī derived scripts also comprises a number of systems used outside India and even the Indian subcontinent. Of special importance are the Tibetan, the Pali, the Old Burmese or Thai and the Kavi (Sinhalese) scripts.

Tibetan   The adaptation to Tibetan of the Gupta alphabet, which is believed to be the immediate forebear of the Tibetan script (Scharlipp 1984), made significant changes necessary because Tibetan is not an Indo-European language and is structurally very different from the Indic languages for which the Gupta script had evolved. As with the Indian scripts, the Tibetan alphabet consists of consonant signs with a weak inherent vowel, which is neutralized by attaching diacritics for other vowels to the consonant signs. However, in contrast to the Indic systems, Tibetan has only one independent vowel letter, for /a/. By extending the principle of diacritical vowel indication, this letter is also used as a base to which diacritics for other vowels are attached to indicate their syllabic occurrence. Ligatures are formed in a way similar to that of Devanagari; however, there is no vowel muting sign. Instead, a dot placed at the upper right corner of a consonant letter indicates syllable closure. Hence, if no dot is placed between two or more consonant letters, the group is to be read as a consonant cluster.

The Tibetan script is hard to read because, while the language has changed considerably, the script has changed very little since its inception some 1,300 years ago. The phonographic match is, therefore, very involved. Moreover, the script has a serious defect. Tibetan is a tone language, but there are no graphic means to indicate tone.

Pali   Yet another subgroup of northern Indian scripts are the *Pali* scripts which came into existence for writing those Prakrit languages most closely associated with Buddhism. The Pali script spread together with this religion, and hence does not have descendants in India, but only in the Buddhist countries of south and south-east Asia (notably in Sri Lanka, Burma, Laos, Thailand and Cambodia) as well as in central Asia and on the Indonesian archipelago, where it served as the model for a variety of new scripts. The Old Thai, or Siamese script, may be mentioned here because it has some interesting features not often found in other scripts.[9]

Old Thai Like Tibetan and Chinese, the Thai language is a tone language but, unlike the scripts of the former two, the Thai script has developed a means of indicating phonemic tone. As a result of sound changes that have reduced the overall number of consonants in the language, some consonant letters have become redundant. These redundant letters were subsequently transformed into tone indicators. In addition, four diacritics placed on the right shoulder of the respective consonant letter are used to indicate tone. When there is a vowel sign on the consonant letter, the tone mark is placed above it.

The Indic method of diacritical vowel indication is not very suitable for a vowel-rich language like Thai where double vowels without any intervening consonants are common. The orthographical device which has evolved for the representation of successions of vowels is the employment of the consonant letters for /ʔ/, /y/ and /w/ as a silent base to which vowel diacritics are attached. Another diacritic is attached to silent letters indicating etymological spelling.

Kavi The influence of northern Indic writing extends as far east as Indonesia where wave after wave of the spread of culture and religion gave rise to a number of new scripts (de Casparis 1975). Historically, Javanese was the most highly cultivated language in Indonesia with the most numerous speech community. It is also the most prominent language to which the Kavi script was applied, a script which was developed on the model of the Old Burmese script. Offshoots of this script are used for Balinese and Madurese. The Kavi script follows the basic Indic principle of vowel indication, but in its Javanese form has developed several peculiar features of its own. Among them are capital letters for proper names and punctuation marks for new paragraphs and for poetry. Most interesting, however, are a number of epistolary signs indicating the writer's social rank as higher, equal or lower than that of his addressee. The Javanese language is well known for its intricate system of honorifics, and it is in keeping that it has honorifics in its writing, too. Moreover, the graphically codified expression of social relationships is a feature that distinguishes the Javanese script from all other Indic derived systems.

The last of the northern scripts which must be mentioned is the Sinhalese script, which is derived from Pali, the Buddhist script. This script also shows the influence of the Malayalam script of the southern Indian group.

The southern group

The division between northern and southern Indian scripts coincides, roughly, with the division between the Aryan and Dravidian languages for which they are used. Both groups, however, include scripts of languages that belong to other language families. The southern group of Indian scripts is comprised of a smaller number than the northern. The most important Dravidian languages are Tamil, Telugu, Malayalam and Kanarese. All of them are written with scripts of the southern group. Several varieties of at least five early systems are attested as being already extant in the fifth century AD. Three of them, the Younger Kalinga, the Western Indian and the Central Indian scripts, did not survive for a long time, however.

More important was the Kadamba script which gave rise to the Old Kanarese script, whose wide distribution over South India resulted in the formation of several distinct systems. As of the middle of the first millennium of the present era, the modern Kanarese, or Kannada, and the Telugu scripts emerged with (by and large) the form in which they are used today. In terms of historical development and their present spread, they are the most important members of the southern group.

The other important type of this group was the Grantha script which in the twelfth century gave rise to the Malayalam script. Apart from the Malayalam language, this script was also used as the southern Indian script for Sanskrit. Nowadays in the south it is only used for Malayalam, but in the west of the subcontinent it is also used for Telugu.

Also derived from the Grantha script is the Tamil alphabet which originated about the eighth century and which occupies a special position in the group of South Indian scripts because it shows shared features with northern systems, pointing to a connection with Nagari. The Tamil system is more economical and easier to read than most

Indian scripts.[10] Having no letters for aspirated consonants or spirants, its inventory of basic signs is rather small, consisting of just over twenty letters,[11] as opposed, for instance, to the forty-odd letters of Old Kanarese, or the fifty-three letters of Malayalam. Moreover, Tamil has no consonant ligatures. The consonants of a cluster are written one next to the other with a dot (*hasanta*) over the letter to be read without its inherent vowel.

The scripts of the southern group share with those of the northern group most features of their structural make-up, in particular the principle of vowel indication by obligatory diacritics to consonant base signs. While certain differences between the various systems are related to structural differences between the languages for which they evolved, the most salient distinctions pertain to the outer form. They are superficial in a systematic sense; but then they are also crucially important in a social sense because it is these most readily noticeable features of a script to which its users attach symbolic values.

Before elaborating this point in some more detail, it should be noted that the foregoing discussion has mentioned only some 10 per cent of all Indian scripts. Brāhmī derived scripts have been applied to hundreds of languages of different affiliations ranging from Indo-European (such as Sanskrit, Hindi, Bengali, Assamese, Rajastani, Punjabi and Sindhi) and Dravidian (such as Tamil, Telugu, Kanarese, Malayalam and Tulu), through Austro-Asiatic (for example, Santhali and Mundari-Ho) and Tibeto-Burman (for example, Tibetan and Burmese) and Austro-Thai (for example, Thai), to Mon-Khmer (for example, Cambodian) and Austronesian (for example, Javanese, Madurese and Balinese). The vastness of the area and the number of the languages in south, south-east and central Asia to which the descendants of the Brāhmī script have radiated is enormous. And on the subcontinent itself the great variety of scripts is a significant part of the literary tradition and the multilingual identity of Indian culture.

SOCIOLINGUISTIC IMPLICATIONS OF WRITING IN INDIA

The availability of writing is one thing; its use and spread in a society is quite a different thing. As pointed out at the beginning of this chapter, the literary tradition of India goes back at least to the fifth century BC when the Kharosthi script and the Brāhmī script appeared on the Indian subcontinent. But how was writing put to use in India, and what were its consequences?

Notice first that a highly conscious and normative attitude towards language was present in India before the advent of literacy. The Vedas and the classical literature in general are thought to have been composed and transmitted orally.[12] The tradition of verbatim transmission was maintained in India well into the period of Classical Sanskrit. In Panini's grammar, for instance, writing is referred to several times, but it does not seem to have played a major role for linguistic studies. On the other hand, once it was available, writing was soon instrumentalized for the already recognized purpose of language cultivation, and it was the cultivated forms of language that were reduced to writing.

Deshpande (1979) has provided ample documentation of terms used by the early Sanskrit grammarians for 'incorrect subnormal' forms of speech that could not lead to *dharma*, 'religious merit'. Such forms could obviously not be *nitya*, 'eternal'. Others could; namely the cultivated varieties that were subjected to the rules of the grammarians. While derived from prestige varieties used by speakers of high social standing, these cultivated forms were bound quickly to cease being native: that is, naturally acquired and spoken varieties. After Panini, Sanskrit became a scholastic language learned from the grammar books rather than in the family setting. Even though the oral tradition based on verbatim repetition was upheld (and even nowadays is an integral part of all learning in south Asia), Sanskrit became a language whose spoken realization depended on the rules that were committed to writing and thus became the prototype of the eternal high prestige variety as opposed to the substandard Prakrits that were corrupted by perpetual change. This was the introduction of diglossia into the linguistic culture of India, a pattern that was reproduced many times as new literary languages were created by consciously selecting and eliminating features found in colloquial usage, and by trying to arrest change and capture the eternal virtues of a language in its written form. As Deshpande (1986: 313) puts it: 'From Katayana (about 300–200 B.C.) onward, the existence of diglossia emerges as a very significant factor in the minds of the Sanskrit grammarians and one detects a number of conceptions relating to it.'

Diglossia[13] is the most consequential effect of the introduction of writing into India, and to this day is one of the most salient features of her literary culture. Diglossia is pervasive. In one form or another most literary languages of India exhibit this characteristic cleavage between the *High* (H) variety, which is based on a codified written standard, and the *Low* (L) variety whose usage is determined in the market place. There is, of course, considerable variation in the spectrum of diglossic situations, and the mass media as well as literacy education are bound to have slow but lasting effects on the diversity of, and relation between, speech varieties of those Indian languages that have a literary tradition. However, even in those languages with respect to which the appropriateness of the notion of diglossia may be questioned, one invariably finds a wide gap between the written style and the spoken style(s). And, on the other hand, there is no diglossia without writing; rather, 'diglossia without writing' is a contradiction in terms (Coulmas 1987c).

For example, with respect to Telugu, Krishnamurti (1979: 20) states that '"diglossia" in the sense in which it obtains in Arabic and Tamil has never existed in Telugu.' Yet he also points out that the relationship between literary and colloquial Telugu was consciously made to conform to the traditional Indian pattern. He writes: 'It appears that language pundits projected the model of the relationship between Sanskrit and Prakrit on to the poetic language and the contemporary modern language within Telugu' (Krishnamurti 1979: 5). The poetic variety alone enjoyed recognition, and grammars were written only for the classical language, keeping the usage of the Kavitraya (poetry from the eleventh to the fourteenth century) as the norm.

Similarly, De Silva (1976: 39) describes Sinhalese as 'a clear case of diglossia, for it shows mutually exclusive domains of use for the two varieties'. Literary Sinhalese obtained its standard in the fourteenth century AD, and this standard is respected by the whole speech community. 'The belief that Literary Sinhalese is superior, more beautiful, more logical and more correct prevails at every level of the society [of Sri Lanka]' (De Silva 1982: 104). This attitude is typical of diglossia. It implies that in a speech community where illiteracy is widespread a large part of the population has very little esteem for the only variety that they speak, because 'High Sinhalese in its full splendor is not a spoken language at all: it is the language of written Sinhalese' (De Silva 1982: 98).

The situation is somewhat different in Tamil for, according to Britto (1986: 115), while the H variety of Tamil has always enjoyed great prestige, 'there is no evidence to suggest that L was demeaned.' Moreover, a feature that distinguishes Tamil from Sinhalese or Telugu is the convention that the classical form of the language must be used in formal speech and is, therefore, less fossilized than the classical varieties of

Sinhalese and Telugu which exist in writing only. This classical form of Tamil is a superposed variety for the whole speech community and recognized as such even by those who have no proficiency in it. As regards the origin of Tamil diglossia, Britto (1986: 100) speculates that 'the ancient writers ... probably ... considered "writing" to be sacred' and did not want to adjust it to colloquial speech (cf. also Annamalai 1986).

Bengali, too, is considered to be a language with diglossia. Although the recent history of Bengali has seen certain reallocations of varieties to functions, Chatterjee (1986) comes to the conclusion that diglossia is still a characteristic feature of Bengali. He writes:

In a culture, such as that in which Bengali is used, where high prestige is accorded to the written word, the linguistic forms that are traditionally encountered in the forms of writing become imbued with feelings of dignity and refinement. In contrast to this, those that are used in day-to-day conversation acquire an inferior status. These levels of usage are learned by natives as part of their total experience. [L] is learned naturally. However, [H] can never be acquired without formal education. (Chatterjee 1986: 301)

Chatterjee goes further, extrapolating from the Bengali example:

I have a feeling that all the Indo-Aryan languages of India, except perhaps Hindi-Urdu, are typically more or less analogous to Bengali ... An educated person, by virtue of his formal schooling, acquires H of the respective community's linguistic repertoire in areas where a non-educated individual knowing only L suffers limitations owing to his inability to control H. (Chatterjee 1986: 301)

In most Dravidian languages the situation is no different. It takes formal instruction to learn H, and traditionally H used to be the only variety deemed fit for writing. Even dialogic prose was phrased according to the standard conventions of H, and only since the beginning of this century have serious attempts been made to write modern varieties closer to colloquial speech. The written varieties of most literary languages of India are still far removed from the vernacular.

More examples could be added, but the above suffice for present purposes.[14] Their brief discussion brings out the following main points. Since antiquity, writing in many languages of India has been used to create and uphold a cleavage between a written H variety and spoken L varieties which has, however, not led to linguistic divergence. The high prestige accorded to the written word, coupled with very restricted literacy that prevented the majority of speakers from being influenced by the written norm in their speech, has led to an often religiously inspired highly normative attitude toward H which came to be recognized as the only worthy incorporation of the language, even though a large part of the speech community was not proficient in it.

In some respects H and L represent different historical stages of a language, as H has preserved the variety of great literary achievement of an earlier period, while L has been allowed to develop (or to be corrupted, as many perceive it). However, it must also be recognized that H is in active use and is not merely a museum piece. Written language and spoken language are functionally distinct; as a result there are structural differences between the spoken and written forms of all languages used in writing. These differences vary considerably in degree. In the diglossic languages of India the gap between the spoken and the written form is very wide. According to those who – such as Diringer (1968), Goody and Watt (1968) or McLuhan (1962), for instance – call alphabetic writing 'democratic', this should not be so, because 'democratic' writing can only truly exist where it represents ordinary speech. However, in spite of the availability of a purely cenemic, in principle alphabetic, script, writing in India for centuries was not supposed to duplicate speech. Rather, if any close relationship between spoken and written language were to be achieved, the former was to be guided (in formal styles) by the latter. Because this attitude is deeply ingrained in the linguistic culture of India, it has proved difficult to promote literacy in L varieties. According to De Silva (1976: 49) the results of a public survey indicate that all Tamils believe that 'literacy' is 'the ability to read and write correctly' – that is, read and write H – rather than 'the mere ability to read and write', namely, the L variety.

The reasons for the coming into existence and preservation of diglossia are many. Norm adherence, esthetic rather than purely instrumental attitudes toward linguistic expression, and social control through restricted literacy seem to be the more significant ones. For, if De Silva is right, the nature of the writing system is also a major factor. According to him, it takes a cenemic writing system to bring about diglossia, because at some point there must have been a close match between the speech form and its written representation which was then

gradually broken up as the spoken language developed while being
upheld in the formal variety (which kept the written standard as its
guideline). The cleavage between spoken and written Chinese, De Silva
(1976: 36) claims, is of a different kind. Since Chinese writing has strong
pleremic elements and only very loosely maps on to the level of speech
sounds, 'it does not motivate the creation of a diglossic situation' (De
Silva 1976). To some extent, the question of whether or not the Chinese
situation should be labeled 'diglossic' is a matter of terminology. It is
apparent, in any event, that both pleremic and cenemic scripts can
produce a wide gap between spoken and written language. Already in
1857, Brown observed that 'Hindu grammarians, like those of China,
neglect the colloquial dialect, which they suppose is already known to
the student' (cited from Krishnamurti 1979: 4). *Wényán*, Classical
Chinese, is as far removed from spoken Chinese as any L from its
respective H in any of the diglossic languages of India. Like H-Sinhalese,
H-Telugu or H-Bengali, it is a scholastic language which has to be
acquired, as it were, letter by letter. To be sure, there are certain functional differences between, for instance, Classical Chinese and Classical
Telugu, but they share the feature which is of greatest interest for the
present discussion: they are book languages that exist in addition to, and
as superposed prestige varieties of, the vernaculars. Without writing
they would not exist.

CONCLUSION

The most important lesson to be learned from the study of writing in
India is that writing is not only the guise or garment of language, but
can have a deep and lasting influence on the development of a language,
since it lends itself as an ideal instrument to the selective cultivation of
one speech variety. By providing a language with a stable and visible
form, writing acquires great symbolic importance. In India, in particular, values of permanence are attached to writing; and the written
varieties of the literary languages are hence accorded higher status than
vernacular speech. Moreover, written languages enjoy higher prestige
than those that have not been reduced to writing. Indeed, it is often
contended that a speech form only acquires the status of a proper
language once it has its own script (Pattanayak 1979: 56). Thus, even
though India still has hundreds of unwritten minority languages, and

even though well over 50 per cent of the population is illiterate, the symbolic and the linguistic implications of writing are nowhere more apparent than in India.

The many Indian scripts are each important symbols of the cultural unity and identity of the groups which employ them. Most scripts are strongly associated with regions, languages and religions. They may, however, also be socially indicative.[15] Many languages are written with more than one, and quite different, scripts. To mention only the most consequential example, apart from the Hindu v. Moslem religious preferences of the native speakers, the differences between Hindi and Urdu are often said to consist largely in the former being written with Devanagari and the latter with Perso-Arabic and in the particular loan vocabulary channeled into each language from either Sanskrit or Arabic, respectively.[16] Many regional scripts vary for the same language according to locality and occupation of their users (Khubchandani 1983: chapter 6). Time and again politicians and linguists have called for a single script for India, but to no avail. 'Today a new script is created in India almost once in three months' (Pattanayak 1979: 43; see below, chapter 12, p. 236). While most of the new scripts, which are produced either for a hitherto unwritten language or as a pan-Indian script, never gain any currency, their constant creation and rejection sheds a vivid light on the symbolic importance of writing which transcends the instrumental value of a recording device.

NOTES

1 See also issue 2.1 of the *Journal of Tamil Studies*, 1970, for further discussion of possible Dravidian connections with the Indus valley script.
2 A puzzling observation concerning the Indus valley script was made by Hevesy (1936) who remarked a striking similarity of some of its characters with those of the Easter Island script. Separated as they are by several millennia and several thousand miles, these two scripts could not be linked in any meaningful way in spite of these graphical similarities.
3 See, for example, Renou 1948; Sheets 1961; Deshpande 1979.
4 Although Devanagari is the most prominent script of Sanskrit literature, Sanskrit of the advanced tradition was written in more than one script. In the Dravidian south, Sanskrit records are found in Malayalam, Grantha and Telugu letters; in the Bhoti script in Tibet; in the Sharada script in Kashmir; in the Bengali and Maithili scripts as well as variations of the Nagari script

in the north-east; and other regional variations of Devanagari in other parts of the subcontinent (cf. Khubchandani 1983: 119).

5 As a learned and consciously regulated language Sanskrit played a role similar to that of Classical Chinese and Latin. Notice, however, that books continue to be published in Sanskrit to this day and that, even though Sanskrit is supposed to have already ceased to exist as a spoken language in Panini's time, there are still speakers who claim Sanskrit as their mother tongue (Central Institute of Indian Languages 1973).

6 Actually, the inherent vowel is more like a schwa, but for reasons of symmetry it is usually transcribed as /a/.

7 In words where nasals are followed by consonants of their own class, they are often indicated by an *anusvāra* rather than by the appropriate consonant (plus inherent vowel) letter. This practice is, however, not in accordance with the established rules.

8 In writing Devanagari, the distinctive portion of each letter is written first, then the perpendicular, and finally the horizontal line.

9 For a detailed account of the Thai writing system see M. Haas (1956). The Thai script has served as the model for the Lao script which is very similar, including the marking of phonemic tone.

10 Notice, however, that this refers to one variety of Tamil only, namely the one which has been the written language of old. Because of the constraints of Tamil orthography, attempts to write the modern language are faced with great difficulties (cf. Britto 1986: 179ff).

11 A distinct system known as 'Tamil Grantha' contains these letters which are needed to write Sanskrit.

12 It must be admitted, however, that some scholars hold the opposite view, viz. that 'to state that all these [Vedic hymns] were composed without aid of writing and without aid of counting each letter is unbelievable' (Wakankar 1983).

13 *Diglossia* is a notion that was first applied to the coexistence of highly divergent spoken and written varieties of one language by Krumbacher (1902) in his book about the modern Greek written language. Later it was applied to Arabic by Marçais (1930). Ferguson (1959) and Fishman (1967) revitalized the discussion of this term in contemporary sociolinguistics. (See Britto 1986, the most extensive account of the literature relating to diglossia to date. See also Coulmas 1988 for a review of Britto 1986.)

14 See, for instance, Nayanak (1967) and Bright (1970) on diglossia in Kannada.

15 For example, the Maithili script, which is derived from, and closely resembles, the Bengali script, is employed only by the Brahmins of Bihar in northern India. Its use is restricted to religious or scholarly manuscripts.

16 In his 1983 book, Khubchandani regularly refers to 'Hindi-Urdu' as one system, while on the other hand listing them as two different languages 'representing the polarization of literary trends and writing systems' (1983: 108). And then again he points out that 'for a native speaker of Hindi to acquire mastery over Urdu, it will suffice to learn another script . . . and add to his repertoire some "high-brow" vocabulary of Perso-Arabic origin' (1983: 153ff).

PART III

Practical Problems

11

From Letter to Sound: Deciphering Written Languages

The main purpose of writing is communication across a spatial or temporal distance separating sender and addressee. Written texts are usually phrased in a language and coded in a writing system known to both the writer and the reader, and therefore the reader has no problem understanding the message conveyed by the text. Sometimes, however, a reader comes across a text of which he or she is not the addressee and may therefore have difficulties reading it. That reader may, indeed, find it impossible to make any sense of it at all. For example, if the finder does not know either the language or the script of the text, he or she does not belong to the group of its potential addressees and readers.

All texts can be read by only a limited number of individuals, just as all utterances can be understood only by those who know the respective language. Some texts can be read by only few readers because they have been deliberately coded in a system not generally known and whose secrecy is carefully guarded by its possessors. More often than not such codes provoke others to try to break them, a task which nowadays usually turns out to be a challenge to experts of electronic data processing programs.[1] There are yet other texts which cannot be read at all, because nobody knows how to relate the written symbols of which they are composed to a meaningful linguistic expression. Before they can be read, these texts need to be deciphered; their code needs to be cracked.

Obviously then, reading is not the same as deciphering. The basic difference between these two kinds of text processing can be summarized in the following matrix shown in table 11.1.

Of the four cases distinguished in the matrix, only the first, where the language and the script are both known, can be considered reading proper; the other three are different forms of deciphering. If the

Practical Problems

TABLE 11.1 *Reading and deciphering*

	Language known	Script known	
(1)	+	+	Reading
(2)	+	−	Deciphering-1
(3)	−	+	Deciphering-2
(4)	−	−	Deciphering-3

language is known but not the script, as in (2), no message can be extracted from the text. Figure 11.1 provides an example which the reader of these pages may use to test his or her skills at deciphering a text which is written in a familiar language but in an unfamiliar script.[2] Number (3) is the case where a familiar script such as the Roman alphabet is used to write a text in a language unknown to the reader: Romaji de kaita kono nihongo no bunsho o wakarimasu ka. Only readers with some knowledge of Japanese will be able to assign any sense to this sentence. Moreover, while others can sound it out, their pronunciation will resemble that of Japanese only to some extent. Again, this is not what ought to be called 'reading'. Finally (4), a situation where neither the language nor the script is known, is obviously the most difficult case

11.1 A cryptogram to be deciphered by the reader

of decipherment. All decipherments belong to one of these three types, although it is not always immediately clear whether a given case falls under (2), (3) or (4), because decipherers may not be aware of the fact that they are ignorant only of the script but not of the language, or they may fail to identify the language of a text written in a familiar script. For example, it took many decades to identify as Semitic certain inscriptions in Greek letters from Crete.

Much more than reading, deciphering is a genuinely linguistic task, and it is quite surprising, therefore, that linguists have taken practically no interest at all in this most challenging activity. The grammarians' task of describing and analyzing a language unknown to them has sometimes been likened to the children's task of acquiring their first language. A more appropriate comparison, it seems to me, is that between first language acquisition and deciphering. Like speechless children, decipherers start out from the assumption that what they are dealing with are signs, and like the former, the latter have the expectation that the sign configurations to which they are exposed can be understood.

However, the analogy cannot be stretched too far. The brains and minds of children are not the same as the brains and minds of adults who acquired their mother tongue long ago and, if they are decipherers, most probably several other languages as well. Also, children may often understand a message before they are able to understand the linguistic units of which it is composed, because communication between mother and infant is not restricted to language but makes use of other channels as well. Moreover, the child gets as much input as necessary. The inductive basis for the child's decoding operation can be expanded almost without limits. Often decipherers do not have this possibility. In many cases their material is extremely limited. The more restricted it is, the more difficult the problems of deciphering.

Furthermore, unlike children, decipherers get no feedback or encouragement relying, as they do, solely on their desire to reveal the secret inherent in an impenetrable text and their conviction that the impenetrability is only temporary and the secret can be revealed. Nobody can tell them whether they are on the right track or pursuing a red herring. A mistaken hypothesis may frustrate their efforts for years. For example, the conviction that the language of Mycenaean texts was not Greek kept Evans and other decipherers for years from finding the right solution. Another difference between first language acquisition and deciphering is that children can start out with simple messages immediately relevant to their existential needs, whereas decipherers are likely to have to deal with messages which are completely unrelated to their lives or even their experiential background.

However, the reward of successful decipherment is considerable. It is a singular achievement which may have major consequences for our understanding of history, as was the case with the decipherment of the various cuneiform systems which provided the key to an entire civilization. The clay tablets of Mesopotamia revealed infinitely more about the civilization of Sumer and Babylon than all other archeological findings combined.

Deciphering a historical script which fell into disuse in the past is very different from breaking the code of modern cryptography. Secret writing for classified communication as used by governments and private agencies is designed to restrict the number of readers and make it difficult for unauthorized readers to extract the message of the text. Forgotten scripts, by contrast, were never meant to defy interpretation, but were intended to be a means of communication which could be used by the entire literate community. It is ironic, therefore, that forgotten scripts are usually more difficult to decipher than deliberately created secret codes. This is so because, however complex they may be, secret codes have to be systematic.[3] Encoding a message would be too difficult if they were not. Forgotten scripts, on the other hand, are historically evolved systems which tend to be characterized in large measure by deviations from systematic principles. The users of these scripts knew the languages for which they were used and could therefore tolerate a great deal of irregularity and imprecision, but decipherers can only hope to achieve their goal by considering the systematic features of a script that allow them to systematically relate its signs and sign configurations to those of another system with which they are familiar.

SOME GENERAL PRINCIPLES OF DECIPHERING

The most fundamental principle of any decipherment is that the meaning is in the document. The decipherer's task is to extract meaning out of the document rather than to put meaning into it. However much knowledge the decipherer supplies to make the document readable, the meaning is part of the text. Hypotheses about the nature and meaning of a document can play a significant role for its decipherment, but eventually every assumption concerning the meaning must be justifiable in terms of systematic relations between written symbols and linguistic units allowing for the translation of the document in question into another system. Only charlatans use an assumed meaning to justify linguistic values of written symbols.

Another important principle guiding the decipherer's work is the necessity of being open and receptive to collateral information of every conceivable kind. Intimate knowledge of the archeological and historical environment of a document may be as important as familiarity with other scripts, the languages which they were used to write and the relations between them, as well as thorough insight into linguistic structures and the various different ways of representing language in writing. Like a detective, astute decipherers do not discard any piece of evidence only because they do not know where or whether it will fit into the pattern. Eventually it may be of unexpected importance. While various different kinds of external or contextual evidence may turn out to be relevant to the decipherment of a given document, it is obviously the document itself that contains the most crucial information.

With Pope (1975), we can distinguish three different kinds of messages that are inherent in every document waiting to be deciphered. These are (1) the frame message, (2) the outer message and (3) the inner message.

The frame message is a meta-message. It says: 'This is a message; it is meant to be read.' Just as infants have to discriminate speech sounds from all sorts of noise in their environment, decipherers must not waste their talents on ornaments, animal traces or accidental cracks on the surface of pottery. While this may seem obvious enough, the frame message of many archeological finds was not immediately understood in the past, and the status of many objects and 'inscriptions' remains a matter of dispute. For example, until recently, the monumental masonry of pre-Columbian Central America was not thought to contain any writing,[4] and for some autochthonous inscriptions of the South American continent it is still not clear how far they represent writing proper. However, the craftsmanship of these monuments leaves no doubt about their being man-made (figure 11.2).

By contrast, the crudeness of early inscriptions in other parts of the world and the sometimes bad state of their preservation often make it difficult for the untrained eye to recognize them as writing: that is, to understand their frame message. Also an inscription may be so short that

11.2 A Maya hieroglyph (from Prem and Riese 1983: 178)

there is very little repetition of signs to suggest they are part of a system. The frame message of an inscription such as the Mycenaean inscription in Figure 11.3 is not exactly compelling at first glance. Understanding the frame message is the first step towards decipherment; it means to understand the need to look for a deciphering method.

Next, the inner message is the content a document is intended to convey. Readers of texts are usually only interested in their inner message and, except for calligraphers, writers too are concerned first and foremost with the meaning they intend to communicate to their readers. The code by means of which this is done is taken for granted and thus of little interest to those using it. Decipherers, on the other hand, may be more interested in the code than in the inner message of the document or documents they are working on. Obviously, to make the inner messages of documents written in forgotten scripts accessible is the ultimate and superordinate rationale of decipherment, but the decipherer may be exhilarated more by the challenge of breaking the code and revealing the secret than by the secret itself which may be a laundry list or a trivial letter whose true value is for the historian to determine. In

11.3 Early Mycenaean inscription from Orchomenos (from Jensen 1925: 94)

order to break the code the decipherer must understand the outer message.

The outer message is an implicit message relating to, and relying on, the outer form of a document. It tells the reader how to decode the inner message. Encoding explicit instructions as to how to decode the outer message is quite impossible, since they would have to be part of the inner message. Hence the outer message is to be viewed as a set of clues which, taken together, constitute the systematic properties of the script.

First of all, a great deal can be said about the script by simply counting the elements and determining how many different signs are present in the data: that is, by determining the type/token quotient of the signs. If thousands of signs can be distinguished, many of which have low frequencies of occurrence – that is, if the system has a high type/token quotient – the system is bound to be logographic. A very restricted set of frequently recurring signs, on the other hand, points towards a phonemic system. If some signs have a very high frequency of occurrence, while that of others is very low, it is reasonable to consider the possibility of a mixed system where different signs serve different functions.

A next step is to look for evidence that might reveal the direction of the script. Different kinds of information can be of help here. Sometimes the physical shape of impressions or incisions indicate the direction of the scribe's hand movement. When a document consists of clearly discernible lines or columns, combinatorial consideration can help to determine the direction of a script. A recurrent group of signs that is split at the end of a line can provide the decisive clue. For example, if the group ABCDE occurs several times in this order and at one point is split in such a way that CDE stands at the left end of one line followed by AB at the right end of the line below it, as in (1), this suggests a left-running system.

(1) XXXXXAB CDE XXXXXXXX
     CDE XXXXXXXXXXXXXXX
     XXXXXXXXXXXXXXXXAB

Or, if ABC occurs at what seems to be the right end of a line followed by ED at the right end of the line below, as in (2), the system might be boustrophedon (that is, changing directions in alternating lines in a plowshare manner).

(2) XXXABCDEXXXXXXXXXX
     XXXXXXXXXXXXXXXXXX
     XXXXXXXXXXXXXXXABC
     XXXXXXXXXXXXXXXXED

In the absence of clearly demarcated lines it is extremely difficult to determine the direction of a script. For example, the direction of the Phaistos script poses great problems because on the only surviving document the individual signs are imprinted with stamps on to a clay disk where they are arranged in a single spiral line circling round the center (figure 11.4). The only not totally arbitrary hypothesis concerning the direction of this script has to do with the directionality of the faces in the pictorial signs. Vargha and Botos (1979) have argued that the text on the disk starts at the outside, because in several other scripts that make use of pictorial signs faces are facing towards the beginning of a line rather than away from the beginning.

Determining the linguistic units of a document is another important part of its decipherment. In some ancient scripts word dividers such as special marks or spaces are employed, which makes the task easier; but if word boundaries are not marked, the decipherer has to apply a distribution analysis and statistical techniques for studying repetitions of sign configurations which can break up the text into its component parts. If the corpus is large enough, words or smaller units can be isolated even though they are not separated in the text. In Akkadian, for instance, words were not separated.

A distribution analysis can reveal certain features of a script such as its

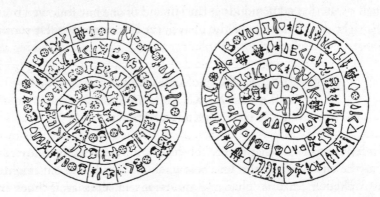

11.4 The Phaistos disk

direction, its systematic type, its elements and the co-occurrence restrictions governing their occurrence. All of this is, however, not sufficient for deciphering an unknown script. Determining the system and deciphering a document written in it are two different steps, the former of which usually precedes the latter. In addition the decipherer needs well-motivated hypotheses based on historical knowledge putting the document(s) in question into a historical and linguistic context. As pointed out above, 'decipherment' does not necessarily mean that the language of the document turns out to be new in the sense that in modern times no one has any knowledge of the language; rather it means to assign correctly linguistic values to written symbols which could not be pronounced or semantically interpreted before. It order to achieve this, decipherers must be both knowledgeable and flexible; they must reckon with the realities of the text to be deciphered and be always ready to explore every new hypothesis. In particular, they must try out probable and possible languages. Such tests often take the form of the 'probable word' of a given configuration of signs. Proper names are of crucial importance in this regard.

Proper names are not always meaningful words, and even those that are do not primarily serve the function of expressing a meaning but rather of designating a person or place. Therefore foreign proper names are not usually translated but represented phonetically.[5] Many of the important decipherments took advantage of this fact. The international contacts of the ancient Near East were recorded in a great variety of languages and documents, and hence archeological findings and historical records often supplied enough collateral information to look systematically for the occurrence of certain names.[6] Herodotus's historical account of the Achaemenid kings and their names provided the crucial data for the decipherment of the cuneiform inscriptions of Persia and Mesopotamia. The names of Ptolemy, Cleopatra and Alexander the Great were the opening wedge needed for deciphering the Egyptian hieroglyphs; and solving the riddle of Linear B was greatly aided by the occurrence of the place names *Knossos* and *Pylos* in texts from Knossos and Pylos, respectively. To the decipherer proper names are thus significant for two different reasons: first because they are the most promising words to look for on the basis of a historically motivated hypothesis, and second they are most likely to supply the data needed for establishing the first phonetic values of elements of the system. Much time and effort has to be spent, however, before such hypotheses lead to successful decipherment. Some exemplary cases are discussed in what follows.

THE DECIPHERMENT OF THE EGYPTIAN HIEROGLYPHS

The decipherment of Egyptian is a textbook example of the powerful influence of a mistaken hypothesis which only the spirit of enlightenment could identify as such. For centuries scholars were misled by the idea, first expressed in Horappolo's treatise *Hieroglyphica* of 390 AD, that the 'sacred' characters were to be interpreted symbolically. The pictorial concreteness and clarity of the glyphs suggested that those were characters which, as it were, directly spoke to the mind. Until modern times those who tried to solve the riddle of Egyptian writing were unable to extricate themselves from this premiss.

In the mid-seventeenth century, Athanasius Kirchner claimed to read whole sentences which later turned out to be single alphabetically written words; and at the beginning of the nineteenth century the great orientalist, Silvestre de Sacy, was still convinced that hieroglyphic characters were representative of ideas rather than language-specific sounds (Pope 1975). The decisive steps toward the decipherment were made by two of Sacy's students, Quatremére (who suggested that Coptic was the successor of ancient Egyptian) and Champollion (who, of course, achieved the breakthrough which, however, would hardly have been possible without the accidental discovery of the Rosetta Stone in the western delta of the Nile by Napoleon's troops).

The Rosetta Stone was invaluable because it is a bilingual document redacted in Greek and Egyptian, the Egyptian text being written in two versions, hieroglyphic and demotic.[7] The Greek text could be read easily so, assuming that it was indeed a bilingual document rather than a collation of different documents in different languages, the remaining task was to find out how the contents of the Greek version were phrased in Egyptian. This was still a formidable challenge.

As the Greek text contains several proper names, it was a reasonable assumption that the same names should show up in the Egyptian text. Sacy pursued this hypothesis and successfully identified proper names in the demotic version. However, he still did not consider the possibility that the demotic and hieroglyphic versions of the text were isomorphic, and moreover worked under the misconception that all demotic words were written alphabetically. Both of these mistakes remained to be corrected by his student, Champollion.

Champollion started out with a very simple but important observation: the Greek text had less than 500 words, while the hieroglyphic text consisted of 1,419 signs. Moreover, the 1,419 tokens were made up of only 66 different types. Both of these observations rule out the possibility of a totally ideographic system; in fact they suggested a basically phonetic system. Working under this hypothesis and assuming that the Greek and Egyptian versions were identical in content, Champollion tried to identify the name of Ptolemy which occurs several times in the Greek version. He correctly assumed that the royal name was graphically distinguished from the rest of the hieroglyphic text and identified a word enclosed in a cartouche as the equivalent of the Greek PTOLE-MAIS. He then gave the signs in the cartouche the following alphabetic values (see figure 11.5).[8]

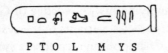

P T O L   M   Y S

11.5 Cartouche with King Ptolemy's name as it appears on the Rosetta Stone with alphabetic equivalents of the Egyptian hieroglyphs

The next step was to test these sound assignments by applying them to other cartouches, thus arriving at new hypotheses of sound assignments which in turn could be tested. By applying this method to as many as eighty cartouches known from other documents and thus moving from one name to another (figure 11.6), Champollion found the basic phonetic signs of the Egyptian hieroglyphs.

His decipherment of name cartouches was convincing, but he had still to demonstrate that hieroglyphs were used phonetically at all times and not for proper names only. The principal difficulty here was that not only was the script unknown but the language too.

Proper names contain very little linguistic information, and hence could only be used to establish the sound values of the signs. Other words whose pronunciation could be approximated on the basis of these tentative sound assignments still could not be understood. However, Champollion was singularly qualified to proceed beyond proper names. He had studied six ancient Near Eastern languages, among them Coptic

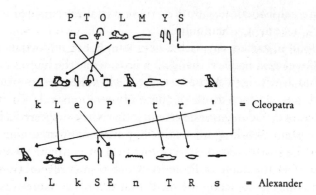

11.6 Testing the sound values assigned to the glyphs in one name cartouche by applying them to another

which turned out to be instrumental for identifying and reconstructing Egyptian words. By applying his knowledge of Greek and Coptic, and by reckoning with inaccuracies, variants in the system and certain systematic inconsistencies, Champollion arrived at a system for the decipherment of the Egyptian hieroglyphs. Thus the key to success was a combination of (1) a thoroughly scientific approach favoring a distribution analysis over unfounded preconceptions; (2) general erudition and knowledge of several languages, in particular a knowledge of Coptic; (3) an understanding of the special nature of proper names; and (4) the availability of a bilingual document.

DECIPHERING CUNEIFORM SCRIPTS

There were certain parallels between the decipherments of Egyptian hieroglyphs and cuneiform. In both cases proper names provided the point of departure for penetrating the system, and bilingual inscriptions enabled the testing of hypotheses (Cottrell 1971). The system of Akkadian/Babylonian writing was by far the most important cuneiform script, because Babylonian was the international language of diplomacy and trade for some 1,000 years. Babylonian documents were discovered everywhere between Mesopotamia, the Old Persian capital of Susa, and the Hittite capital, Chattusha. The system of this script is so involved that its decipherment would certainly have been impossible without a bilingual inscription. However, the code of another cuneiform script, Old Persian, was broken without the aid of a bilingual document. This script was well suited for such an achievement because it is the simplest of all cuneiform systems, consisting of only 40 signs (cf. chapter 5 above).

The decipherment of Old Persian proceeded through the following stages. First, a method was sought to identify proper names. To this end, Grotefend, one of the decipherers, set up a hypothetical formula which was known from Greek sources to refer to Persian kings, mentioning their names and titles: 'X, king of kings, son of Y'. In the great rock inscription of Darius several occurrences of sign configurations were found that could fit this pattern, and on the basis of Greek historical records they were identified as referring to the Achaemenid kings, namely Xerxes, the king, son of Darius, the king, son of Hystaspes (who was not a king). This was a great success and promising for a beginning, but not quite sufficient to assure correct sound assignments for all letters.

Next, a linguistic argument paved the way for further improvements. Rasmus Rask in 1826 suggested that the genitive plural ending in the phrase 'king of kings' should be *-anam* rather than *-ačao* as had been assumed by Grotefend. This amendment was very consequential because *-anam* happens to be the ending of the genitive plural in Sanskrit. Naturally, at a time when comparative philology was rapidly developing into a new and very active scientific field, this suggestion was eagerly discussed since it implied the possibility, if not likelihood, that Old Persian and Sanskrit were related languages. This hypothesis was systematically pursued by comparing words which had been tentatively assigned sound values – beginning with the word for 'king' – with Sanskrit and Avestian words. Modifications of the sound assignments were suggested on the basis of these comparisons, which eventually yielded the most likely pronunciations of the Old Persian words.

A more meticulous investigation of the system as a whole and a careful distribution analysis then led to a better understanding of the conventions governing the script and its use. It was shown that certain characters occurred in restricted contexts only, namely before certain vowels. Since independent vowel signs had been stipulated for /a/, /i/ and /u/, it was concluded that the system was partly syllabic (that is, that the consonant letters had a potential inherent vowel). This explained the apparent polyvalency of several of the consonant signs.

In sum, the decipherment of Old Persian could be achieved because

(1) the writing system was simple, (2) historical records were available and (3) the language could be linked to other well-known languages.

The decipherment of Old Persian was, however, only the beginning of the struggle to unlock the world of cuneiform writing. Since Old Persian cuneiform is the simplest of all cuneiform scripts and makes use of characters which differ considerably from those of common cuneiform writing, and since other languages written in cuneiform (such as Elamite and Babylonian/Akkadian) are not related to Old Persian, the results of the Old Persian decipherment were of only limited help for penetrating the other system. The one point that made Old Persian very valuable for the decipherments of Babylonian, Elamite and even Hittite was that it was used in bilingual documents, but the underlying systems of the other cuneiform scripts had to be deciphered all the same.

The great number and multiformity of cuneiform signs found in the excavated documents of Mesopotamia prompted many skeptics to doubt that a system could ever be discovered in this seemingly infinite variety. However, the persistence of dedicated scholars such as Talbot, Hinck, Rawlinson and Oppert[9] proved the skeptics wrong. The basis of their work were bilingual or polylingual inscriptions, such as the Darius-rock inscription in which the achievements of Darius and Xerxes were recorded in Old Persian, Elamite and Babylonian/Akkadian.

Babylonian/Akkadian was extremely difficult, because it was necessary not only to find the correct sound values for many hundreds of signs, but in addition the decipherers had to realize that many characters were used in multiple functions serving as syllable signs and as logograms, and sometimes as determinatives as well. The system had been used for many centuries and, as a result, the spelling conventions were much more involved than those of Old Persian. If they followed any logic at all, it was the logic of historical development. Viewed synchronically, the script had more inconsistencies, redundancies, ambiguities and homophone signs than it had systematic features. Spelling conventions seemed to be intolerably loose. Nevertheless, even this intricate script could not resist the onslaught of determined code breakers who were prepared to tackle the problem in a rational and linguistically informed manner.

If parallel texts exist, it is possible to determine the translation relation holding between them, however complex it may be. Provided that the text corpus is large enough and that it contains some proper names enabling initial sound assignments, the underlying system of the script to be deciphered can be discovered. And even if some uncertainties concerning the exact sound values of the signs remain, the code can be broken and the contents of documents written in that script can be made accessible. Exactly how Babylonian words were pronounced is bound to remain an open question; and the same is true of many other ancient languages such as Elamite, Hittite, Hurrian or Mycenaean Greek. This does not mean, however, that texts written in these languages cannot be read and understood. This is so because writing is not, and never was, a means of transcribing speech sounds, but is rather an instrument of visually representing language by means of relating visual signs in various different ways which are more or less faithful to the speech sounds of a given language at a given time.[10]

THE DECIPHERMENT OF LINEAR B

Judging from the time span that elapsed between the discovery and the deciphering of Linear B, breaking this code was very difficult. The first inscriptions were found at Knossos on Crete in 1900, but it took more than half a century before texts written in Linear B could be read. In 1953, the British architect Michael Ventris presented his decipherment which he had achieved with the help of John Chadwick, a classicist. The progress of this decipherment is well documented by twenty 'Notes' which Ventris sent out to several scholars in the field between 1951 and 1952 (cf. Chadwick 1958).

The decipherment of Linear B was a decipherment without a 'bilinguis'. Since historical records about the culture of ancient Crete in other languages were extremely scarce, there was no collateral evidence that could have clarified the linguistic affiliation of the many texts excavated at Knossos. In the absence of a bilinguis, the decipherer has to rely exclusively on combinatorial methods: that is, a distributional analysis.

Ventris started out with some basic assumptions concerning both the texts and the writing system. As for the former, he hypothesized that the documents discovered at Knossos were inventories, accounts and receipts. With respect to the latter, the number of different signs led him to believe that Linear B was a syllabic system. It contains an indeterminate number of pictorial signs which, Ventris assumed, served the function of classifiers, and which he interpreted from their pictorial form. In addition, the system consists of a set of 88 recurrent signs which Ventris analyzed on the analogy of the Cypriot syllabary as syllable signs of the form CV or V. It was, of course, unclear how such syllable signs corresponded to the syllable structure of the language (that is, how faithfully they represented the language).

Some linguistic observations helped to clarify this point. In particular, the use of vertical strokes as word boundary markers proved very helpful because it enabled the calculation of distributions and frequencies of syllables on two structural levels, the text and the word. One of Ventris's hypotheses was that signs occurring with high frequency in word initial position indicated vocalic syllables. Using this as a starting point, he constructed a grid which was designed to determine, by trial and error, the sound values for the signs of Linear B.

The indication of word boundaries was also useful in that they made it possible to establish what were presumably paradigms. By observing variation in the final sign of a group, Ventris concluded that the differences indicated inflectional endings of the type of Latin *bo-ni*, *bo-no*, *bo-na*. However, while this turned out to be a correct assumption, the absence of any reference point that could confirm individual sound assignments prevented an early solution. Ventris's 'Notes' show several unsuccessful attempts to arrange the signs of Linear B in a grid that yielded useful results. The eventual breakthrough was brought about by the interpretation of place names and their grouping in paradigms.

This was possible because Ventris applied a device that was known from the Cypriot syllabary. This writing system has no signs for isolated consonants and therefore cannot represent consonant clusters directly. Rather, clusters are written by two signs consisting of the consonant and the vowel of the following consonant: that is, a group such as -V1C1C2V2- was written as -V1-C1V2-C2V2-. The first name that was deciphered on the basis of assuming this principle was *Amnisos* which appeared as *A-mi-ni-so*. This name was known from Homer. *Ko-no-so*, readily recognized as *Knossos*, followed. Other forms of these names were *A-mi-ni-si-io-* (*Amnisio-*), *A-mi-ni-si-ia-* (*Amnisia-*), and *Ko-no-si-io-* (*Knosio-*), respectively. These variations forced Ventris to conclude that the language of Linear B was indeed Greek, an insight which ran counter to his original assumptions, but which turned out to be the key to the decipherment.

The identification of words was still quite difficult because the archaic variety of Greek recorded in the documents of Knossos was unknown and differed considerably from Classical Greek. At this stage, Ventris drew on Chadwick's expertise in the Greek language, and Chadwick helped to solve many problems by reconstructing and thus identifying Greek words in Linear B texts. For example, the two forms *po-me*, *po-me-no* could be identified with the classical word for 'shepherd', *poimen* (nominative) and *poimenos* (genitive). With ever more words being identified and entire passages of text becoming understandable, Ventris and Chadwick's supposition that Linear B represented a Greek dialect used between 1400 and 1200 on Crete and in southern Greece became a certainty.

The fact that, none the less, some documents remain obscure has a variety of reasons that do not call into doubt the correctness of Ventris and Chadwick's solution.

1 Not all syllable signs have been determined conclusively.
2 Some words could not be related to any words of a later period of Greek and neither could their meaning be inferred from the Linear B texts themselves.
3 The writing system was imprecise and defective in representing the language, leaving gaps that could not be filled by philological reconstruction. Most probably the syllabic system had been taken over from another language.
4 Documents were fragmentary.

However, these deficiencies notwithstanding, the decipherment of Linear B produced evidence of a pre-alphabetic literate culture on Greek soil, which was the most sensational achievement in the area of decipherment in recent times.

CONCLUSION

All the decipherments that have been achieved since the enlightenment demonstrate the value of a linguistic approach which from the beginning takes into account the segmentation of linguistic units, their organization on several structural levels and the various possible ways for graphic signs to relate to these levels. With this in mind, the successful decipherer looks for a systematic method of mapping the units of the unknown code on to those of one that is familiar. No decipherment is possible without ultimately referring to a language whose system is known. This is particularly true of phonetically based writing systems.

Another important point decipherers have to reckon with is that ancient writing systems may not only be highly intricate but also defective. Linear B, for instance, does not indicate all the phonemes of the Greek language it represents. On the other hand, it is redundant and inflexible as regards the representation of certain sound configurations. The speaker of the language thus represented can easily tolerate such deficiencies; but for the decipherer they often present considerable obstacles. For the reconstruction of a phonological system other sources have to be tapped, notably related languages and dialects. Yet decipherers may never find enough evidence to close every gap in the system. As Segert (1983) has pointed out, some rare phonemes may escape their grasp, and even if the phoneme's position in the system can be determined, its actual sound value often remains unclear. However, the decipherer can live with this kind of underdeterminacy because establishing a relation between letter and sound is important only to the extent that the phonological structure of the language is revealed which, in turn, provides access to other structural levels and eventually to meaning.

NOTES

1 Gordon (1971: 15ff) provides a good overview of the basic principles of producing and solving secret codes.
2 When I gave this piece of text to a class of graduate students at Georgetown University as an assignment with the intent that they should find out as many of the systematic properties of the system, frequencies of occurrence and distribution of letters, etc., I was quite surprised when one of the students presented me with the complete decipherment the following week. The students did not know that the language of the text was English, and I had given them only two hints: (1) proper names are distinguished by a 'namer dot', and (2) what look like punctuation marks are punctuation marks. I do not consider it a coincidence that the successful decipherer was Japanese. Rather it seems to me that the early exposure to minute graphical differences in writing accompanying the acquisition of the Japanese writing system is an excellent training for every visual task.

Since not every reader of this book may have enough patience or time to decipher the text on p. 206, a key to the solution is provided after the last note to this chapter.

3 Because secret writing is systematically related to a language, any code used extensively is vulnerable, for in any language, phonemes, syllables and words have certain frequencies of occurrence which provide the code-breaker with a lever for statistical analysis.

4 Prem and Riese comment on the story of the decipherment of Maya writing as follows: 'Until recently the linguistic decipherment of Maya writing has suffered from lack of a well defined theoretical framework. Thus highly eclectic and phantastic speculations and claims have discredited this approach for a long time ... More explicit theoretical attempts about the nature of Maya writing combined with strictly methodological linguistic attempts in decipherment have brought a break-through' (Prem and Riese 1983: 178).

5 Notice that this is true only of proper names in phonetically based scripts. In the context of the Chinese writing system, proper names are incorporated in their respective characters rather than in a particular pronunciation. Chinese names are represented with their original characters in Korean and Japanese while the pronunciation of these characters is very different.

6 Leibniz was probably the first to recognize the importance of proper names for the decipherment of ancient scripts. In a letter of 1714 he wrote (concerning documents from Palmyra and Syria) that many inscriptions exist in two versions, one in Greek and one in another script and language. In the Greek version occur proper names, 'and their pronunciation must have been approximately the same in the native language as in Greek' (Leibniz 1923).

7 The Rosetta Stone dates from 197 BC. It is a decree passed by a general council of Egyptian priests assembled at Memphis on the occasion of the first commemoration of the coronation of King Ptolemy V. Since Alexander, many documents in Egypt were provided in Greek and Egyptian because the ruling house and the chief administrators were Greek. The Rosetta Stone was the first such document to be discovered in modern times. For more details on the historical background and the contents of the document see Andrews (1981).

8 The individual glyphs are here linearized for greater clarity. In the cartouche on the Rosetta Stone they are arranged in non-linear clusters.

9 In the 1850s these four scholars participated in a public experiment designed to demonstrate that Assyrology, as the new field came to be called, was a serious discipline not to be belittled as charlatanry. By agreeing to independently decode and translate a newly excavated document and submitting their translations for comparison, they provided the opportunity to examine the reliability of their method. The result was convincing, since the translations exhibited remarkable concurrence (cf. Pope 1975).

10 To what extent the reconstruction of the phonology of a dead language is possible on the basis of written documents alone is demonstrated for several Semitic languages in Wilhelm (1983).

The text on p. 206 is from Lincoln's speech at Gettysburg. It is written with the Bernard Shaw Alphabet, also known as *Shavian*, which represents an attempt at radical spelling reform for English. For historical details and a discussion of the special features of the system see McCarthy (1969).

Figure 11.7 presents a reading key of the Shaw Alphabet. The letters are classified as 'tall', 'deep', 'short' and 'compound'. (Notice the phonologically motivated symmetries inherent in the system.) Beneath each letter is its name with the pronunciation indicated in bold type.

11.7 A reading key of the Shaw Alphabet

12

From Sound to Letter: Creating Alphabets

Inscriptions or documents that were handed down through the ages to the present or were recently rediscovered are often our only source of knowledge of the tongues of speakers long silenced. Other tongues we know, so to speak, only by word of mouth; for their native speakers never knew, or today have not yet learned, that language can be written, and their words preserved in writing. These unrecorded languages are the subject of this chapter; curiously, they are the majority of the languages of the world. While some of them most probably will never be used in writing, others are still felt to have a chance of becoming written languages, at least to a limited extent. For this to be accomplished, each must be provided with both a suitable script and a suitable orthography.

Selecting a script and constructing an orthography for a language that never had one is a form of encoding the language visually in such a way that it can be used efficiently in written communication. What are the principal difficulties of this endeavor, and what are the principal demands on such a code? The following discussion of some of the more important issues offers some suggestions for the solution of the problems and difficulties involved in devising a writing system, even if it cannot treat the subject exhaustively. The problems of script selection and orthography design are obviously not the same, but neither are they completely independent of each other, for the first may have repercussions on the other. This is particularly evident where a choice must be made between different writing systems such as the Roman alphabet, the Chinese writing system or a Devanagari-type syllabic alphabet. Moreover, in addition to the systematic considerations pertaining to script selection and orthography design, both of these processes have socio-linguistic implications which transcend the limits of linguistic analysis in the narrow sense. This is so because writing a language and recording it are two quite different things; or, to put it differently, a viable orthography is not the same as a transcription system.

Implementing a writing system, either for a language that never had one or for one that used to be written by means of another system, is not usually a process that is judged dispassionately and on the grounds of the systematic merits and shortcomings alone. To what extent new orthographies should and can be based on phonetic transcription is therefore only one of the questions that needs to be considered. Systematic soundness, precision and economy, however important they may seem to the orthography maker, are known to determine the success of a proposed orthography only to a quite limited extent at best (Berry 1958, 1977); for there are no systematic choices that are socioculturally neutral for those concerned. As the most visible items of a language, scripts and orthographies are 'emotionally loaded', indicating as they do group loyalties and identities. Rather than being mere instruments of a practical nature, they are symbolic systems of great social significance which may, moreover, have profound effects on the social structure of a speech community.

Thus there are linguistic aspects as well as social aspects to the endeavors of script choice and orthography design. Both kinds of aspects are reflected in Smalley's (1964) five criteria for an optimal new writing system. These criteria are:

1 maximum motivation for the learner;
2 maximum representation of speech;
3 maximum ease of learning;
4 maximum transfer;
5 maximum ease of reproduction.

Each one of these criteria seems unobjectionable by itself, but it is far from obvious to what extent the choices involved in its realization can be reconciled with similar choices made to achieve maximum realization of the other criteria on the list. A brief discussion of the items on Smalley's list may help to clarify some of the problems.

MOTIVATION FOR THE LEARNER

It is interesting to note that the first criterion, maximum motivation for the learner, is not a linguistic criterion; rather, it recognizes the fact that a systematically elegant orthography is worthless if it is rejected by the community for extrasystemic reasons. It has been observed more than once that the users of orthographies do not always agree with linguists in evaluating the suitability of an orthographic system for a given language (see, for example, Nida 1953; Garvin 1954; Sjoberg 1964; Winter 1983). Thus, unless the orthography makers are going to be content with what otherwise may prove to have been a purely academic exercise, they must be prepared to compromise their analytic principles for the sake of acceptance, however irrational the requirements may be that force them to deviate from a systematically motivated representation of the language. Language attitudes such as the desire to have an orthography which makes the language in question graphically similar to another or, conversely, makes the language dissimilar to another, may be irrational but they are social facts which often strongly influence the success of a proposed system.

For example, Sjoberg (1964: 268) reports that in Bolivia the Aymara allophones of /u/ and /i/, [o] and [e] respectively, came to be represented in writing because Spanish orthography includes the letters ⟨o⟩ and ⟨e⟩ which correspond to Spanish phonemes. Leaving these sounds unrepresented in Aymara would be, from a strictly linguistic viewpoint, systematically reasonable because allophones are morphophonologically predictable. However, from a sociolinguistic viewpoint, to some Aymaras the Aymara orthography would look defective and less dignified if it had fewer letters than the prestige language Spanish.

Another typical example of externally motivated spelling is the use of both ⟨l⟩ and ⟨r⟩ in New Guinea Pidgin orthographies, although most Pidgin dialects have only one sound, an alveolar flap, which corresponds to both of these letters. The spelling is determined by the use of ⟨l⟩ and ⟨r⟩ in the English source words (cf. Wurm 1977).

Reverse reactions have also been observed – that is, opposition against the introduction of special symbols which are linguistically well motivated but do not occur in the orthographies of the major Western languages – as for instance ⟨ŋ⟩ rather than ⟨ng⟩ for /ŋ/.

Depending on the colonial history, a Western orthography may be either a prestige model to imitate or a standard to be avoided and deviated from. Smalley (1964) mentions the case of some speech communities in Cameroon who were opposed to writing their languages with letters whose sound values are those given them in French.

The implications of these and similar observations are clear. Linguistic adequacy and motivation for the learner (that is, acceptability) are separate criteria. The former cannot simply be treated as one factor of the latter because both criteria seem to be largely independent. A linguist is, nevertheless, obliged to take the standards of systemic adequacy as the starting point, but must also be prepared to reckon with externally motivated deviations.

REPRESENTATION OF SPEECH

Smalley's second criterion, maximum representation of speech, is the proper domain for strictly linguistic considerations. That an orthography should be designed to represent speech as faithfully as possible seems obvious enough; but it is not so clear what exactly this implies for unwritten languages. First of all, there is the problem of language-internal dialect variation and selecting a dialect or variety of the language which the orthography is supposed to represent.

Venezky (1970) has surmised that, in the design of new orthographies, dialect differences pose a greater problem in theory than in practice. However, in support of this claim, he refers to English where considerable dialect differences, according to him, do not impair the learning of the orthography because English orthographies do not map on to a level of shallow phonological representation. English, of course, is a standard language which has been used in writing for several centuries and whose written norm has affected the development of the language, bringing about linguistic convergence[1] and a clear understanding of what is standard and what is dialectal deviation from it. It is doubtful, therefore, that conclusions drawn from observations about English can easily be transferred to hitherto unwritten languages.[2]

Linguistic history provides ample evidence of the importance of choosing one dialect rather than another for representing a given language in writing. For example, the emergence of Dutch as a separate language can be attributed in large measure to the choice of a High German variety rather than a Low German variety as the standard for written German (cf. Feldbusch 1985), and to the decision to establish a written standard in its own right for Dutch, one of the Low German varieties (cf. Van der Plank 1988). More recently, dialect choice was a crucial issue in making Faeroese a written language (Ferguson 1983). The importance of making the proper dialect choice for an orthography is documented by Smalley (1964) and Ansre (1974) for several African languages.

Theoretically it can be argued that if all occurrences of phone A in one dialect correspond to phone B in another, then the two dialects are isomorphic and it should thus be immaterial which one becomes the base of a new orthography. However, this is a very theoretical argument indeed with little practical relevance, because dialects are not usually so regularly related to each other. As Haugen (1966) has pointed out, the notion of dialect is a relational one which is used sensibly only when every dialect, D_n, is understood as a dialect of a language, L_m, which serves as a point of reference for all dialects of a dialect family. For unwritten languages – or rather, for an unwritten dialect family – it is not always easy to determine the point of reference: that is, the variety of which the others can be said to be dialects. In some cases such a point of reference is being created by choosing one variety rather than another as the base for written representation. Before the alphabet maker can start to work on the technical details, he or she thus has to answer a twofold question and answer it in a sociolinguistically informed way: namely, (1) is there a social consensus as to which dialect would be the natural choice as the model for graphically representing the language in question, and (2) in the absence of such a consensus, which variety is most likely to be generally accepted as a model and to bring about dialect convergence?

Assuming that these questions have been answered,[3] the orthography designer then has to decide what features of the phonetic representation of the language should be taken into account in its written representation. To Smalley it seems obvious that the criterion of maximum representation of speech is best realized by a phonemic orthography operating, by and large, on the principle of having a single representation for each phoneme of the language. To aim at a phonemic-like transcription-type orthography presupposes a dependency relation between speech and writing which assigns to writing a preponderantly derivative character only. As pointed out repeatedly in previous chapters, this attitude toward writing has been criticized on the grounds that it fails to recognize the dynamic force which writing introduces into linguistic evolution.

However, there is no reason to discard completely either the principle or employment of a phonemic-like transcription when creating an orthography. Rather, one ought to consider how the phonemic-like representation of a given language might be modified to satisfy the criterion of the 'maximum representation of speech'. Since transcriptions, in any event, cannot give more than a rough idea of the actual pronunciation of a language, phonological distinctions with a low functional load may well be left unrepresented for the sake of economy because they can be inferred from the context. On the other hand, it may be desirable to supplement the phonemic representation by certain higher-level distinctions. Recent reading research has accumulated ever more evidence that words and morphemes are the critical units for the proficient reader, whereas grapheme–phoneme correspondences seem to be of lesser importance[4] (Ehri 1979; Frith 1979).

If anything can be learned from the history of extant alphabetic orthographies, it is that as they increase in age, they tend to move away from simple phonemic representation. This can be described as a historically conditioned deviation from the phonemic principle; but at the same time it also represents a process of accommodating in the written representation of a given language information from other systemic levels. In other words, thanks to the multi-level structure of natural languages, violating the prototypical alphabetical principle of using a single letter or combination of letters for one phoneme is not just destructive but also, in a sense, productive because deviations from, or shifts in, phoneme–grapheme correspondences do not happen randomly; more often than not they occur in a way that lets other structural units and patterns become more apparent (hence Bolinger's notion in 1946 of 'visual morphemes' in alphabetic orthographies). Indeed, mature alphabetic orthographies encode morphological and lexical information in addition to phonemic information; and mature readers make use of this information more than they do of letter–sound correspondences.[5]

These observations give rise to the question of the extent to which the alphabet maker should try to anticipate historical 'corruptions' of a strictly phonemic representation by incorporating lexical and morphological information from the start. To do so, of course, presupposes a very thorough morphological, syntactic and lexical analysis of the language in question. This is a formidable task because, when the decisions are being made to provide previously unwritten languages with an orthography, those languages have usually not yet been studied for a long time. Even the segmentation of words can pose considerable problems (cf., for example, Beck 1964; Gudschinsky 1970). As has been argued in chapter 3, the orthographic word is, partly at least, an artefact,

yet the one who designs the orthography has to make non-arbitrary segmentations which will become orthographic words once the orthography is accepted and employed.

To attempt to incorporate more information than has been described
above in an orthography for a hitherto unwritten language may be too
ambitious. For one thing, it is difficult to predict how a new orthography influences the linguistic awareness of its users. Also, it is likely
that, in a language newly reduced to writing, there will remain patterns
and units not yet clearly understood. Therefore it seems wiser, easier
and more economical at the initial stage to be content with a valid
phonological transcription as the way to introduce a new orthography.

Another issue which cannot be ignored by one who is designing an
orthography which will employ the Roman alphabet is how to represent
phonemes which the Roman alphabet was not designed to represent.
Indeed, the same problem is faced by those designing orthographies
which employ other orthographies or writing systems, if that particular
system does not have a way of representing a given sound of the
language to be provided with the new orthography.

For those orthographies which employ the Roman alphabet the following are the most obvious options available when dealing with this
issue.

1 IPA signs such as æ or ʃ can be introduced as additional letters.
2 Letter combinations can be given singular sound value definitions, for instance ⟨dh⟩ for /θ/.
3 Superfluous letters can be redefined using, for instance, ⟨x⟩ for a
   palatal fricative rather than for /ks/.
4 Letters can be used in different sizes as sub- or superscripts, as in
   ⟨kʷ⟩ or ⟨k_y⟩.
5 The basic letters can be augmented with diacritics, for example,
   by accent marks, whether acute, grave or circumflex, tilde,
   breath marks, tone signs, umlaut or diaeresis dots, cedilla, juncture marks, macron or breve.
6 Different typefaces can be used to differentiate, for example,
   long and short vowels or stressed and unstressed syllables.

Many current Roman orthographies make use of one or several of these
devices which serve to improve the accuracy of representing a language
considerably. The necessity of using them is evidence of the limitations
of the alphabet in its simple form.

EASE OF LEARNING

To maximize the ease of its learning, an orthography has to be simple. From this apparently trivial postulate one might be tempted to jump to the conclusion that a shallow phonemic transcription is the easiest orthography to learn. This is not quite so because the phoneme itself is already a highly abstract unit, perceptible to the native speaker, but whose concrete realization may be difficult to describe or represent. To track the sound stream in terms of phonemic segments, identify each segment with a letter, and then relate groups of segment-letters to individual meanings is not an easy task, even given a highly regular system. Some segments are, moreover, impossible to isolate as separate sounds, so that even an ideal phonemic orthography is bound to be marred by inconsistencies of sound–letter relations which would be easier to avoid in non-phonemic syllabic transcriptions, for instance. A syllabic transcription, however, inevitably means an increase of the number of basic signs to be learned. It depends on the syllabic structure of the language which is being encoded whether a syllabic orthography is even worth considering from the point of view of ease of learning. If the syllabic structure is intricate, the greater ease of grasping syllables as opposed to phonemes is likely to be outweighed by the great number of necessary signs which a syllabic system must employ.

Maximum ease of learning, moreover, is a criterion which refers to two skills, both to reading and to writing. It is uncontroversial that these skills are not the reverse of each other. Each involves very different psychological, perceptual and linguistic skills, capacities and processes. What makes for ease in learning to read may not make for ease in learning to write, and vice versa.

For example, reading words which are homophones and not homographs, words that sound alike but are not spelled alike, is not difficult and rarely causes mistakes in pronunciation. In contrast, having to differentiate homophone words in writing is the source of many spelling mistakes and hence appears to be difficult. Consequently Frith (1979) suggests that sound in reading plays a secondary role only, but is very important in writing. Different spellings of homophone words makes for easier access to meaning when reading but, when writing, different spellings for homophone words force the writer to make a choice for mapping sounds on to letters. That is to say, a multiple phoneme to grapheme correspondence may be an advantage for reading, but an obstacle for writing. Consequently, when the designer of an orthography considers the criterion of 'maximum ease for learning', he or she has to strike a balance between the needs of the reader and those of the writer. However, if the needs and ease of the reader are favored and satisfied to a somewhat greater extent, this may be justified by the fact that many more people read than write.

TRANSFER

Languages that in modern times are being provided with their first orthography are unlikely to have a very wide communicative range. One of the main reasons for reducing them to writing is the generally held belief that becoming literate is more difficult in a foreign or second language than it is in one's mother tongue (Gudschinsky 1976; Srivastava et al. 1978).[6] Rather than expecting that recently graphicized languages will in their written form suddenly assume a wide range of communicative functions, the dominant and practical rationale behind such a complex and costly effort is the expectation that having become literate in the mother tongue first will facilitate becoming literate in a language of wider communication later. Given that this is a major objective of designing an orthography for a hitherto unwritten language, it is highly desirable that the new orthography differ as little as possible from that language of wider communication which is of greatest functional value for the speech community in question.

This requirement puts severe restrictions on the design of new orthographies. Easy transfer can be hoped for only if the orthography to be created makes use of the same script as that of the major contact language in the environment. This precludes many choices. A Roman orthography for an Indian language, for example, would facilitate transfer to English but not to any of the orthographies of the major regional languages which are much more important in rural India (Jalaluddin 1983). Although in the southern part of the Soviet Union there is some overlap of cultural spheres of influence in places where the Arabic alphabet has for centuries served as a link with the Islamic world, the Cyrillic alphabet is the obvious basis of new orthographies. Similarly, in Africa, the Roman and Arabic alphabets compete in some

countries where both Arabic and a European colonial language play a
significant role (Tucker 1971).

Script choice is, of course, only one aspect of ease of transfer. Once a
script has been chosen, there are still numerous options for the orthography to be designed. The greatest transfer to an existing orthography
is achieved if the letters of the script in question are given the same
sound values in the new orthography. This is what European travelers in
former times did naïvely whenever they recorded exotic languages
which they came to know in other parts of the world. They used the
alphabet according to the conventions of the orthography of their
mother tongue. The result is articulately illustrated by the following
remarks one writer made early in the nineteenth century about the
language specificity of alphabetic writing:

When, for example, a mere English reader finds the familiar names of the
Creeks and the *Choctaws*, the *Wabash* and the *Washita*, with many others, dis-
guised by the French writers under the strange garb of *Kriques*, and *Tchactas*,
Ouabach and *Ouachita*, &c.; and among the German authors, the letters G, J, T,
and Z used to denote sounds which we should denote by C, Y, D, and TS, as in
the words *Ganata* for *Canada*, *Japewi* for *Yapewi*, *N'mizi* for *N'meetsee* ... he
will at first view suppose that they are the names and languages of so many different tribes of Indians. (Pickering 1818, quoted in Kemp 1981: 24).[7]

In the nineteenth century, missionaries and scholars became keenly
aware of the fact that it was difficult not to impose the orthographic
conventions of their mother tongue on to the new orthographies they
were trying to construct. Transfer was achieved, as it were, by default.
However, greater familiarity with ever more languages also led to the
insight that the orthographic conventions of one language might not do
justice to the sounds of another. Serious efforts at overcoming the
language specificity of the alphabet were the result. Several schemes
were proposed for a 'universal alphabet' capable of representing the
relevant sound distinctions of all languages.[8] The eventual outcome of
this quest was, of course, the IPA which was thought to be rich enough
to offer for all languages a sufficient selection of letters for the sounds
that are phonemic, and in which letters are used with uniformly defined
sound values. Certain problems remain, in particular the representation
of length, tone and stress (Garvin 1954); but in principle IPA is a viable
universal transcription system, though it is by no means accepted
throughout the world.[9]

The whole point of having an international phonetic alphabet is, of course, not to tie it to any particular language. It is not meant to be used as an orthography, because as such it could not guard against the sound changes that constantly occur in all languages and which either require periodic adjustments in the way a given orthography records the sounds of a particular language or lead to the corruption of the originally designed fit between certain graphic symbols and phonetically defined sound values. For this very practical reason, the IPA has not been used as the orthography for any major language, so to use it for new orthographies does not offer any advantage in terms of transfer.

Consequently, to maximize transferability means in effect to model a new orthography as closely as possible on that of the major contact language, while at the same time avoiding obvious distortions such as the marking of distinctions that are present in the contact language but do not occur in the language for which an orthography is being designed. For the new orthography this means that it should use the orthography of the contact language as the starting point and matrix to be adapted to the structural requirements of its own new needs. More specifically, the new orthography should observe the following principles.

1 It should make use of the grapheme inventory of the major contact language with the same or similar sound values where correspondences exist.
2 It should not use any graphemes of the contact language for which there are no corresponding values in the phonology of the as yet unwritten language.
3 For phonemic units with a high functional load which have no counterpart in the major contact language and are thus not represented in its orthography, the new orthography should introduce graphemic distinctions by using digraphs, trigraphs, diacritics or, where necessary, additional letters.

EASE OF REPRODUCTION

This criterion is a purely technical one which is, none the less, of considerable importance. Standard typewriters and typesetting machines are designed for a handful of European languages and hence accommodate only their orthographic distinctions. Every additional letter or diacritic mark is a serious problem for mechanically reproducing texts which make use of such signs. While all this has somewhat changed with dozens of fonts and typefaces, and practically unlimited possibilities of designing new characters in computer-assisted word processing equipment, this kind of equipment is not typically available to speech communities at the threshold of literacy, and neither can these conditions be expected to change for some time to come. Therefore technical considerations will continue to be of great importance for the design of any new orthography whose purpose and intent is to promote literacy.

SYNTHESIZING LINGUISTIC AND EXTRA-LINGUISTIC REQUIREMENTS

From the discussion of Smalley's five criteria for the design of new orthographies it should be obvious that in some respects they are in conflict with each other. Maximizing one often goes at the expense of others. For example, in a community that entertains strong feelings about its new orthography as a symbol of self-identity, the motivation for the learner is likely to be reduced to the extent that transfer to the orthography of the dominant contact language[10] is increased by using the dominant contact language as a model. In India where, according to Pattanayak (1979: 43), 'a new script is created ... almost once in three months', this is a serious problem because, despite persistent demands for new systems, the general policy is to adopt for unwritten languages the script and orthography of the dominant regional language rather than proliferate the already confusing number of Indian scripts and writing systems (cf. chapter 10). Such a policy, which emphasizes transfer and ease of reproduction, is often resented by speakers of non-literate languages because it is perceived as threatening their linguistic identity[11] (Srivastava and Gupta 1983).

Other conflicts can occur between an effort faithfully to map speech and virtually every other criterion. To indicate the relevant phonetic or phonemic distinctions of a language accurately may be costly, cumbersome in reproduction, detrimental to transfer and unnecessarily difficult for the learner, and hence thwart any effort to motivate. Where the phonology and other structures of a particular language differ very much from those of the major contact language, every feature that favors transferability frustrates faithful mapping. The Cyrillic orthography for

Karakalpak, a Turkic language of central Asia, is a typical example. At a linguistic conference in 1954 it was condemned for its inadequacy: 'The great shortcoming of current Karakalpak orthography, as many speakers mentioned, is the fact that it does not reflect the phonetic structure of the Karakalpak language' (Henze 1977). In spite of great differences between Russian and Karakalpak, the Cyrillic alphabet was used in a way very similar to the Russian orthography. Transferability was high, but the faithful representation of speech was low.

Similarly, ease of reproduction may conflict with high accuracy in representing speech. This is a particular problem for phonemes that do not have equivalents in the Roman, Cyrillic or Arabic alphabets. Phonemic tone, clicks, vowel length and stress are features of this kind. It is often difficult to find for them satisfactory solutions which combine accuracy and ease of reproduction. For West African languages this has long been recognized (Meinhof 1931). Vietnamese, a tone language, for instance, has more than ten different diacritics for some vowel letters. In handwritten script they are easily and often omitted; and in print they make for a cluttered appearance.

In some cases transfer considerations interfere with ease of learning. For example, in the Devanagari script the schwa vowel is not indicated in consonant initial syllables. This is a well-known problem for those learning to read Hindi, yet new orthographies continue to be modeled on the orthography of Hindi, including this feature.

It must be kept in mind that 'faithful mapping of speech' can refer to different structural levels. Informed decisions as to which units and levels should be incorporated in a new orthography can only be made on the basis of a thorough analysis of the entire language system. Such decisions are necessarily language specific. For example, an orthography for a language which has a relatively simple phonology but an intricate morphology should be more morphophonemic than one for a language with a very complex phonology and a simple morphology. Thus the same single criterion for measuring the aptness of a new orthography for one language is likely to imply something quite different when applied to another language.

This is also true for the extra-linguistic criteria which vary so greatly from one speech community to another. Yet whoever designs an orthography must reckon with the reality that social pressure overrides all other considerations. Prestige, resistance to national integration or submission to a dominant language and culture, local customs, the level of technological development; these are variables which time and again have been shown to affect in significant ways both the design and development of orthographies for previously unwritten languages. This does not mean that linguistic, psychological and pedagogical factors are unimportant. Berry (1977: 4) is overstating the case when he writes that 'acceptance or rejection of an orthography has little to do with its linguistic adequacy.' It is certainly true that systemic elegance and flexibility are not often perceived as good arguments *for* accepting a script or orthography, but a new system may well be rejected for reasons of linguistic inadequacy.

What follows is that, to harmonize the linguistic and the extra-linguistic requirements for a new orthography, those who design a successful new orthography must have not only analytic insight into the linguistic levels of the language in question, but they must also be ready and willing to apply those insights within the social, political and cultural confines of the external requirements imposed by the prospective users of the new orthography. Linguistic analysis can be of great service and should be the foundation of any new orthography but it can only serve, it cannot dominate; and its suggestions must be attuned to the variety of factors which constitute sociocultural reality.

In sum, a new orthography should be: (1) based on a variety of the language which is acceptable to the majority of the speech community; (2) easy to learn; (3) easy to write; (4) easy to read; (5) founded on a phonemic analysis of the language while affording access to the morphophonemic and lexical levels; (6) transcending the limitations of the sign inventory of the orthography of the respective major contact language as little as possible; and (7) in as much agreement with the available printing technology as the internal consistency of the system and the requirement of indicating the basic repertoire of phonemes will permit.

NOTES

1 See, for instance, Pawley and Syder (1983) for some references on the impact of writing on the evolution of language.
2 It should also be noted that the claim that dialect differences are no impediment to learning the English orthography is not uncontested (cf. Shuy 1973). For a discussion of some points concerning dialect influences in writing, see Whiteman (1981).

3 There may be a geographically motivated choice of a centrally located variety which is equidistant from all others, or an elite variety or a functionally specialized variety used for formal or poetic purposes, as for instance the variety of Somali which was taken as the basis for the new orthography (cf. Labahn 1982).

4 One sort of evidence comes from dyslexia research. A syndrome known as 'phonological dyslexia' indicates that in reading (alphabetic scripts) there is a direct 'route' from print to meaning which does not depend on letter-to-sound conversions. Patients with this syndrome have lost the ability of carrying out even the simplest letter-to-sound conversions but still can understand written words. Evidence of this sort cannot be taken to mean that relating letters to phonemes plays no part in reading, but it does show that this level of structural correspondence can be bypassed if necessary (cf. Ellis 1984: 15ff).

5 A useful discussion of the most important results of recent research about the psycholinguistics of reading that underscores the importance of meaning rather than sound is found in Steinberg (1982: chapter 10). See also Underwood and Underwood (1986).

6 The growing awareness of functional illiteracy as a major problem in industrialized societies has yielded a flood of literature on literacy and mother tongue education in the 1970s and 1980s. Some useful titles are Bisseret (1979), Fiore and Elsasser (1982) and Wallerstein (1984).

7 In the preceding chapter mention has been made several times of proper names and their special status with respect to the reconstruction of the phonology of a forgotten language. In the present context, the special nature of proper names again helps to highlight the point at issue. Since their sound is a crucial part of their meaning, they cannot simply be translated. Rather, it is important to represent their form as faithfully as possible by means of another language and script.

8 Richard Lepsius' *Standard Orthography for Reducing Unwritten Languages and Foreign Graphic Systems to a Uniform Orthography in European Letters* was one of the better known and well-construed of such systems. It gained some recognition, especially in Africa, but never became widely accepted, let alone universal as its creator had hoped. The history of universal alphabets is documented in Kemp (1981).

9 For an account of the development of IPA see R. W. Albright (1958).

10 Although a substantial part of the world population is still illiterate, there are no major languages that remain unwritten today. Orthography making thus invariably concerns languages of small speech communities which are spoken in a multilingual environment with at least one dominant literate language (cf. Coulmas 1984b). The latter is here referred to as the 'dominant' or 'link language', a term often used in the sociology of language

to refer to languages employed for inter-speech community communication.

11 For some communities the policy of enhancing transferability creates special problems because, on the basis of this policy, they are obliged to adopt more than one script/orthography for their language. A well-known case is that of the Santhali, a speech community distributed over four Indian states with distinctly different scripts (Bengali, Oriya, Hindi and Assamese). Not surprisingly, opposition against the use of four different scripts for writing Santhali led to the development of a Santhali script, known as *Ol Chiki*, which attempts to combine features of Hindi, Bengali and Roman. In West Bengal Ol Chiki was recognized in 1981 as the medium of instruction on the primary level (Jalaluddin 1983: 521).

13

Writing Reform: Conditions and Implications

The standard of excellence of a good writing system, whatever it may be, can be applied to both the creation of new systems and the revision of existing ones, but the tasks of reducing an unwritten language to writing, on the one hand, and reforming an existing orthography, on the other hand, nevertheless differ in important respects. Mention was made earlier of the conservatism of writing in general and of individual orthographies in particular. Once written norms are established, they attract emotional attachment, and hence discussions about the reform of a given orthography or script often resemble a religious war[1] more than a rational discourse, generating more heat than light. The question of whether a system should or should not be reformed therefore tends to be debated with more zeal than that of how it should be changed if it should be changed.

There are four philosophical positions that are familiar in any discussion of societal norms. First, from a *norm-positivistic* point of view, it is more important that there is a norm than that there is a good norm, whereas the adherents of a *rational-normative* view insist that a norm should be well motivated in order to be accepted. Plain *conservatives*, on the other hand, hold the opinion that the tradition is worth preserving as a value in its own right, no matter how cumbersome or irrational it may appear from a synchronic point of view. Finally, there is the *anarchistic* position which holds that norms are unnecessary constraints of individual freedom and creativity.

In writing reform discussions such underlying philosophical attitudes are not always made explicit; rather the discussants tend to invoke technical arguments in support of their positions. It is more difficult than one might think, therefore, to separate scientific and political interests in such disputes, and evaluate the research findings that are presented in support of, or as evidence against, a given position. While it can be argued that the necessity of reform is more apparent in some cases than in others, there is always an element of belief and conviction in answering the question of whether a given system should be subjected to a reform. It is not our purpose here to advocate or combat a particular reform project. Instead of addressing the *whether*, this chapter thus deals with the *why* and *how* of writing reforms and tries to explain some of the technical difficulties involved in such a project.

It must be noted that, no matter how trivial a proposed change may seem in substance – such as spelling *honour* with or without the ⟨u⟩ – a writing reform is always an undertaking of some consequence because it concerns a speech community as a whole. Like a reform of traffic regulations, a writing reform must be enacted in a way that ensures general adherence and not just conformity of the majority. Of course, reforms differ greatly in extent and result. In particular, changes involving the script rather than only the spelling conventions have more weighty consequences for the society, since they entail a much more drastic break with a tradition. Adjustments of spelling conventions may inconvenience the writer, but they do not usually cause great problems to the reader who can still read texts written according to the old rules. A new script, however, makes a literary tradition practically inaccessible to subsequent generations of writers and readers. The following account will focus first on the conditions and implications of script reforms and then go on to examine the key issues of orthography reforms.

SCRIPT REFORMS

Script reforms usually consist of two steps, (1) script choice and (2) orthography formation. Only in some cases does a script reform not entail the selection of a script, but consist of the reduction or elimination of a system or part of a system. The abolition of Chinese characters in North Korea is a case in point. Until the coming into existence of the two Korean states, Chinese characters were used in combination with Han'gul as part of the Korean writing system. In the interest of facilitating the learning of the written language, the government of the Peoples Republic of Korea decided to dispense with Chinese characters and write the Korean language exclusively with Han'gul. Since Chinese characters are the basis of a cultural bond among the educated elites in north-east Asia, and since South Korea continues to use the Han'gul-plus-characters system, this was a reform of some consequence, yet it did not involve the selection of a new script (as did the replacement of Chinese characters by a Roman orthography for Annamese, the intro-duction of a Cyrillic alphabet instead of the Arabic for Uigur in the Soviet Union or the substitution of Arabic by Roman letters for Hausa).

The North Korean case is rather unique, but script reforms involving the shift from one system to another have been proposed and carried out often. Egyptian was written in the autochthonous hieroglyphic, hieratic and demotic scripts which were eventually supplanted by the Greek (Coptic) script. In India a large number of languages in the course of his-tory have been written in different scripts, and for many of them the dis-cussion about a linguistically appropriate and culturally acceptable script continues (Pattanayak 1979).² In the 1920s many minority languages of the Soviet Union underwent changes in their scripts from Arabic to Latin and then Cyrillic (Henze 1977). In what was probably the most successful reform in this century, Turkey also changed from the Arabic script to a Romanized orthography.

Turkish

The Turkish script reform was part of a larger cultural and political reform by means of which Kemal Atatürk, a strong nationalistic leader, set his country on a course of Westernization. It was coupled with a movement to rid Turkish of Arabic and Persian words and to bring the written language into line with the spoken. The delicate point was the association of the Arabic script with the Islamic faith whose representa-tives Atatürk did not want to antagonize unnecessarily. That the shift from Arabic to Roman was accomplished successfully can be attributed to two factors. First, at the time of the reform, literacy was very low in Turkey, and hence only a small part of the population was required to change from one system to another. Second, in the ideological discus-sion nationalistic slogans were emphasized at the expense of arguments pertaining to religion. The declared aim of the reform was 'to bring out the genuine beauty and richness of the Turkish language and to elevate it to the high rank it deserves among world languages' (quoted in Heyd 1954: 14). Thus Romanization was sold to the public as a means of authentification. The Arabic alphabet was depicted as being unsuitable for the representation of the Turkish language, a strait-jacket preventing the language from unfolding its full potential.

This was true only to some extent, because obviously the Arabic script could have been amended to suit the Turkish language better than it did. However, owing to the great importance of vowels in Turkish, substantial changes would have been necessary which, precisely because of the association of the Arabic script with Islam and with a long literary tradition, might have been more difficult to implement than the introduction of a new script. The Roman alphabet, too, had to be adjusted to the phonology of Turkish, but here no resistance had to be overcome that was grounded in tradition. Three letters of the Roman alphabet, ⟨q⟩, ⟨w⟩ and ⟨x⟩, were discarded; ⟨Z⟩ was designated as a lengthening sign; a cedilla was used as a diacritic for ⟨ç⟩ and ⟨ş⟩, a hook for ⟨ğ⟩ and, optionally, also over ⟨ĭ⟩ and ⟨ŭ⟩. Further diacritics are ⟨ö⟩, ⟨ü⟩ and ⟨ı⟩. ⟨'⟩ is used as a juncture mark.[3]

With these additions the Roman alphabet was introduced for the writing of Turkish in 1928. A year later the use of Arabic and Persian as languages of instruction in high school was phased out. Although the literati, especially scholars involved with the study of texts, naturally continued to use the Arabic script for some time, and although its role for religious purposes was preserved, the introduction of the new Turkish orthography with Roman letters was accepted rapidly.

Not all details of Turkish spelling with Roman letters are completely settled yet. In particular, there is no general agreement about the spelling of words of Arabic origin. Arabic /b/ and /d/, for instance, are written alternatively as ⟨b⟩, ⟨d⟩ or ⟨p⟩, ⟨t⟩, as in *ibtida, idhal* as against *iptida, ithal*, the former representing the etymology and the latter the pronunciation in Turkish. Moreover, there is considerable variation in the spelling of vowels. Common variations include ⟨u⟩ and ⟨ü⟩, ⟨ü⟩ and ⟨ö⟩, ⟨i⟩ and ⟨ı⟩. Since the authoritative Romanized Turkish dictionary is yet to be written, this state of affairs is likely to continue. However, in spite of some remaining uncertainties, the Turkish script reform must be evaluated as a complete success.

Chinese

If the length of a literary tradition is any indication of the problems of a writing reform, then the reform of the Chinese script can be expected to be excruciatingly difficult both to conceive and to enact. Of course, there are also other reasons why the 'reform of the Chinese written language', as it is known in China, is a complicated matter. The sheer magnitude of the project makes it an awesome task. The size of the speech community is enormous, and the nature of the Chinese writing system implies that a reform involves a review of practically the entire vocabulary of Chinese. Attempts at reforming the Chinese script go back to the 1890s (DeFrancis 1977) and to the 'literary revolution of 1918–1919' (Konrad 1977), but the present discussion is limited to more recent developments in the People's Republic of China.

The reform program consists of three main tasks, all of which were mentioned by Premier Chou En-lai in a speech delivered in 1959 (Chou 1959). They are (1) the standardization and simplification of Chinese characters, (2) the creation of a romanized orthography, and (3) the nationwide promotion of the standard language. The Committee for Reforming the Chinese Written Language is responsible for designing the details of this policy.[4]

The first measure has involved the simplification of the internal structure of *Hanzi* and the exclusion of variants. Since 1956, when the first standardization scheme was issued, 2,238 *Hanzi* have been simplified and 1,055 variants have been ruled out. Character simplification is achieved on the basis of several principles. Some many-stroked *Hanzi* were replaced by simpler ones. In other cases complex *Hanzi* were reduced to one of their compound parts. The most prolific principle is, however, to linearize cursively handwritten *Hanzi* or parts thereof and to adopt these as the standard printed forms. The simplification of *Hanzi* is a reform that caters more to the writer than to the reader. While it is certainly true that a character becomes easier to write if the number of its compound strokes is reduced, it must also be noted that its distinctness decreases by the same measure. As opposed to the obvious benefit of reducing the number of variant characters in current use, the advantage of simplified characters is thus hard to assess, which is perhaps why the Committee has abstained of late from publishing any further lists of simplified *Hanzi.* In the beginning the simplified *Hanzi* were rapidly accepted in China, but they have not completely replaced the old ones in public life. Figure 13.1 lists some simplified *Hanzi* with their original forms shown in brackets.

The second measure was implemented after thorough research and deliberation when, in 1958, the People's Congress adopted the Chinese phonetic alphabet, *hànyǔ pīnyīn*, as the standard system of writing the

迠	〔建〕	旦	〔蛋〕
江	〔豇〕	[illegible]	〔弹〕
[illegible]	〔酱〕	[illegible]	〔蹈〕
交	〔跤〕	[illegible]	〔稻〕
茭	〔椒〕	辺	〔道〕
亍	〔街〕	[illegible]	〔懂〕
井	〔阱〕	斗拱	〔枓栱〕
垪	〔境〕	[illegible]	〔短〕
[illegible]	〔镜〕	[illegible]	〔蹲〕
艽	〔韭〕	炖	〔燉〕

13.1 Some simplified Hanzi and their original forms in square brackets

Chinese language with Roman letters. Since the seventeenth century numerous Romanized systems had been developed and used, resulting in a rather chaotic situation in which a variety of systems coexisted. Pinyin is a phonemic orthography which marks the four tones of the standard language with accent marks on the tone bearing vowel. It makes use of the following letters with straightforward values for vowels, semivowels and consonants:

vowels: ⟨a⟩, ⟨e⟩, ⟨i⟩, ⟨o⟩, ⟨u⟩, ⟨ü⟩
semivowels: ⟨y⟩, ⟨w⟩
consonants: ⟨b⟩, ⟨p⟩, ⟨d⟩, ⟨t⟩, ⟨z⟩, ⟨c⟩, ⟨s⟩
⟨j⟩, ⟨q⟩, ⟨x⟩, ⟨g⟩, ⟨k⟩, ⟨h⟩, ⟨l⟩, ⟨r⟩

In addition, three digraphs are used for retroflex stops and fricatives, ⟨zh⟩, ⟨ch⟩ and ⟨sh⟩. The tones are marked as follows: ⟨ā⟩, ⟨á⟩, ⟨ǎ⟩ and ⟨à⟩. Analytically the new Roman orthography is clearly superior to the older systems, and its international acceptance has been rapid and successful. The UN has adopted it as the standard system of Romanization of Chinese names, which is why Peking, Nanking, Taipei, Sinkiang, etc., are now generally spelled *Beijing*, *Nanjing*, *Taibei* and *Xinjiang.* In China, the functions of the Pinyin are, however, still very limited. Some recent dictionaries are arranged in alphabetical order, and it is used for annotating *Hanzi*, especially for a foreign readership. It is also taught at the elementary school level, but although there are some periodicals that are published in *pinyin*, it has not captured a place in everyday life as a medium of the written language.

The question is whether this is ever going to happen: that is, whether Pinyin is ever going to replace rather than supplement *Hanzi.* Some politicians and linguists have at times advocated a full-fledged Romanization program leading to the destruction of character literacy. Mao Zedong is said to have spoken of the 'need to abandon' *Hanzi* (Snow 1968: 446) in the interest of promoting literacy and development,[5] and eminent linguists such as Wang Li and Lyu Shuxiang have argued for a gradual extension of Pinyin into an independent orthography competing with, and eventually supplanting, *Hanzi* as the popular medium of written Chinese. What the actual course of the development of Pinyin literacy in China will be is still hard to predict, but at present it seems as unlikely as ever that *Hanzi* will be replaced by Pinyin.

The third measure of the reform of the Chinese written language should be mentioned here briefly: the promotion of the standard language. If Romanization is a serious goal, then a systematically well-conceived alphabetic orthography is obviously only the first step. As a phonemic script Pinyin depends to a greater extent than do Chinese characters on the phonology of the standard language, *pǔtōnghuà*, and is hence of little use to those who do not understand this language. Obviously Pinyin, or a variant thereof, could also be used to write Cantonese, Wu, Hakka or any other Chinese dialect, but this would destroy the unity of the Chinese written language which *Hanzi* have served for so many centuries to preserve. Knowledge of the standard language throughout the country is thus a precondition for employing Pinyin as an efficient means of written communication in China. Accordingly, the official promotion of Pinyin is coupled with that of the standard language. To date, the standard language is not used in everyday life throughout the country, and as long as this is the case, Pinyin cannot be expected to gain ground in public communication.

It is clear that general knowledge of the standard language and Pinyin would drastically change the linguistic situation in China. If this is ever going to be achieved, it is bound to take many decades rather than years, and the consequences of shifting to a sound-based writing system in so vast a speech community are hard to predict. The significant point is that the dialect distinctions become highlighted by a script which represents one dialect only, namely the standard language which is basically the Beijing dialect of Mandarin. Since dialect distinctions are slight on the morphemic level having to do mainly with divergent pronunciations, the speakers of other dialects do not have more difficulties learning *Hanzi* than speakers of standard Mandarin. For them to learn to write Mandarin with a phonographic script, however, is a major feat, which in effect requires them to learn to speak Mandarin first. In a sense, the speakers of non-Mandarin varieties of Chinese have to adapt their pronunciation to the norm of the standard language first in order to be able to use the phonographic script which is based on this norm. Far from mapping their speech, the alphabetic script thus for them is a pronunciation guideline.

Clearly then, much more is involved in the pronunciation of Pinyin than introducing to the Chinese speech community a simple phonographic script which is adjusted to their speech. To what extent it will be accepted by the various dialect groups, and how it will affect their speech ecology, only careful observation in the future can show.

SPELLING REFORM OR PRONUNCIATION REFORM?

Spelling reforms are deemed necessary wherever the prolonged use of an orthographic system has led to major complications and/or corruptions of the fundamental relations holding between its graphic signs and the linguistic units they represent. The proper way of correcting and simplifying the relations between spoken and written signs is usually considered to be a reform of the rules governing the latter rather than the former. Writing reforms are official acts carried out on the basis of expert deliberation and advice. In view of the great social prestige attributed to writing, this is by no means a matter of course. Theoretically, the misfit between orthography and pronunciation could also be corrected by bringing the pronunciation into line with the spelling, and this is what speech communities in many instances do. Spelling pronunciation is just that: an unofficial pronunciation reform that takes the spelling of certain words as the model for their pronunciation.

However, officially implemented pronunciation reforms are almost unheard of, whereas spelling reforms – or, at least, debates about such reforms – are fairly common. In spite of the social prestige of writing, the Western tradition by and large adheres to the surrogationalist view which considers writing as a substitute of speech. It is writing that should represent speech rather than the other way round. Therefore, adulterated relationships between sound and letter are to be rectified by adjusting the spelling rather than the pronunciation.

Ad litteras

The most obvious of the reasons that make pronunciation reforms impractical is that general literacy is a very recent achievement. Where literacy is restricted to a small part of the speech community, pronunciation reforms must lead to diglossia or linguistic divergence. The story of Latin is a case in point. As part of his educational reforms, Charlemagne demanded that the corruption of the language of the church should be checked and that Latin should be pronounced *ad litteras*: that is, articulating each word so that each letter could be 'heard' in a way that was thought to have been the pronunciation of those letters in Classical times. This officially coordinated attempt to interfere in the development of the language under the guidance of members of the social and intellectual elite such as Alcuin of York became known as *reparatio* (Fleckenstein 1953). Charlemagne's pronunciation reform was very successful with respect to its declared intention, but it had unforeseen consequences. Through *reparatio* (through the re-establishment of a close correspondence of spoken and written Latin), the relation between speech and writing reversed for this language: the image became the model; the language was henceforward guided by its written representation which, however, could provide guidance only to the literati who constituted a very small part of the speech community. As a consequence, by being subjected to the authority of the letter, Latin degenerated into a written language only and gradually lost its native speaker community.[6]

Since the pronunciation of the common people remained unaffected by the reform, the vernacular varieties of Latin continued to evolve, eventually emerging as languages in their own right. Thus while for Latin the reform narrowed the gap between the spoken and the written form, the discrepancy between spoken and written language became even wider since for some time Latin remained the only proper written language. This cannot be the purpose of a language reform that is intended to remedy corruptions of sound–letter correspondences. Even in fully literate communities it would be all but impossible to employ the written norm as the yardstick of speech because such a measure will inevitably subdue the development of the language. Hence, assuming that a close and simple correspondence between the spoken and written forms of language is desirable, a spelling reform is the only practical means of bringing such a correspondence about where it has been upset in the course of historical change.

A MATTER OF DEGREE

A crucial issue for every spelling reform project is the question concerning to what extent the new system should deviate from the old one. Spelling reform proposals fall into two broad categories: (1) those remedying the deficiencies of the alphabet as it is used for the language in question by adding new symbols and diacritics; and (2) those trying to ameliorate the system by deleting irregularities and systematizing the existing spelling conventions. Some of the particulars and difficulties of both types can be illustrated with English, since more spelling reform proposals have been made for English than for almost any other language (Scragg 1974), and they differ from each other most obviously in the degree to which they depart from the established system.

English

It seems likely that the spelling conventions of English were once based on much closer phoneme–grapheme correspondences than they are now (Vachek 1973). In their major characteristics these conventions were established more than 400 years ago and, apart from minor features, have changed very little ever since (Stubbs 1980: 70). Occasional moderate modifications could have avoided the often lamented misfit between the forty-odd phonemes of English and the some 200 ways of spelling them. English has sixteen vowel phonemes and twenty-four consonant phonemes, as shown below:

vowels: /i/, /iː/, /e/, /eː/, /æ/, /a/, /ɔ/, /o/, /uː/, /u/, /ɛ/, /ə/, /ai/, /ɔi/, /au/, /əu/

consonants: /p/, /b/, /t/, /d/, /č/, /ǰ/, /k/, /g/, /f/, /v/, /θ/, /ð/, /s/, /z/, /š/, /ž/, /m/, /n/, /ŋ/, /l/, /r/, /j/, /w/, /h/

If it were only a matter of numerical underdetermination of letters relative to phonemes, the problem of representing these phonemes with the available letters would be a minor one. The rate of vowel phonemes to vowel letters is 3 : 1, and the corresponding rate for consonants is even less troublesome. However, the problem is not restricted to the necessity of using letters in a multifunctional way. The reverse phenomenon, the use of different letters for the representation of one and the same phoneme, is also common. Yet English spelling has never been fundamentally reformed, in spite of the recommendations of two learned societies, the (American) Simplified Spelling Board of 1906 and the (British) Simplified Spelling Society,[7] and although numerous proposals for a better spelling have been advanced by individuals that, from a purely systematic point of view, had much to commend them.[8]

One reform project which has been widely discussed is Pitman's Initial Teaching Alphabet (ITA). It belongs to the first category of proposals mentioned above since it comprises twenty-one new letters for those phonemes which in traditional English spelling are not indicated unambiguously. This alphabet, which was designed as a transitional orthography intended to facilitate the initial acquisition of literacy, was taught experimentally in some schools in Britain and the United States (Downing 1967). While these experiments were a remarkable success for the spelling reform lobby, they remained without any serious consequences.

The same can be said of other reform projects of this type. One which aroused considerable interest by the public is *Shavian*, or the Bernard Shaw Alphabet (cf. figure 11.7). Shavian was designed by Kingsley Read in accordance with the requirements laid down in G. B. Shaw's will. Shaw was so dissatisfied with the uneconomical English spelling system that he bequeathed a large sum of money to be used for designing and propagating a new alphabet for English consisting of at least forty letters.[9] Shaw's will was carried out to the letter, so to speak, but in spite of its systematic beauty and superiority over the conventional English orthography,[10] the new system never had a chance of being adopted. Shavian is a complete break not only with the old system, but with the entire literary tradition of Europe. Its symbols are all new, and therefore nobody can read anything written in it even approximately without having learned the new symbols with their sound values. Shavian was not taken seriously by many, therefore, and those who were engaged in the project were most probably more intrigued by the challenge of meeting Shaw's requirements than they were interested in improving the writing of English.

Yet another proposal of the first category is UNIFON, an alphabet consisting of forty letters which was invented in 1959 by John Malone, an economist from Chicago. As shown in figure 13.2, UNIFON makes

13.2 UNIFON, a transitory alphabet for English (from The Ambassador *10/1986)*

use of eighteen new letters and eliminates two old ones, ⟨q⟩ and ⟨x⟩. It is a phonemic transcription system which, like ITA, is intended to facilitate the learning of English in first and second language class rooms. The idea is to use it as a pronunciation key in English dictionaries, thus bridging the gap between speech and spelling. This 'non-imperial English' is then supposed first to supplement and then to compete internationally with British English and American English. The chances of an early success of UNIFON seem slim in spite of its simplicity, if only because it would require international agreement and cooperation.

One important point that can be learned from the above and other reform projects belonging to the first category is that a spelling reform that breaks with a tradition, without putting another in its place, has practically no chance of being accepted, at least not in a highly literate society. Consequently reform projects of the second category which are designed to redress obvious imperfections without changing the existing system beyond recognition are more realistic and interesting.

The most successful such project which is also the most successful modification of the spelling of English ever put into practice was brought about in the New World by Noah Webster. It is no coincidence that this happened at the time of the American independence movement. The waves of the new patriotism went high, and everything that underlined the differences with the colonial motherland had a good chance of being welcomed. That Webster was driven by the fever of American nationalism is evidenced in his own testimony. His proposals for a reform of the spelling system of English were set forth in an appendix to his *Dissertations on the English Language*, published in 1789, where he wrote that 'a capital advantage would be that it would make a difference between the English orthography and the American.'[11]

Although he was a reformer, Webster was a fundamentally conservative and rather philistine thinker who entertained very conventional ideas about the relation between speech and spelling. While he could not fail to realize the discrepancies between the canonical sound values of the letters of the alphabet and their pronunciation in English words which he intended to eliminate by reforming the orthography, he nevertheless thought that the best pronunciation was that which accorded most closely with the spelling. He also believed that it was possible to arrest language change if only a sound spelling system was available. He was very concerned therefore with the elimination of elements whose relation to pronunciation could not be determined easily. The following are some of the simplifications he proposed:

> *bred* for *bread*
> *bilt* for *built*
> *giv* for *give*
> *laf* for *laugh*
> *arkitecture* for *architecture*

These proposals did not survive, but many others did. As a matter of fact, virtually all characteristically American spellings resulted from Webster's innovations. Some of the most apparent American spellings are ⟨-or⟩ for ⟨-our⟩ as in *savior*, *labor*, etc.; ⟨-er⟩ for ⟨-re⟩ as *center*, *meter*, etc.; ⟨-ize⟩ for ⟨-ise⟩ as in *organize*, *idealize*, etc. Some of Webster's other innovations are less conspicuous at present because they were also accepted in England. *Music* and *public* spelt with a ⟨c⟩ instead of ⟨ck⟩, or ⟨-ection⟩ for ⟨-exion⟩ as in *connection*, *reflection*, etc. are two examples.

Webster was not the only advocate of a spelling reform in the North American colonies, but he was in the most favorable position to promote his suggestions. With his dictionary and his spelling book (for which he received backing from several government officials) he reached a large readership. Since many of his readers were immigrants from non-English speaking countries, his spelling changes did not amount to a reform for them but rather to a first exposure. They had no particular feelings about upholding a tradition. Together with the reform-minded literate establishment they contributed greatly to the success of

Webster's innovations. It is noticeable, however, that his more radical proposals, which would have meant a drastic departure from the British standard, were not adopted. His innovations did not amount to the great reform so often called for in order to make the spelling of English more systematic and easier to learn. American spelling is no significant improvement over the English norm, but it is what Webster wanted it to be: a symbol of a separate national identity. The net benefit is very questionable because there are two standards now instead of one, which hardly simplifies matters.

Another reform project was advanced by a famous contemporary of Webster's. In 1768, Benjamin Franklin proposed a new alphabet for English which in many respects was more sophisticated than Webster's, since it came closer to a phonemic notation. Franklin used some diacritics and a couple of new characters which, however, closely resemble familiar Roman letters (figure 13.3). For example, he created the letter *ish* to replace the digraph ⟨sh⟩ as well as its voiced counterpart ⟨j⟩. Franklin used his alphabet in some personal correspondence from which it becomes clear that his motivation was to provide a system which would prove easier than the standard orthography for poor spellers who, according to him, tend to spell phonetically. Furthermore, he was concerned that because of the change of English over the centuries, 'our words will gradually cease to express sounds, they will only stand for things as the written words do in Chinese' (Willcox 1972: 174).

Viewed systematically, Franklin's alphabet was superior to Webster's amendments to the English orthography, and he must have been aware of this because he did not lend his support to Webster's efforts, even though Webster had dedicated his 'Dissertations' to him. However, Franklin's many other responsibilities also kept him from doing much to promote his own system. Since it involved rather major disturbances of the existing spelling conventions it did not stand a good chance of being accepted.

Most spelling reform proposals in the past had been based on the principle that a closer correspondence should be achieved between sounds and letters, but they did not agree on the structural level on which the orthography should operate. Zachrisson's (1930) system, for example, was largely phonetic. Rather than spelling the plural morpheme in all its phonetic realizations as ⟨-s⟩, he suggested differentiating /z/ from /s/ and thus spelled *trublz* but *shoks*. Similarly, the past participle suffix was to be spelled according to its phonetic forms, for

Characters	Sounded as now in	Names of the letters expressed in the reformed sounds and characters
o	old	o
a [ɑ]	John, Folly	a
a	man, can	a
e	mane, lane	e
i	een, seen	i
u	tool, fool	u
ɥ [ɣ; Ӵ]	um, un, as in umbrage, unto, &c.	ɥ
h	hunter, happy, high	huh
g	give, gather	gi
k	keep, kick	ki
s [ʃ]	sh, ship, wish	ish
ŋ [ŋ]	ng, ing, reaping, among	ing
n	end	en
r	art	ar
t	teeth	ti
d	deed	di
l	ell, tell	el
ħ [ħ]	th, think	eħ
dħ [ð; Ð]	dh, thy	edħ
s	essence	es
z	ez, wages	ez
f	effect	ef
v	ever	ev
b	bees	bi
p	peep	pi
m	ember	em

13.3 Benjamin Franklin's reformed alphabet (from The Papers of Benjamin Franklin, *vol. 15*, 1972, New Haven: 175)

example, *konseevd* but *advaanst*. From the point of view of conventional English spelling which, by and large, ignores predictable morpho-phonemic alternations, this seems very uneconomical. Yet there is an underlying rationale, namely the assumption that an orthography should be based on only one principle rather than mixing principles. It is certainly one of the conspicuous features of the English spelling system that it incorporates various competing principles and rules. Thus the question every reformer has to answer is which principles should be eliminated and which ones should be kept.

Modern theoreticians recognize the 'polydimensionalism' (Vachek 1973: 67) of orthographic problems and concede that a spelling reform of English oriented exclusively on one principle would be unrealistic and impractical (Venezky 1970: 122). For instance, if the principles of morphemic invariance, etymology, homograph avoidance or deviant proper name spelling, all of which play an important part in present English spelling, were discarded for the sake of a rigorously phonemic orthography, the result would be too strange and involve too many changes in the established spelling habits to be accepted by the literate part of the speech community. Some reformers have, therefore, decided to advocate moderate simplifications instead of comprehensive systematic reforms. Wijk's (1959) *Regularized English* is an example of this approach which is further pursued in Carr (1969). Some of Carr's principles are as follows:

1 the alphabet should not be augmented with non-Roman letters;
2 diacritics should be restricted to a minimum;
3 present regularities should be preserved where they do not conflict with other regularities;
4 irregular spellings should be limited to some of the most frequent words such as *by*, *one*, *too*, *to*, etc.;
5 personal names should be exempted from general rules;
6 silent letters in initial position should be dropped from words of Anglo-Saxon origin, but retained in Greek and Latin origin words (hence *nife* and *rite*, but **seudonym* and **sychology*);
7 the competing spellings of diphthongs such as *ai/ay*, *oi/oy* should be regularized so that one is used in morpheme initial position and the other in morpheme final position.

This is but a selection of Carr's suggestions which suffices, however, to exemplify the principle of bringing about greater systematicity and coherence without departing too much from established practice. The following passage from Lincoln's Gettysburg Address (which is identical with that written in Shavian on p. 206) illustrates the result.

But, in a larger sense, we can not dedicate – we can not consecrate – we can not hallow – this ground. The brave men, livving and ded, who struggled here, hav consecrated it, far abuv our poor pouer to ad or detract. The world will little note, nor long remember what we say here, but it can never forget what they did here. It is for us, the livving, rather, to be here dedicated to the graet task remaining before us – that from these onnord ded we take increased devotion to that caus for which they gave the last full mesure of devotion – that we here hiely resolv that these ded shall not hav died in vain – that this nation, under God, shall hav a new birth of freedom – and that guvernment of the peeple, by the peeple, for the peeple, shall not perish from the earth. (Adapted from Carr 1969: 37ff)

SOME IMPLICATIONS

Obviously, *semiregularized* English, as Carr calls his system, does not deviate drastically from the current standard(s), but deviate it does, and as long as a spelling system is perceived as a deviation it is impractical, because even if it is more systematic than the standard the public will simply regard it as 'bad' spelling. Like standard speech, spelling in literate societies is regarded as a social shibboleth. Without official recognition and promotion, spellings not conforming to established practice are often taken as indicating ill-breeding and thus lower the writer in the reader's eye. Since the writer has fewer means at his or her disposal for correcting false impressions than the speaker, the social pressure of norm adherence in writing is particularly strong. It is also efficient because, where a norm is well established, spellings cannot be changed unnoted like gradual changes in pronunciation.

Usually, reform projects meet with some resistance and are difficult to effect, because for the generation that has to enact the reform it implies more inconvenience than relief. Therefore, it is usually easier to argue against 'tampering with the national othography' than pleading for sensible reforms. As a result, reform projects are often protracted by endless discussions. For instance, an orthography reform for German has been under discussion for many years (Augst 1974). One of the questions which has been discussed as if it were a matter of grave national importance is whether the characteristically German use of capital letters should be discontinued and, if so, how capital letters should be used instead.[12]

German

The protagonists of a reform point out that revising the rules for using capital letters would bring the orthography of German closer to those of the neighboring languages, none of which use capital letters in the way German does. By contrast, the antagonists argue that there is not only nothing wrong with a characteristically German feature of the spelling system, but that this is in fact highly desirable and in accord with tradition. Of course, the reasons for both keeping and discarding capital letters are strictly scientific. Much ink and paper, money and energy has been spent to show this. That capitals are a matter of taste would be an offensive proposition to most discussants who rely on the authority of scientific arguments about possible correlations between orthographic systems and speed and ease of reading and writing, the necessary time and effort of learning to read and write or the linguistic motivation of given conventions. The whole matter is thus taken away from the domain of taste, and those who want to argue on grounds of taste are excluded from the discussion.[13]

The proponents of a reform argue that discarding capital letters is a simplification of the German orthography which will hence be easier to learn. Generations of school children will save thousands of hours which otherwise they would have to waste learning the difficult and often arbitrary conventions for using capital letters. The opponents, however, point out that while it is true that learning the rules of capitalization requires some extra effort, it is insignificant if matched against the great advantages for reading. Because capital letters in the German system provide additional grammatical information, they greatly facilitate the processing of written texts.

As it stands, the system of capitalization in German spelling is like this: capital letters are used (1) at the beginning of each sentence, (2) for proper names, (3) for nouns, (4) for abbreviations, and (5) for the formal pronoun *Sie* in direct address. This looks simpler than it is, because proper names and nouns are hard to define as grammatical classes, and the spelling system is full of inconsistencies in this regard. An often quoted example is *radfahren*, 'to bicycle' as against *Auto fahren*, 'to drive a car', but *Ich fahre Rad* and *Ich fahre Auto*, which is held against the keepers of capital letters. The rule about writing nouns with initial capitals is, moreover, easily circular when a noun is defined simply as a word that is spelled with a capital letter. It is obviously arbitrary (that is, only for historical reasons) that *radfahren* is lexicalized as a compound verb, while *Auto fahren* counts as a verb phrase with a noun in object position. On systematic grounds this distinction is hard to defend. Most of the rather contrived examples of the alleged merits of capitalization are not much more convincing.

Moderate reformers want to keep capital letters for proper names only, while abolishing them for common nouns. This would bring the German system into accord with other European spelling systems, such as the English, but the problem with this proposal is that proper names are not a natural class which can be distinguished easily from common nouns. As an example consider the words *Sonne*, 'sun' and *Mond*, 'moon'. Should *die Sonne* be spelled with a capital ⟨S⟩, but *eine sonne* with a small ⟨s⟩? *Sun* and *moon* can be used both as proper names and as common nouns. In a sentence such as 'Do you know how many moons Saturn has?' *moon* is not a proper name, but in 'Who was the first man to set foot on the moon?' it is. It is hard to avoid the conclusion that the only way to define the class of proper names to be capitalized in the new spelling system is by enumerating them in lists, a solution which does not look like a significant improvement on the present convention.

Political aspects of spelling reforms

The debate over a possible reform of the German orthography has a profound political dimension. There are four German-speaking countries: the Federal Republic of Germany, the German Democratic Republic, Austria and Switzerland. On one hand, there is a desire to keep a common spelling system across political boundaries but, on the other, a reform scheme that all of the four parties can accept is difficult to find, since every proposal tends to be associated with the country of its author.

Political implications of spelling reforms often interfere with their systematic aspects. The roman orthography of Malay is another example. It developed on the basis of two European orthographies, the British in Malaya/Malaysia, and the Dutch in the Dutch East Indies (that is, Indonesia). As a result, many loan words as well as indigenous words are spelled differently in Malaysia and Indonesia: for example, Malaysian *station* as against Indonesian *stasion*. In 1959, a committee was founded for the creation of a unified orthography of Bahasa Indonesia/Malay.

Proposals were worked out carefully by linguists, but when in 1967 the Indonesian government tried to implement the reform, it provoked public resistance because many people regarded the changes as a sell-out to Malaysia (Rubin 1977), although the new orthography had been created largely by Indonesians. The Indonesian government hence felt compelled to withdraw the reform and made a new effort to implement it only five years later, in 1972, when the political tensions between the two countries had eased.[14]

In nationally divided speech communities it is not uncommon that political differences and inclinations are reflected in the difficulties of maintaining or achieving a common orthographic norm. The spelling reform discussion across the Dutch-Belgian border is a well-known case. In principle, the Flemings and the Dutch agree that a uniform standard for written Dutch is desirable. In 1944 a Dutch–Belgian commission was established whose task it was to form a uniform orthography in order to make the Dutch language valid on both sides of the border. With respect to many details, however, the members of the commission found them-selves in disagreement because the desire to create unity was countered by a desire to be different; different, that is, not with respect to each other, but with respect to neighboring languages. Geerts et al. (1977: 234) mention the example of words such as *kultuur* which the Flemings prefer to spell with a ⟨k⟩ because ⟨c⟩ is too similar to French, while in the Netherlands many prefer the ⟨c⟩ spelling because ⟨k⟩ is too reminiscent of German.[15]

Such matters are trifling, to be sure, but so are most of the details con-cerning innovations, alternations and normalizations of orthographies which on systematic grounds are found wanting. Taken together, they form a subsystem of language which occupies a special position in the language ecology of a community. Since it is an artefact, the spelling system of a language is more susceptible to deliberate intervention than other subsystems. Nevertheless spelling habits are hard to change because, concrete as they are, they constitute the most obvious part of language to which loyalty can be tied.

This is only one of the paradoxical aspects of spelling reform. Another, more disquieting, one is that, to the extent that a reform is satisfactory in the sense that its result is a simple and well-motivated orthography, it sets a standard from which it is bound to deviate. The question that every spelling reform raises is that of how long it can last. How soon will it need another revision? And is it possible to uphold the fundamental representational relations of a script by making occasional adjustments? The fact of the matter is that our historical experience with successful spelling reforms is too limited, and general literacy is too recent a phenomenon to warrant any general statements about what kind of effects are brought about by what kind of measures.

Every writing reform is a social experiment on a large scale, and since there are always sociolinguistic factors which interfere with the ideal solution from a strictly systematic point of view, the results are to some degree unpredictable; however, this only means that more research is needed about the interaction between code-specific and sociolinguistic factors in determining the outcomes of writing reforms.

NOTES

1 This is not just hyperbolic or metaphorical. The ideological and, more specifically, religious associations of different scripts are well known and were mentioned in previous chapters several times. Arabic/Islam, Devanagari/Hinduism, Pali/Buddhism, Hebrew/Judaism, Roman/Christian and Cyrillic/Orthodox are only the most prominent examples. The linguistic differences between Serbian and Croatian are relatively minor, and most scholars therefore refer to one language, Serbo-Croatian. However, the fact that the largely Roman Catholic Croatians use Latin letters, whereas the Orthodox Serbians have written their variety since the tenth century in the Cyrillic alphabet, underscores the differences rather than the common ground.

   To name but three instances of religiously inspired changes, the Arabic script spread across central Asia in the wake of Islam competing with Buddhist scripts such as the Tibetan and Mongolian (Henze 1977). The Romanization of several African languages earlier written in Arabic was effected largely by Christian missionaries (Gregersen 1977). Writing reforms in the USSR that replaced the Arabic with the Roman or Cyrillic alphabet have been interpreted as an attempt by the communist government (under Stalin) to cut the ties of the respective speech communities with the Islamic world (Lewis 1983).

2 Since state boundaries in independent India have been changed in order to create linguistically more homogeneous states, some minor language groups were integrated administratively into a script area to which they did not belong earlier. It is because of these new affiliations and because recently created scripts have turned out to be maladjusted that 'there is a

constant demand of script reform in almost all of the major script areas'
(Pattanayak 1979: 46).

3 Cf. Steuerwald (1963/4) for a detailed account of the modern Turkish
   phonology and orthography.

4 Cf. DeFrancis (1977), Seyboldt and Chiang (1979) and Coulmas (1983) for
   more detailed accounts of the tasks of the Committee and the Chinese
   writing reform.

5 The idea that an alphabetic script would be a great social benefit for China
   and, by implication, that *Hanzi* are a great burden, is also very popular
   among Western linguists and Sinologists. Giving expression to this conviction (for which I cannot see any convincing evidence) DeFrancis, for
   instance, in his recent book (1984: 286ff) states that 'China's modernization, to say the least, is impeded by sole reliance on a script that has shown
   itself unsuccessful in producing mass literacy and meeting other needs of a
   modern society.' The high literacy rate in Japan, on the one hand, and the
   low literacy rate in countries such as India that have used alphabetic scripts
   for centuries make it very doubtful that it is scripts which are successful or
   unsuccessful in producing mass literacy.

6 The development of Latin as a written language and its importance as the
   source of the 'bookish lexicon common to the Western world' is lucidly
   described in Kahane (1986).

7 Vachek (1973) discusses the proposals of both societies in some detail.

8 Cf. W. Haas (1969) for an overview of the literature on English spelling
   reform and the issues at hand, and Follick (1965) for a modern proposal for
   a reform.

9 Shaw used to mock the supposedly irrational character of English spelling
   with the rather misleading example of *ghoti* which, according to him, is a
   possible spelling for the English word fish /fiš/: ⟨gh⟩ as in *enough*, ⟨o⟩ as in
   women, and ⟨ti⟩ as in *nation*. Without suggesting that Shaw actually meant
   that such a spelling would be in agreement with the standard orthography,
   Stubbs (1980) explains why the rules of English do not allow for a spelling
   like that: ⟨gh⟩ is never realized as /f/ in word initial position; ⟨o⟩ for /i/ as in
   women does not conform to any productive rule, but is an exceptional
   spelling which came into existence thanks to typographical considerations; and ⟨ti⟩ cannot be separated from ⟨on⟩ because it never stands for /š/
   except in the syllable /šən/ or /šn/ which is then written ⟨tion⟩.

10 For details see McCarthy (1969).

11 For more details of Webster's 'linguistic Declaration of Independence' cf.
   Mencken (1919/49: 9ff).

12 For a thorough discussion of other theoretical aspects of German orthography cf. Kohrt (1987).

13 Geerts et al. (1977) call this process the 'scientification' of the spelling

reform discussion. It cannot be denied that rational arguments are to be preferred over indulgence in arbitrary predilection, but it must also be realized that, where social norms are concerned, it is difficult to prevent that scientific arguments are exploited for given purposes.

14 For more details on the standardization of Bahasa Indonesia/Malay see Alisjahbana (1984).

15 These varying preferences are one of the reasons why the official spelling of Dutch admits variants to a much greater extent than, for instance, the French or German orthographies. Cf. Van de Craen and Willemijns (1988) for more details.

PART IV

Conclusion

14

What Writing Means for Linguistics

The past decade has seen the publication of numerous linguistic books and research papers concerned with written language, spoken language and the relations between them. This can be taken to indicate that, ever since de Saussure, linguists have only paid lip service to the so-called priority of speech. Why would anyone call for the study of spoken language, and how could terms such as 'spoken language' and 'written language' gain sudden currency if linguists had been occupied with the study of speech all along? In fact, mainstream linguists have largely ignored the relation between spoken and written language as well as that between speech and writing. The many recent publications dealing with specific properties of language in its spoken and written forms are beginning to correct this oversight.[1]

The present book is presented to the reader in the belief that this is a healthy and necessary development, and that the exclusion of writing from the realm of modern linguistics was one of the fallacies accompanying the establishment of the structuralist paradigm which was bound to be corrected. There are many things that linguists should know about writing: more, in any event, than can be suggested in passing. In most introductory linguistics textbooks writing is relegated to a brief final chapter or an appendix. Yet, in a very real sense, students of language do not know what they are talking about and have no grasp of their subject matter before they have developed an understanding of the relationships between writing, speech and language. After all, there is no linguistic research that can dispense with written signs on a durable surface which relate to linguistic units in a conventional way (cf. chapter 2, p. 17). Since written language is what linguists usually deal with, it is imperative that they understand the complex ways in which written units relate to units of language.

Every writing system is an abstraction, and every transcript is an arte-fact. Speech can be represented by graphical means only very imper-fectly. Every linguist who has ever tried to reduce the continuous sound stream of recorded speech data to the necessarily discrete units of a written representation knows this. Moreover, proficient transcribers also know that it is highly unlikely that they will be satisfied with the segmentations they made in their transcriptions the next time they listen to the recording. These are well-known and perhaps trivial problems hav-ing to do with limited attention spans and the difficulty of distinguishing what one hears from what one expects to hear, as well as the technical shortcomings of recording devices; but they give rise to the not so trivial question regarding in what sense the linguist ever deals with speech rather than with writing. Obviously not every linguist can be expected to contribute to the solution of this question. However, since a fundamental methodological problem of the science of language is involved here, every linguist should at least be aware of it, rather than assume, naïvely, that it is possible to study speech simply by writing it down.

Apart from this most obvious but hardly insignificant reason, which makes the study of writing indispensable to linguistic work, there are several others of no less importance. Some of them were referred to explicitly more than once in the foregoing chapters; others were dealt with in a more implicit manner. By way of concluding this book, they are reviewed here once again, however briefly. Clearly, the linguist's interest in writing is not the same as that of the psychologist, the epi-grapher, the historian or the archeologist. To be sure, linguists can learn much from what these other scholars know about writing, but the linguistic point of view is different; which is also why the classical works about writing by such profound scholars as Jensen, Gelb, Diringer, Friedrich and others do not necessarily provide the information the linguist needs to know about writing. This is not to diminish the value of these books; they are invaluable sources of knowledge. However, their authors have a background in Classical or Orientalist studies and do not always ask, let alone answer, the questions the linguist should be inter-ested in.

One of the most general of these questions has to do with the history of linguistics and the products of linguistic scholarship. The most eminent results of linguistic work in the past, the dictionary and the grammar, were always based on written language. The monolingual dictionary which, as Harris (1980) has demonstrated in his brilliant book, is one of the important achievements of the Renaissance, relied on the language of the most respected writers of the time for delimiting the corpus; and the grammar was similarly based on, and intended to guide, the written language. The positivistic orientation in the social sciences at the turn of this century brought about a change of paradigm from a prescriptive to a descriptive orientation in the study of language. In the interest of establishing their scientific credentials grammarians voluntarily relinquished the traditional prerogative of their profession, namely that of setting standards and defining norms. It is more than doubtful, however, that this conversion from normativism to descriptivism was accompanied by the development of purely descriptive concepts and methods. Both Harris (1980) and Linell (1982) have argued convincingly that descriptive linguistics is pervaded by notions originating in normative grammar. And normative grammar is based on written language.

The important point here is that, if this is true – that is, if the theoretical concepts and the methods that linguists apply in their work are derived from language as it manifests itself in writing – then the standard argument justifying the disregard of writing in linguistics, namely that speech is much older than writing and acquired earlier by the individual, is entirely beside the point. Linguists cannot afford to disregard writing, because the notions by means of which they profess to analyze language independent of writing are themselves shaped by the written language and the units distinguished by the writing system. Writing systems are artefacts, but linguists have not usually been involved in their creation. No writing system is ideal in the sense that it maps the units of language as the linguist would if he or she were able to uncover the underlying structure of the language in question without being influenced, however slightly, by the categories of a writing system. Bloomfield (1933: 21) once stated the problem very neatly: 'The most difficult step in the study of language is the first step. Again and again, scholarship has approached the study of language without actually entering upon it.' According to Bloomfield, this deplorable deficiency of linguistics could only be amended by ridding linguistic analysis of the entirely secondary accretions of writing attached to the phenomenon of language. It is more than doubtful, however, whether Bloomfield or his many disciples really succeeded in providing the notions and methods by means of which the linguist can enter the territory of language without unwittingly being affected by writing.

The treatment in traditional and modern grammars of what (for lack of a term not betraying the written language perspective) is called 'supra-segmental features' such as stress, tone, intonation, melody and rhythm, illustrates the influence of writing on grammatical description most clearly. In traditional grammars prosody is often ignored, and in modern ones it is treated in a separate chapter. In both cases it is abstracted from the discrete units that are distinguished in writing: sentences, words and letters. These units are treated as if they had an independent existence to which intonation is added in speech. But where does the intonationless sentence occur? On the printed page.

In linguistic parlance, certain sentences have different 'readings'. Rather than being an empty figure of speech, this metaphor is very indicative of the way linguists usually look at language. A decontextualized sentence which is committed to, or has been composed on, paper can be read in several different ways. In speech it is much less common that sentences are perceived as being ambiguous. Again this kind of approach is evidence of the linguist's dependency on written language. It is like saying that the Chinese syllable *wu* becomes disambiguated in speech when spoken with a certain tone. The catch is that in speech there is no Chinese syllable without a tone.

Other notions that exhibit the influence of written language on linguistic theorizing could be added here: for instance, those of 'literal' meaning or the fixed word meaning which only echo the dictionary definition. But the above suffice to illustrate the point. The units of linguistic analysis are derivative of the units of written language.

This is not surprising because, after all, every writing system deserving of that name is a device for representing language; and in order to be able to fulfil this function, a writing system has to segment the object of its representation. In this sense every writing system incorporates a linguistic analysis. Many linguists are quick to denounce this kind of implicit analysis as obscuring rather than disclosing the underlying linguistic structure, without sparing much time to reflect on the problem of devising a representational system that does not impose but only maps linguistic structures. Writing systems operate on different levels and emphasize different units of language. As should have become apparent in the chapters of this book, this is so because all writing systems have come into existence in the context of a given language whose structural peculiarities have left more or less noticeable traces. This fact alone makes writing systems an object of prominent linguistic interest.

Much more research is needed to reach a better understanding of the intricate mutual relations between writing systems and languages but, even though writing systems can be employed for different languages and many languages have been written with different writing systems, there are such relationships. One subset of questions under this heading concerns the adaptation of writing systems to languages other than those for which they had first been developed. Studying this question, one cannot fail to notice a strong influence of the spoken language on the development of writing and written language. The adaptation of Sumerian cuneiform to Akkadian and other Semitic languages shows this well, as does the adaptation of the Phoenician consonant script to Greek or the Chinese morphosyllabic script to Japanese. In each of these cases, as well as in several others, the adaptation process resulted in a fundamental change in the make-up of the writing system. A language hitherto unwritten thus forced some of its structural features on to the writing system.

On the other hand, the development of writing systems also shows processes that do not depend on, or correspond to, developmental processes of language. The introduction of determinatives into Egyptian hieroglyphics or the formation of semantic–phonetic compound characters in Chinese writing do not reflect any processes in Egyptian and Chinese, respectively. Similarly, that the English orthography nowadays, by and large, maps on to the morphophonemic level does not reflect an adaptation of the spelling system to certain changes of the language, but rather the fact that spelling and language develop in asynchronous ways. This could not be otherwise, because there is a perennial tension between the sounds of speech which disappear with the air waves that carry them and the written traces which suggest permanence.

To what extent writing interferes with the 'natural' development of language is not so clear yet, and general hypotheses about such an effect are hard to justify because widespread literacy is such a recent phenomenon. However, today it is well understood that speech habits are subject to social pressure and that speakers adjust their speech for purposes of social prestige, thus bringing to bear a cultural influence on linguistic development. Artificial written styles had been cultivated in Sumerian times. In all kinds of speech communities the written language incorporates a prestigious norm which in one way or another serves as a model. Thus writing must be reckoned with as a factor of the historical development of languages, and it must be assigned its proper place in a diachronic theory of language.

It is arguable that the dichotomy of diachrony as against synchrony – another holy cow of modern linguistics – is also an outgrowth of the influence of writing on linguistic theorizing. The written sentence does not change. It is a spatial structure, not a temporal one, and offers itself to inspection as long and as often as is necessary for the analyst's purposes. But the spoken sentence is never the same when uttered again. On the basis of these differing physical preconditions, spoken and written language differ in several respects, to investigate which is hardly anybody's task if not the linguist's.

Writing systems are semiotic systems which have properties not found in speech. Yet there is no denying that writing systems are systems for the materialization of language. That they are phylogenetically younger than speech and that speech is natural and universal, whereas writing is artificial and present in only some speech communities, are hardly good reasons to ignore them in linguistic research. Written language is a form of language, and if it is a form that is present only in some languages but not in others, it is nevertheless a potential for all languages. It is a form of language which is neither more nor less perfect than spoken language, but which differs from spoken language in some important respects because, naturally, writing serves functions that are different from those of speech. If this were not the case, there would be no good reason for writing to have come into existence at all. The invention of writing is the answer to the limitations of speech to the here and now. Thus, by acquiring a written form, the expressive power of a language is realized to a greater extent than it is in speech only.

That both speech and writing are communicative activities is just as evident as the fact that both written and spoken language are forms of language. But how they differ from each other, and what the differences between them mean for our understanding of language, is not all that clear. Among the contrasts between spoken and written language that have been discussed in the literature are the effervescence of the former as opposed to the relative stability of the latter; the age and mode of acquisition; the speed of planning and production; the mode of transmission and reception; the availability of immediate feedback; complementary situations for speech and writing; as well as lexical and syntactic devices that are specialized for speech and writing. It can be argued that both speech and writing draw on the same expressive potential of language but in so doing make different selections. If this is so, these differences are to be documented and methods are to be devised which can assess the respective properties of different writing systems in this regard. How can a description of a language and an analysis of its structures be complete if the range of their variation is not accounted for?

Writing is not language. This is an axiom of modern linguistics. Those who advocate that writing should none the less be included into the core of a linguistics curriculum do not want to argue this point. However, granted that writing must not be confused with language, it is still not a foregone conclusion that it has no place in the study of language. Writing systems relate to linguistic structures, and where they are adopted for a given language, they develop into linguistic subsystems (orthographies). Their use, moreover, leads to the development of a special form of language (styles). What position this subsystem and this form occupy within the complex whole of language, and what role they play in its development and functioning, the linguist can only hope to understand by studying writing, not by ignoring it.

NOTE

1 Many of these publications were referred to in previous chapters. Among the more important monographs and collections of articles are Stubbs (1980), Linell (1982), Henderson (1982, 1984), Feldbusch (1985), Frith (1980), W. Haas (1982), Coulmas and Ehlich (1983), Günther and Günther (1983), Augst (1986). Another excellent book is Sampson (1985).

References

Abercrombie, David. 1949. 'What is a "Letter"?' *Lingua* 2: 54–62.

Akinnaso, F. Niyi. 1982. 'On the Difference between Spoken and Written Language', *Language and Speech* 25/2: 97–125.

Albright, R. W. 1958. *The International Phonetic Alphabet: Its Backgrounds and Development.* Indiana: Indiana University Research Center in Anthropology, Folklore and Linguistics.

Albright, W. F. 1934. *The Vocalization of the Egyptian Syllabic Orthography.* New Haven, Conn.: Yale University Press.

Albright, W. F. 1966. *The Proto-Sinaitic Inscriptions and their Decipherment.* Cambridge, Mass.: Harvard University Press.

Albrow, K. H. 1972. *The English Writing System: Notes Towards a Description.* London: Longman.

Alexander, R. P. 1951. Supplement to W. P. Lehman and L. Faust. *A Grammar of Formal Written Japanese.* Cambridge, Mass.: Harvard University Press.

Alisjahbana, S. Takdir. 1984. 'The Concept of Language Standardization and its Application to the Indonesian Language'. In: Coulmas (1984b): 77–98.

Allchin, Bridget and Allchin, Raymond. 1982. *The Rise of Civilization in India and Pakistan.* Cambridge: Cambridge University Press.

Allen, W. S. 1962. *Sandhi: The Theoretical, Phonetic and Historical Basis of Word-junction in Sanskrit.* The Hague: Mouton.

Alleton, Viviane. 1970. *L'écriture chinoise.* Paris: Presses universitaires de France.

Andrews, Carol. 1981. *The Rosetta Stone.* London: British Museum Publications.

Annamalai, E. 1986. 'Some Syntactic Differences between Spoken and Written Tamil'. In: Bh. Krishnamurti (ed.), *South Asian Languages. Structure, Convergence and Diglossia.* Delhi: Motilal Banarsidass: 289–93.

Ansre, Gilbert. 1974. 'Language Standardisation in Sub-Saharan Africa'. In: J. A. Fishman (ed.), *Advances in Language Planning.* The Hague, Paris: Mouton: 369–89.

Augst, Gerhard. 1974. 'Ergebnisse eines projektseminars "rechtschreibung und rechtschreibreform"'. *Mitteilungen des Deutschen Germanistenverbandes* 21: 38–41.

Augst, Gerhard (ed.) 1986. *New Trends in Graphemics and Orthography*. Berlin, New York: de Gruyter.

Ball, C. J. 1913. *Chinese and Sumerian*. London: Oxford University Press, H. Milford.

Barnard, Noel. 1978. 'The Nature of the Ch'in "Reform of the Script" as Reflected in Archeological Documents Excavated under Conditions of Control'. In: David T. Roy and Tsuen-hsuin Tsien (eds), *Ancient China: Studies in Early Civilization*. Hong Kong: Chinese University Press.

Bauer, H. 1937. 'Der Ursprung des Alphabets'. *Der Alte Orient* 36, 1/2.

Beaugrande, R. de and Dressler, W. 1981. *Introduction to Text Linguistics*. London: Longman.

Beck, H. 1964. 'Problems of Word Division and Capitalization'. In: W. A. Smalley et al. (1964): 156–60.

Becker, A. L. 1983. 'Literacy and Culture Change: Some Experiences'. In: R. W. Bailey and R. M. Fosheim (eds), *Literacy for Life*. New York: Modern Language Association.

Benvéniste, Emile. 1966. *Problèmes de linguistique générale*. Paris: Gallimard (Bibliothèque des sciences humaines).

Bernal, J. D. 1954. *Science in History*, 4 vols. London: C. A. Watts. Reprinted 1971: Cambridge, Mass.: MIT Press.

Berry, Jack. 1958. 'The Making of Alphabets'. In: *Proceedings of the Eighth International Congress of Linguists*. Oslo: Oslo University Press: 752–64.

Berry, Jack. 1977. '"The Making of Alphabets" Revisited'. In: J. A. Fishman (1977): 3–16.

Bieber, Douglas. 1986. 'Spoken and Written Textual Dimensions in English: Resolving the Contradictory Findings'. *Language* 62/2: 384–414.

Bierwisch, Manfred. 1972. 'Schriftstruktur und Phonologie'. *Probleme und Ergebnisse der Psychologie* 43: 21–44.

Birnbaum, S. A. 1971. *The Hebrew Script*. Edinburgh: Neil.

Bisseret, Noelle. 1979. *Education, Class Language and Ideology*. Boston: Routledge & Kegan Paul.

Bloomfield, Leonhard. 1933. *Language*. New York: Holt, Rinehart & Winston.

Bolinger, Dwight. 1946. 'Visual Morphemes'. *Language* 22: 333–40.

Boodberg, Peter. 1940. '"Ideography" or Iconolatry?' *T'oung Pao* 35: 266–88.

Bork, F. 1924. 'Das Sumerische, eine kaukasische Sprache'. *Orientalische Literatur-Zeitung* 27 (Leipzig).

Bottéro, Jean. 1987. 'The Culinary Tablets at Yale'. *Journal of the American Oriental Society* 107/1: 11–19.

Bouda, K. 1938. 'Die Beziehungen des Sumerischen zum Baskischen,

Westkaukasischen und Tibetischen'. *Mitteilungen der Altorientalischen Gesellschaft* 12 (Leipzig).

Breasted, James H. 1926. *The Conquest of Civilization.* New York and London: Harper.

Bright, W. 1970. 'Phonological Rules in Literary and Colloquial Kannada'. *Journal of the American Oriental Society* 90.1: 140–4.

Britto, Francis. 1986. *Diglossia: A Study of the Theory with Application to Tamil.* Washington: Georgetown University Press.

Burrows, M. 1955. *The Dead Sea Scrolls.* New York: Viking Press.

Burrows, M. 1958. *More Light on the Dead Sea Scrolls.* New York: Viking Press.

Carr, Denzel. 1969. 'The Semiregularization of English Spelling'. In: R. Jakobson and S. Kawamoto (eds), *Studies in General and Oriental Linguistics. Presented to Shiro Hattori on the Occasion of his Sixtieth Birthday.* Tokyo: TEC (Corporation for Language and Education Research).

Central Institute of Indian Languages. 1973. *Distribution of Languages in India in States and Union Territories.* Manasagangotri, Mysore.

Chadwick, J. 1958. *The Decipherment of Linear B.* Cambridge: Cambridge University Press.

Chafe, Wallace. 1979. 'The Flow of Thought and the Flow of Language'. In: T. Givon (ed.), *Syntax and Semantics*, vol. 12, *Discourse and Syntax.* New York: Academic press: 159–81.

Chang Kwang-chih. 1963. *The Archeology of Ancient China.* New Haven, Conn.: Yale University Press.

Chao, Yuen Ren. 1948. *Mandarin Primer.* Cambridge, Mass.: Harvard University press.

Chao, Yuen Ren. 1968. *Language and Symbolic Systems.* Cambridge: Cambridge University Press.

Chatterjee, Suhas. 1986. 'Diglossia in Bengali'. In: Bh. Krishnamurti (ed.), 1986. *South Asian Languages. Structure, Convergence and Diglossia.* Delhi: Motilal Banarsidass: 294–303.

Chiera, Edward. 1938. *They Wrote on Clay.* Chicago and London: University of Chicago Press.

Childe, Gordon. 1941. *Man Makes Himself.* London: Watts.

Childe, Gordon. 1982. *What Happened in History.* Harmondsworth: Penguin (first published 1942).

Chomsky, N. and Halle, M. 1968. *The Sound Pattern of English.* New York: Harper & Row.

Chou En-lai. 1959. 'Current Tasks of Reforming the Written Language'. *Reform of the Chinese Written Language.* Peking: Foreign Languages Press.

Civil, Miguel. 1973. 'The Sumerian Writing System: Some Problems'. *Orientalia* 42: 21–34.

Cohen, Marcel. 1958. *La grande invention de l'écriture et son évolution.* Paris: Imprimerie nationale. (Quote taken from 2nd edn 1969)

Cohen, Marcel. 1964. *Essai comparative sur le vocabulaire et la phonétique du chamito-sémitique.* Paris: Honoré Champion.

Copperman, Paul. 1980. 'The Decline of Literacy'. *Journal of Communication* 30/1: 113–22.

Cottrell, Leonard. 1971. *Reading the Past. The Story of Deciphering Ancient Languages.* New York: Crowell-Collier Press.

Coulmas, Florian. 1981a. 'Conversational Routine'. In F. Coulmas (ed.), *Conversational Routine.* The Hague: Mouton.

Coulmas, Florian. 1981b. *Über Schrift.* Frankfurt am Main: Suhrkamp.

Coulmas, Florian. 1983. 'Writing and Literacy in China'. In: F. Coulmas and K. Ehlich (eds) (1983): 239–54.

Coulmas, Florian. 1984a. 'Arbitrariness and Double Articulation in Writing'. In: Henderson (1984) 57–66.

Coulmas, Florian. 1984b. *Linguistic Minorities and Literacy.* Berlin, Amsterdam, New York: Mouton.

Coulmas, Florian. 1987a. 'Overcoming Diglossia: The Rapprochement of Spoken and Written Japanese'. In: Nina Catach (ed.), *Pour une théorie de la langue écrite.* Paris: Centre National de la Recherche Scientifique.

Coulmas, Florian. 1987b. 'Review of E. Feldbusch, "Geschriebene Sprache"'. Berlin, New York: De Gruyter (1985). *Linguistics* 25/4: 792–7.

Coulmas, Florian. 1987c. 'What Writing can do to Language'. In: S. Battestini (ed.), *Georgetown University Roundtable on Languages and Linguistics 1986.* Washington, DC: Georgetown University Press: 107–29.

Coulmas, Florian. 1988. 'Review of "Diglossia" by Francis Britto'. *International Journal of the Sociology of Language* 74: 148–53.

Coulmas, F. and Ehlich, K. (eds) 1983: *Writing in Focus.* Berlin, Amsterdam, New York: Mouton.

Cowgill, Warren. 1963. 'Universals in Diachronic Morphology'. In: J. Greenberg (ed.), *Universals of Language.* Cambridge, Mass.: MIT Press: 114–41.

Coyaud, Maurice. 1985. *L'ambiguïté en japonais écrit.* Paris: Pour l'analyse du Folklore.

Creel, Herrlee G. 1936. 'On the Nature of Chinese Ideography'. *T'oung Pao* 32: 85–161.

Creel, Herrlee G. 1938. 'On the Ideographic Element in Ancient Chinese'. *T'oung Pao* 34: 265–94.

Creel, Herrlee G. 1943. *Chinese Writing.* Washington, DC: American Council on Education.

Crofts, Alfred and Buchanan, Percy. 1958. *A History of the Far East.* New York, London: Longman, Green.

Dani, Ahmed Hasan. 1983. 'Enigma of the Indus Valley Script'. *Third World International* 7/1: 33–6 (Karachi).

de Casparis, J. G. 1975. *Indonesian Palaeography.* Leiden: Brill.

de Rooij, J. and Verhoeven, G. 1988. 'Orthography Reform and Language

Planning for Dutch'. *The Sociolinguistics of Dutch*, ed. J. Stalpers and F. Coulmas, *International Journal of the Sociology of Language* 73: 65–84.

De Silva, M. W. Sugathapala. 1976. *Diglossia and Literacy.* Manasagangotri, Mysore: Central Institute of Indian Languages.

De Silva, M. W. Sugathapala. 1982. 'Some Consequences of Diglossia'. In: W. Haas (1982): 94–122.

DeFrancis, John. 1977. 'Language and Script Reform in China'. In: J. A. Fishman (1977): 121–48.

DeFrancis, John. 1984. *The Chinese Language. Fact and Fantasy.* Honolulu: University of Hawaii Press.

Deshpande, Madhav M. 1979. *Critical Studies in Indian Grammarians.* Ann Arbor, Mich.: The Michigan Series in South and Southeast Asian Languages and Linguistics, No. 2.

Deshpande, Madhav M. 1986. 'Sanskrit Grammarians on Diglossia'. In: Bh. Krishnamurti (ed.), *South Asian Languages. Structure, Convergence and Diglossia.* Delhi: Motilal Banarsidass: 312–21.

Dhorme, E. 1948. 'Déchifferement des inscriptions pseudo-hiéroglyphiques de Byblos'. *Syria* 1946–8. Paris.

Diringer, David. 1943. 'The Origin of the Alphabet'. *Antiquity* 17: 77–90.

Diringer, David. 1968. *The Alphabet: A Key to the History of Mankind.* New York: Funk & Wagnalls (third revised edition).

Downing, John. 1967. *Evaluating the Initial Teaching Alphabet.* London: Cassell.

Driver, G. R. 1976. *Semitic Writing. From Pictograph to Alphabet.* London: Oxford University Press (newly revised edition; first published 1948).

Duggan, Joseph J. (ed.) 1975. *Oral Literature.* New York: Barnes & Noble.

DuPonceau 1838. *A Dissertation on the Nature and Character of the Chinese System of Writing.* Philadelphia.

Ehlich, Konrad. 1983. 'Development of Writing as Social Problem Solving'. In: F. Coulmas and K. Ehlich (eds), *Writing in Focus.* Berlin, Amsterdam, New York: Mouton: 99–129.

Ehri, Linnea C. 1979. 'Linguistic Insight: Threshold of Reading Acquisition'. In: T. G. Waller and G. E. Mackinnon (eds), *Reading Research, Advances in Theory and Practice.* vol. I. New York: Academic Press: 63–114.

Eisenberg, Peter. 1983. 'Writing System and Morphology: Some Orthographic Regularities'. In: F. Coulmas and K. Ehlich (eds), *Writing in Focus.* New York, Berlin, Amsterdam: Mouton: 63–80.

Ellis, Andrew W. 1984. *Reading, Writing and Dyslexia: A Cognitive Analysis.* Hillsdale, NJ: Erlbaum.

Evans, Arthur. 1909. *Scripta Minoa I.* Oxford: Clarendon Press.

Falkenstein, A. 1964. *Das Sumerische.* Reprint from 'Handbuch der Orientalistik'. Leiden: Brill.

Feldbusch, Elisabeth. 1985. *Geschriebene Sprache. Untersuchungen zu ihrer Herausbildung und Grundlegung ihrer Theorie.* Berlin, New York: De Gruyter.

Ferguson, Charles A. 1959. 'Diglossia'. *Word* 15: 325–40.

Ferguson, Charles A. 1983. 'Language Planning and Language Change'. In: J. Cobarrubias and J. A. Fishman (eds), *Progress in Language Planning.* Berlin, New York, Amsterdam: Mouton: 29–40.

Fiore, Kyle and Elsasser, Nan. 1982. 'Strangers No More: A Liberatory Literacy Curriculum'. *College English*, February: 115–28.

Firth, J. R. 1930. *The Tongues of Men.* London: Watts.

Fishman, Joshua A. 1967. 'Bilingualism with and without Diglossia; Diglossia with and without Bilingualism'. *Journal of Social Issues* 23: 29–38.

Fishman, Joshua A. (ed.) 1977. *Advances in the Creation and Revision of Writing Systems.* The Hague, Paris: Mouton.

Fleckenstein, Josef. 1953. *Die Bildungsreform Karls des Großen als Verwirklichung der norma rectitudinis.* Freiburg/Br.: Albert.

Follick, M. 1965. *The Case for Spelling Reform.* London: Pitman.

Friedrich, Johannes. 1954. *Entzifferung verschollener Schriften und Sprachen.* Berlin: Springer.

Friedrich, Johannes. 1966. *Geschichte der Schrift.* Heidelberg: Carl Winter, Universitätsverlag.

Fries, Charles C. 1952. *The Structure of English.* New York: Harcourt, Brace.

Frith, Uta. 1979. 'Reading by Eye and Writing by Ear'. In P. A. Kolers, M. E. Wrolstad and H. Bouma (eds), *Processing of Visible Language.* New York: Plenum, 379–90.

Frith, Uta (ed.) 1980. *Cognitive Processes in Spelling.* London: Academic Press.

Gardiner, A. H. 1916. 'The Egyptian Origin of the Semitic Alphabet'. *Journal of Egyptian Archeology* 3: 1ff.

Gardiner, A. H. 1957. *Egyptian Grammar.* Oxford: Oxford University Press (third revised edition).

Garvin, Paul. 1954. 'Literacy as a Problem in Language and Culture'. *Georgetown University Monograph Series on Language and Linguistics* 7: 117–29.

Geerts, G., Van den Broeck, J. and Verdoodt, A. 1977. 'Successes and Failures in Dutch Spelling Reform'. In: J. A. Fishman (1977): 179–245.

Gelb, Ignace J. 1931. *Hittite Hieroglyphs.* London, Chicago: University of Chicago Press.

Gelb, Ignace J. 1963. *A Study of Writing.* Chicago, London: The University of Chicago Press (revised edition, first published 1952).

Gelb, I. J. 1980. 'Principles of Writing Systems within the Frame of Visual Communication'. In: P. A. Kolers, M. E. Wrolstad and H. Bouma (eds), *Processing of Visible Language 2.* New York: Plenum Press.

Gibson, E. J. and Levin, A. 1975. *The Psychology of Reading.* Cambridge, Mass.: MIT Press.

Goody, Jack. 1977. *The Domestication of the Savage Mind.* Cambridge: Cambridge University Press.

Goody, Jack and Watt, Ian. 1968. 'The Consequences of Literacy'. In: Jack Goody (ed.), *Literacy in Traditional Societies.* Cambridge: Cambridge University Press: 27–68.

Gordon, Cyrus H. 1971. *Forgotten Scripts. The Story of their Decipherment.* Harmondsworth: Penguin.

Graff, Harvey J. 1979. *The Literacy Myth: Literacy and Social Structure in the 19th Century City.* New York: Academic Press.

Green, M. W. 1981. 'The Construction and Implementation of the Cuneiform Writing System'. *Visible Language* 15/4: 345–72.

Gregersen, Edgar A. 1977. 'Successes and Failures in the Modernization of Hausa Spelling'. In: J. A. Fishman (1977): 421–40.

Gudschinsky, Sarah C. 1970. 'More on Formulating Efficient Orthographies'. *The Bible Translator* 21: 21–5.

Gudschinsky, Sarah C. 1976. *Literacy: The Growing Influence of Linguistics.* The Hague: Mouton.

Günther, K. B. and Günther, H. (eds) 1983. *Schrift, Schreiben, Schriftlichkeit.* Tübingen: Niemeyer.

Haas, Mary. 1956. *The Thai System of Writing.* Washington, DC: American Council of Learned Societies.

Haas, W. (ed.) 1969. *Alphabets for English.* Manchester: Manchester University Press.

Haas, W. 1970. *Phono-Graphic Translation.* Manchester: Manchester University Press.

Haas, W. 1976. 'Writing: The Basic Options'. In: W. Haas (ed.), *Writing without Letters.* Manchester: Manchester University Press: 131–208.

Haas, W. (ed.) 1982. *Standard Languages, Spoken and Written.* Manchester: Manchester University Press.

Haas, W. 1983. 'Determining the Level of a Script'. In: F. Coulmas and K. Ehlich (eds), *Writing in Focus.* Berlin, Amsterdam, New York: Mouton: 15–29.

Harris, Roy. 1980. *The Language Makers.* Ithaca, NY: Cornell University Press.

Haugen, Einar. 1966. 'Language, Dialect, Nation'. *American Anthropologist* 68: 922–35.

Havelock, Eric. 1982. *The Literate Revolution in Greece and its Cultural Consequences.* Princeton, NJ: Princeton University Press.

Havelock, Eric. 1986. 'Orality, Literacy, and Star Wars'. *Written Communication* 3/4: 411–20.

Hayashi Okii (ed.) 1982. *Zusetsu nihongo* [Graphic Japanese]. Tokyo: Kadokawa Shoten.

Hembram, N. 1982. *Austric Civilization of India.* Calcutta: Hari Pada Sahoo.

Henderson, L. 1982. *Orthography and Word Recognition in Reading.* London, New York: Academic Press.

Henderson, L. (ed.) 1984. *Orthographies and Reading.* London: Erlbaum.

Henze, Paul B. 1977. 'Politics and Alphabets in Inner Asia'. In: J. A. Fishman (1977).

Herdner, Andrée. 1963. *Corpus des tablettes en cunéiformes alphabétiques découvertes à Ras Shamra - Ugarit de 1929 à 1939.* Paris: Imprimerie nationale.

Herslund, M. 1986. 'French External Sandhi: The Case of Liaison'. In: H. Anderson (ed.), *Sandhi Phenomena in the Languages of Europe.* Berlin, Amsterdam, New York: Mouton de Gruyter, 85–92.

Hevesy, M. G. de. 1936. 'Sur une écriture océanienne paraissant d'origine néolithique'. *Bulletin de la societé préhistorique française* 7/8.

Heyd, Uriel. 1954. 'Language Reform in Modern Turkey'. *Oriental Notes and Studies* 5 (Jerusalem).

Ho Fing-ti. 1976. *The Cradle of the East.* Chicago: University of Chicago Press.

Hockett, Charles F. 1963. 'The Problem of Universals in Language'. In: J. H. Greenberg (ed.), *Universals of Language.* Cambridge, Mass.: MIT Press: 1–29.

Householder, Fred. 1972. *Linguistic Speculations.* New York, London: Cambridge University Press.

Jacobson, Thorkild. 1970. 'Early Political Development of Mesopotamia'. *Toward the Image of Tammuz and Other Essays on Mesopotamian History and Culture.* Oslo.

Jalaluddin, A. K. 1983. 'Problems of Transition of Rural Indian Society from Oral to Written Tradition through Adult Education'. In: F. Coulmas (ed.), *Linguistic Problems of Literacy. Special Issue, Journal of Pragmatics* 7/5: 517–31.

Jensen, Hans. 1925. *Geschichte der Schrift.* Hannover: Orientbuchhandlung H. Lataire.

Jensen, Hans. 1969. *Die Schrift in Vergangenheit und Gegenwart.* Berlin: VEB Deutscher Verlag der Wissenschaften (reprint of third edition). (*Sign, Symbol and Script.* New York: Putnam's, 1969.)

Jordan, Julius. 1932. 'Uruk, vorläufige Berichte'. *Abhandlungen der Preussischen Akademie der Wissenschaften, philosophischhistorische Klasse.* Berlin.

Kahane, Henry, 1986. 'A Typology of the Prestige Language'. *Language* 62/3: 495–508.

Kannaiyan, V. 1960. *Scripts in and around India.* Madras.

Karlgren, Bernhard. 1923. *Analytic Dictionary of Chinese and Sino-Japanese.* Paris: Geuthner.

Kemp, J. Alan (ed.) 1981. *Richard Lepsius' Standard Alphabet for Reducing Unwritten Languages and Foreign Graphic Systems to a Uniform Orthography in European Letters.* Amsterdam: John Benjamins.

282   References

Kennedy, George A. 1951. 'The Monosyllabic Myth'. *Journal of the American Oriental Society* 71: 161–6.

Khubchandani, Lachman M. 1983. *Plural Languages, Plural Cultures.* Honolulu: University of Hawaii Press.

Kindaichi, Haruhiko. 1957. *Nihongo* [The Japanese Language]. Tokyo: Iwanami.

Klima, Edward S. 1972. 'How Alphabets Might Reflect Language'. In: J. F. Kavanagh and I. G. Mattingly (eds), *Language by Ear and by Eye.* Cambridge, Mass.: MIT Press: 57–80.

Kohrt, M. 1987. *Theoretische Aspekte der deutschen Orthographie.* Tübingen: Niemeyer.

König, Friedrich Wilhelm. 1965. *Die elamischen Königsinschriften.* Graz: Archiv für Orientforschung.

Kôno Rokurô. 1969. 'The Chinese Writing and its Influence on the Scripts of the Neighboring Peoples with Special Reference to Korea and Japan'. *Memoirs of the Research Department of the Tôyô Bunko* 27: 84–140.

Konrad, N. J. 1977. 'On the Literary Languages in China and Japan'. In: P. A. Luelsdorff (ed.), *Soviet Contributions to the Sociology of Language.* The Hague, Paris: Mouton: 31–73.

Kramer, Samuel Noah. 1981. *History Begins at Sumer.* Philadelphia: University of Pennsylvania Press (third revised edition).

Krishnamurti, Bh. 1979. 'Classical or Modern – A Controversy in Education in Telugu'. In: E. Annamalai (ed.), *Language Movements in India.* Manasagangotri, Mysore: Central Institute of Indian Languages: 1–24.

Krumbacher, K. 1902. *Das Problem der neugriechischen Schriftsprache.* München: Königliche Bayerische Akademie.

Labahn, Thomas. 1982. *Sprache und Staat. Sprachpolitik in Somalia.* Hamburg: Buske.

Larfeld, W. 1907. *Handbuch der Griechischen Epigraphik.* Leipzig: D. R. Reisland.

Ledyard, Gari K. 1966. *The Korean Language Reform of 1446: The Origin, Background, and Early History of the Korean Alphabet.*

Lee Sangbaek. 1970. 'The Origin of Korean Alphabet "Hangul"'. In his: *A History of Korean Alphabet and Movable Types.* Seoul: Ministry of Culture and Information.

Leibniz, Gottfried Wilhelm. 1923ff. *Sämtliche Schriften und Briefe.* Berlin: Preussische Akademie der Wissenschaften.

Levenson, Joseph R. and Schurmann, Franz. 1969. *China: An Interpretive History.* Berkeley, CA: University of California Press.

Lévi-Strauss, Claude. 1955. *Tristes Tropiques.* Paris: Plon.

Levitt, J. 1978. 'The Influence of Orthography on Phonology: A Comparative Study (English, French, Spanish, Italian, German)'. *Linguistics* 208: 43–67.

Lewis, Glyn. 1983. 'Implementation of Language Planning in the Soviet Union'.

In: J. Cobarrubias and J. A. Fishman (eds), *Progress in Language Planning*. Berlin, Amsterdam, New York: Mouton: 309–26.

Linell, Per. 1982. *The Written Language Bias in Linguistics*. Linköping: University of Linköping Studies in Communication.

Liu Shi-hung. 1969. *Chinese Characters and their Impact on other Languages of East Asia*. Taipei, MA thesis.

Lüdtke, H. 1969. 'Die Alphabetschrift und das Problem der Lautsegmentierung'. *Phonetica* 20: 147–76.

Ludwig, Otto. 1983. 'Writing Systems and Written Language'. In: F. Coulmas and K. Ehlich (eds), *Writing in Focus*. Berlin, Amsterdam, New York: Mouton: 31–43.

Lyons, John. 1977. *Semantics*, vol. I. Cambridge: Cambridge University Press.

Mahadevan, I. 1970. 'Dravidian Parallels in Proto-Indian Script'. *Journal of Tamil Studies* 2/1:

Mahadevan, I. 1986. 'Study of the Indus Script: A Bi-Lingual Approach'. In: Bh. Krishnamurti (ed.), *South Asian Languages. Structure, Convergence and Diglossia*. Delhi: Motilal Banarsidass: 113–19.

Mahmoud, Youssef. 1979. 'The Arabic Writing System and the Sociolinguistics of Orthography Reform'. Ph.D. Dissertation, Georgetown University.

Makita, K. 1968. 'The Rarity of Reading Disability in Japanese Children'. *American Journal of Orthopsychiatry* 38: 599–614.

Mallery, Garrick. 1893. 'Picture Writing of the American Indians'. *Tenth Annual Report of the Bureau of Ethnology*. Washington, DC: Smithsonian Institution.

Marçais, W. 1930. 'La diglossie arabe'. *L'enseignement public* 97: 401–9.

Marcus, Joyce. 1980. 'Zapotec Writing'. *Scientific American* 242/2: 46–60.

Martin, Samuel. 1975. *A Reference Grammar of Japanese*. New Haven, Conn.: Yale University Press.

McCarter, P. Kyle Jr. 1975. *The Antiquity of the Greek Alphabet and the Early Phoenician Scripts*. Missoula: Scholars Press (for Harvard Semitic Museum).

McCarthy, P. A. D. 1969. 'The Bernard Shaw Alphabet'. In: W. Haas (1969): 105–17.

McIntosh, Angus. 1956. 'The Analysis of Written Middle English'. *Transactions of the Philological Society*: 26–55.

McLuhan, Marshall. 1962. *The Gutenberg Galaxy*. Toronto: University of Toronto Press.

Meinhof, Carl. 1911. 'Zur Entstehung der Schrift'. *Zeitschrift für Ägyptische Sprache* 49: 1–14.

Meinhof, Carl. 1931. 'Principles of Practical Orthography for African Languages'. *Africa* 1: 228–39.

Mencken, H. L. *The American Language*. New York: Knopf. (First published 1919.)

Miller, G. A. and Johnson-Laird, P. N. 1976. *Language and Perception.* Cambridge, Mass.: Harvard University Press.

Miller, Roy Andrew. 1967. *The Japanese Language.* Chicago and London: University of Chicago Press.

Miyajima Tatsuo. 1977. 'Kindai nihongo ni okeru kango no chii' [The Position of Sino-Japanese Words in Modern Japanese]. In: Suzuki Yasushi (ed.), *Kokugo kokujimondai no riron.* Tokyo: Mugi no kyôiku bunko 12: 135–86.

Morais, J., Cary, L., Alegria, J. and Bertelson, P. 1979. 'Does Awareness of Speech as a Sequence of Phones Arise Spontaneously?' *Cognition* 7: 323–31.

Morioka Kenji. 1968. 'Mojikeitaisôron' [A Morpheme Theory of *Kanji*]. *Kokugo to kokubungaku* 45/2: 8–27.

Mulugeta Seyoum. 1988. 'The Emergence of the National Language in Ethiopia: An Historical Perspective'. In: F. Coulmas (ed.), *With Forked Tongues. What are National Languages Good for?* Ann Arbor, Mich.: Karoma.

Naveh, J. 1973. 'Some Semitic Epigraphical Considerations in the Antiquity of the Greek Alphabet'. *American Journal of Archeology* 77: 1–8.

Navon, D. and Shimron, J. 1984. 'Reading Hebrew: How Necessary is the Graphemic Representation of Vowels?' In: L. Henderson (1984): 91–102.

Nayanak, H. M. 1967. *Kannada, Literary and Colloquial: A Study of two Styles.* Mysore: Rao & Ragavan.

Needham, Joseph. 1978. *The Shorter Science and Civilization of China.* (Abridged edition by C. A. Ronan.) Cambridge: Cambridge University Press.

Nida, Eugene. 1953. 'Practical Limitations to a Phonemic Orthography'. *Bible Translator* 5. (Reprinted in Smalley et al. 1964: 22–30.)

O'Donnell, R. C. 1974. 'Syntactic Differences between Speech and Writing'. *American Speech* 49: 102–10.

Olson, David. 1977. 'From Utterance to Text: The Bias of Language in Speech and Writing'. *Harvard Educational Review* 47, 3: 257–81.

Ong, Walter J. 1977. *Interfaces of the Word. Studies in the Evolution of Consciousness and Culture.* Ithaca, NY, and London: Cornell University Press.

Ong, Walter J. 1982. *Orality and Literacy. The Technologizing of the Word.* London, New York: Methuen.

Oppenheim, A. L. 1964. *Ancient Mesopotamia.* Chicago: University of Chicago Press.

Oxenham, John. 1980. *Literacy. Writing, Reading and Social Organisation.* London, Boston and Henley: Routledge & Kegan Paul.

Paradis, Michel, Hagiwara, Hiroko and Hildebrandt, Nancy. 1985. *Neurolinguistic Aspects of the Japanese Writing System.* Orlando, Fla., Tokyo: Academic Press.

Park, S. and Arbuckle, T. Y. 1977. 'Ideograms versus Alphabets: Effects of Scripts on Memory in "Biscriptual" Korean Subjects'. *Journal of Experimental Psychology: Human Learning and Memory* 3: 631–42.

Pattanayak, D. P. 1979. 'The Problem and Planning of Scripts'. In: G. Sambasiva Rao (ed.), *Literacy Methodology*. Manasagangotri, Mysore: Central Institute of Indian Languages: 43–59.

Pawley, Andrew and Syder, Frances Hodgetts. 1983. 'Natural Selection in Syntax: Notes on Adaptive Variation and Change in Vernacular and Literary Grammar'. *Journal of Pragmatics* 7/5: 551–79: special issue on Linguistic Problems of Literacy (ed. F. Coulmas).

Pope, Maurice. 1975. *The Story of Decipherment. From Egyptian Hieroglyphic to Linear B*. London: Thames & Hudson.

Powell, Marvin A. 1981. 'Three Problems in the History of Cuneiform Writing: Origins, Direction of Script, Literacy'. *Visible Language* 5/4: 419–40.

Praetorius, Franz. 1906. *Über den Ursprung des kanaanäischen Alphabets*. Berlin: Reuther und Reichard.

Prem, Hans and Riese, Berthold. 1983. 'Autochthonous American Writing Systems: The Aztec and Maya Examples'. In: F. Coulmas and K. Ehlich (eds), *Writing in Focus*. Berlin, Amsterdam, New York: Mouton: 167–86.

Pritchard, J. B. 1958. *Archeology and the Old Testament*. Princeton: Princeton University Press.

Pulgram, Ernst. 1976. 'The Typologies of Writing Systems'. In: W. Haas (ed.), *Writing without Letters*. Manchester: Manchester University Press: 1–27.

Ray, Punya Sloka. 1960. 'A Single Script for India'. *Seminar*, July 1960.

Reiner, Erica. 1966. *A Linguistic Analysis of Akkadian*. London, The Hague, Paris: Mouton.

Reiner, Erica. 1973. 'How We Read Cuneiform Texts'. *Journal of Cuneiform Studies* 25: 3–58.

Renou, L. 1948. *La grammaire de Panini*. Paris: Payot.

Rubin, Joan. 1977. 'Indonesian Language Planning and Education'. In: J. Rubin et al. (eds), *Language Planning Processes*. The Hague, Paris: Mouton: 111–29.

Russell, Bertrand. 1922. *The Problem of China*. London: George Allen & Unwin.

Rüster, Christel. 1972. *Hethitische Keilschrift-Paläographie*. Wiesbaden: Harrassowitz.

Saeki Kôsuke. 1966. 'Kanji to sono shûhen' [Chinese Characters and their Context], *Izumi* 66.

Sampson, Geoffrey. 1985. *Writing Systems: A Linguistic Introduction*. London: Hutchinson.

Sansom, George. 1928. *Historical Grammar of Japanese*. Oxford: Hutchinson.

Sasanuma, S. 1975. 'Kana and Kanji Processing in Japanese Aphasics'. *Brain and Language*: 369–83.

Sato Habein, Yaeko. 1984. *The History of the Japanese Written Language*. Tokyo: University of Tokyo Press.

Saussure, Ferdinand de. 1972. *Cours de linguistique générale*. (Edition préparée par Tuliio de Mauro.) Paris: Payot.

Sayce, A. H. 1910. *Proceedings of the Society of Biblical Archeology* 32: 217ff.

Scharlipp, Wolfgang-Ekkehard. 1984. *Einführung in die tibetische Schrift.* Hamburg: Buske.

Scheerer, Eckart. 1986. 'Orthography and Lexical Access'. In: Gerhard Augst (1986): 262–86.

Schenkel, Wolfgang. 1983. 'Wozu die Ägypter eine Schrift brauchten'. In: Aleida and Jan Assmann and Christof Hardmeier (eds), *Schrift und Gedächtnis.* München: Wilhelm Fink Verlag: 45–63.

Schmandt-Besserat, D. 1978. 'The Earliest Precursors of Writing'. *Scientific American* 238: 50–9.

Schmandt-Besserat, D. 1979. 'Reckoning before Writing'. *Archeology* 32: 23–31.

Schmandt-Besserat, D. 1980. 'The Envelopes that Bear the First Writing'. *Technology and Culture* 21: 371–4.

Schmandt-Besserat, D. 1981. 'From Tokens to Tablets: A Re-evaluation of the so-called "Numerical Tablets"'. *Visible Language*, 15/4: 321–44.

Schmitt, Alfred. 1938. *Die Erfindung der Schrift.* Erlanger Universitätsreden 22. Erlangen: Deichert.

Scragg, D. G. 1974. *A History of English Spelling.* Manchester: Manchester University Press.

Segert, Stanislav. 1983. 'Decipherment of Forgotten Writing Systems: Two Different Approaches'. In: F. Coulmas and K. Ehlich (eds), *Writing in Focus.* Berlin, New York, Amsterdam: Mouton: 131–56.

Segert, Stanislav. 1984. *A Basic Grammar of the Ugaritic Language.* Berkeley, CA: University of California Press.

Sethe, K. 1939. *Vom Bild zum Buchstaben. Die Entstehungsgeschichte der Schrift.* Untersuchungen zur Geschichte und Altertumskunde Ägyptens 12. Leipzig: J. C. Hinrichs.

Seyboldt, Peter, and Chiang, Gregory K. 1979. *Language Reform in China. Documents and Commentary.* White Plains, NY: Sharpe.

Sheets, B. 1961. *Grammatical Method in Panini.* New Haven, Conn.: Yale University Press.

Shuy, Roger W. 1973. 'Nonstandard Dialect Problems: An Overview'. In: James L. Laffey and Roger W. Shuy (eds), *Language Differences: Do they Interfere?* Newark, NJ: International Reading Association.

Sjoberg, André F. 1964. 'Writing, Speech and Society: Some Changing Interrelationships'. In: *Proceedings of the Ninth International Congress of Linguists.* The Hague: Mouton: 892–7.

Smalley, William A. 1964. 'Dialect and Orthography in Gipende'. In: W. Smalley et al. (1964): 138–44.

Smalley, William A. et al. 1964. *Orthography Studies: Articles on New Writing Systems.* London: United Bible Societies.

Smith, Frank. 1973. 'Alphabetic Writing – A Language Compromise?' *Psycholinguistics and Reading*, 117ff.

Smith, P. T. 1980. 'Linguistic Information in Spelling'. In: Frith (1980), 33–49.

Snow, Edgar. 1968. *Red Star over China.* New York: Grove Press (first revised edition).

Sobelman, H. 1961. 'The Proto-Byblian Inscriptions'. *The Journal of Semitic Studies.*

Sommer, F. E. 1942. *The Arabic Writing in Five Lessons, with Practical Exercises and Key.* New York: Frederick Ungar.

Soothill, W. E. 1942. *The Student's Four Thousand Character and General Pocket Dictionary.* London: Kegan Paul (first published 1899).

Speiser, E. A. 1939. 'The Beginnings of Civilization in Mesopotamia'. *Supplement to Journal of the American Oriental Society* 4.

Srivastava, R. N. et al. 1978. *Evaluating Communicability in Village Settings.* Delhi: UNICEF.

Srivastava, R. N. and Gupta, R. S. 1983. 'A Linguistic View of Literacy'. *Journal of Pragmatics* 7/5: 533–49.

Steinberg, Danny D. 1982. *Psycholinguistics. Language, Mind, and World.* London: Longman.

Steuerwald, Karl. 1963/4. *Untersuchungen zur türkischen Sprache der Gegenwart.* 2 vols. Berlin, Schöneberg.

Stratton, Jon. 1980. 'Writing and the Concept of Law in Ancient Greece'. *Visible Language* 14, 2: 99–121.

Street, Brian V. 1984. *Literacy in Theory and Practice.* Cambridge: Cambridge University Press.

Stubbs, Michael. 1980. *Language and Literacy.* London: Routledge & Kegan Paul.

Stubbs, Michael. 1983. 'Can I have this in Writing, Please? Some Neglected Topics in Speech Act Theory'. *Journal of Pragmatics,* 7/5: 479–94, Special Issue 'Linguistic Problems of Literacy' (ed. F. Coulmas).

Suzuki Takao. 1977. 'Writing is not Language, or is it?' *Journal of Pragmatics* 1: 407–20.

Sznycer, Maurice. 1973. 'Les inscriptions pseudo-hiéroglyphiques de Byblos'. In: *Colloque du 29e Congrès des Orientalistes, Paris 1973.* Paris: 'Asia-thèque: 75–84.

Taylor, Insup. 1981. 'Writing Systems and Reading'. In G. E. Mackinnon and T. G. Weller (eds), *Reading Research. Advances in Theory and Practice*, vol. 2. New York: Academic Press: 1–51.

Taylor, Isaac. 1899. *The History of the Alphabet. An Account of the Origin and Development of Letters*, 2 vols. London: Edward Arnold.

Thompson, J. Eric S. 1968. 'Deciphering Maya glyphs'. In: *Cranbrook Institute of Science Newsletter.*

Tsuen-hsuin Tsien. 1962. *Written on Bamboo and Silk.* Chicago: University of Chicago Press.

Tucker, A. N. 1971. 'Orthographic Systems and Conventions in Sub-Saharan

Africa'. In: T. A. Sebeok (ed.), *Current Trends in Linguistics 7: Linguistics in Sub-Saharan Africa.* The Hague: Mouton, 618–53.

Tzeng, O. J., Hung, D. L. and Wang, W. S.-Y. 1977. 'Speech Recoding in Reading Chinese Characters'. *Journal of Experimental Psychology: Human Learning and Memory* 3: 621–30.

Tzeng, O. J., Hung, D. L., Cotton, B. and Wang W. S.-Y. 1979. 'Visual Lateralisation Effect in Reading Chinese Characters'. *Nature* 282: 499–501.

Underwood, Geoffrey and Underwood, Jean. 1986. 'Cognitive Processes in Reading and Spelling'. In: Asher Cashdan (ed.), *Literacy; Teaching and Learning Language Skills.* Oxford: Blackwell.

Ungnad, A. 1927. 'Sumerische und chinesische Schrift'. *Wiener Zeitschrift für die Kunde des Morgenlandes* 34.

Vachek, J. 1973. *Written Language. General Problems and Problems of English.* The Hague: Mouton.

Van de Craen, Pete and Willemijns, Roland. 1988. 'Orthography Reform and Language Planning for Dutch'. In: J. Stalpers and F. Coulmas (eds), *The Sociolinguistics of Dutch. International Journal of the Sociology of Language* 73: 45–64.

Van der Plank, Pieter H. 1988. 'Growth and Decline of the Dutch Standard Language Across the State Borders'. In: J. Stalpers and F. Coulmas (eds), *The Sociolinguistics of Dutch. International Journal of the Sociology of Language* 73: 9–28.

Vargha, D. and Botos, J. 1979. *An Attempt at Homophony-free Deciphering of the Phaistos Disc.* Budapest: Hungarian Academy of Sciences.

Venezky, R. 1970. 'Principles for the Design of Practical Writing Systems'. *Anthropological Linguistics* 12/7: 265–70.

Venezky, R. L. 1972. *The Structure of English Orthography.* The Hague: Mouton.

Voegelin, C. F. and Voegelin, F. M. 1961. 'Typological Classification of Systems with Included, Excluded and Self-sufficient Alphabets'. *Anthropological Linguistics* 3/2: 55–94.

Vollemaere, Anton L. 1971. 'Nouvelles interprétations de l'écriture des codex mayas'. Doctoral thesis, Sorbonne.

von Soden, W. 1936. 'Leistungen und Grenzen babylonischer und sumerischer Wissenschaft'. *Die Welt als Geschichte* 2: 411–64, 509–77.

Wakankar, L. S. 1983. 'Writing in India – Ignorance and Reality'. *CALTIS 83.* Pune: Institute of Typographical Research.

Wallerstein, Nina. 1984. *Language and Culture in Conflict: Problem-Posing in the ESL Classroom.* NJ: Addison-Wesley.

Wang, William S.-Y. 1980. 'Speech and Script in some Asian Languages'. Symposium on Bilingual Research – Asian/American Perspectives, 3–5 September, Los Alamitos.

Watanabe Kiruyon and Suzuki Takao. 1981. *Chôsengo no susume* [Recommendation of Korean]. Tokyo: Kôdansha.

Wen-Pu Yao, Suzanne. 1981. *Ostasiatische Schriftkunst.* Berlin: Museum für Ostasiatische Kunst.

Whiteman, M. F. 1981. 'Dialect Influence in Writing'. In: M. F. Whiteman (ed.), *Writing: The Nature, Development, and Teaching of Written Communication*, vol. 1. Hillsdale, NJ: Erlbaum: 153–66.

Wieger, Léon. 1932. *Caractères Chinois. Etymologie, graphies, lexiques.* (Fifth edition.) Taichung: Kuangchi Press.

Wieseman, D. J. 1970. 'Books in the Ancient World'. In: P. R. Ackroyd and C. F. Evans (eds), *The Cambridge History of the Bible*, vol. 1. Cambridge: Cambridge University Press.

Wijk, Axel. 1959. *Regularized English.* Stockholm: Almqvist & Wiksell.

Wilhelm, Gernot. 1983. 'Reconstructing the Phonology of Dead Languages'. In: F. Coulmas and K. Ehlich (eds), *Writing in Focus.* Berlin, New York, Amsterdam: Mouton: 157–66.

Willcox, William B. 1972. *The Papers of Benjamin Franklin*, vol. 15. New Haven, Conn.: Yale University Press.

Winter, Werner. 1983. 'Tradition and Innovation in Alphabet Making'. In: F. Coulmas and K. Ehlich (eds), *Writing in Focus.* Berlin, Amsterdam, New York: Mouton: 227–38.

Wurm, Stephen A. 1977. 'The Spelling of New Guinea Pidgin (Neo-Melanesian)'. In Fishman (1977): 441–57.

Zachrisson, R. E. 1930. *Anglic, a New Agreed Simplified English Spelling.* Stockholm: Almqvist & Wiksell.

Appendix I
Ancient Near Eastern Chronology

	Mesopotamia	Anatolia	Iran	Egypt
3500 BC	Uruk 3500–3100	Troy	Susa II	
	Jemdet Nasr 3100–2900			Archaic period
3000 BC	Early dynastic period 2900–2300		Susa III	
			Sumero-Elamite period	Old Kingdom 2680–2160
	Akkadian period 2300–2150			
	Neo-Sumerian period 2140–2120		Akkadian rule	
				Middle Kingdom 2060–1786
2000 BC	Old Assyrian period 1900–1750		Old Elamite period 1900–1500	
	Old Babylonian period 1890–1600	Old Hittite period 1650–1400		New Kingdom 1570–1085

	Mesopotamia	Anatolia	Iran	Egypt
	Middle Assyrian period 1300–1000	Hittite Empire period 1400–1200		
1000 BC				
	Neo-Assyrian period 880–610	Phrygian period 775–690		Late Dynastic period 650–330
	Neo-Babylonian period 625–539			

Alexander the Great 331–23

Appendix II
Far Eastern Chronology

	China	*Korea*	*Japan*	*Vietnam*
2200 BC	Xia dynasty			
1523 BC	Shang dynasty (oracle bone inscriptions)		Jômon period	
1027 BC	Zhou conquer Shang			
550 BC	Confucius			
255 BC	Qin dynasty Li Su (small seal script, block printing)	Kokuryo becomes part of Qin realm		
206 BC	Han dynasty (*Shuo wen* dictionary)	Chinese colonies in Korea	Yayoi period	Annam invaded by Chinese
220 AD	Six dynasties of Nanjing		Chinese script used by government	Annamese revolt crushed by Chinese
618 AD	Tang dynasty	*Idu* writing systematized by	*Manyôgana*	
710 AD			Nara period	

	China	Korea	Japan	Vietnam
794 AD		Solch'ong	Heian period *onnade* (*Hiragana*)	Annam gains independ-ence from China
907 AD	Five dynasties	Korea unified	*Katakana*	
960 AD	Sung dynasty (movable type)	under Wang dynasty	Genji	
1004 AD			Monogatari	Annamese script *chũ*
1300 AD		(movable metal type)		*nôm*
1446 AD		Korean script	Japan united	
1550 AD	Portuguese settle in Macao	*Han'gul*	under Nobunaga	
1644 AD	Ching dynasty			Alphabet for
1730 AD		Grand Reform at court in Seoul		Annamese

Index

Abercrombie, D. 167
abstractness of writing 41, 46f
acrophonic principle 32, 35, 140, 156, 164, 166
adaptation of Chinese characters 114, 123
adaptation of a script 42f, 45, 72, 80, 82f, 89,
    112, 115, 145, 157, 162, 185, 190, 271
agglutinative language 115, 124
Ahiram epitaph 141
Akinnaso, F. V. 53
Akkadian 72, 80, 125, 137, 157, 212
  decipherment of 218
Albright, R. W. 239
Albright, W. F. 68, 140
Albrow, K. H. 171
Alexander, R. P. 129
Alisjahbana, S. T. 263
Allchin, B. 180
Allchin, R. 180
Allen, W. S. 188
Alleton, V. 102, 104, 109, 110
alphabet 33f, 37, 108
  Arabic 148, 150–2, 233
  Greek 37
  hieroglyphic 63f
  of human thought 104
  order of 88, 156, 166
  Roman 37
  Russian 37
  Ugaritic 88, 138f
  uniqueness of 177
  universality of 45, 47, 167, 176
alphabetic hypothesis 160
alphabetic orthography 168–75
alphabetic writing, origin of 138
American spelling 253f
Amharic 155
Andrews, C. 61, 63, 223
Annamalai, E. 196
Annamese 43f, 112–15, 116, 243

Ansre, G. 229
aphasia 134
Arabic 137, 145
  script 144, 150–2, 243f
Aramaic 137, 142f, 182
Arbuckle, T. Y. 134
Aristotle 35
Asoka inscriptions 181f
Assamese 189
Assyrian 72, 138
Ateji 128f
Augst, G. 257
Aymara orthography 227
Aztec writing 31f

Babylonian 72, 218
Bahasa Indonesia 259
Ball, C. J. 93
Barnard, N. 94
Bauer, H. 141, 156
Beaugrande, R. de 39
Beck, H. 53, 230
Becker, A. L. 135
Bengali 189, 196
Benvéniste, E. 107
Berber 150
Bernal, J. D. 8
Bernard Shaw Alphabet 224, 251
Berry, J. 226, 238
Bieber, D. 52
Bierwisch, M. 40
bilingual inscriptions 214, 216, 217
Birnbaum, S. A. 157
Bisseret, N. 239
Bloomfield, L. 62, 269
Bodberg, P. 105
Bolinger, D. 178, 230
Bork, F. 90
Botos, J. 212

Bouda, K. 90
Brahmi derived scripts 182, 193
Brahmi script 54, 166, 181f
Bright, W. 200
Britto, F. 195, 200
Buchanan, P. 113
Burrows, M. 157
Byblos script 139, 156

calligraphy 14, 95, 109
Canaanite 142
Carr, D. 256f
cenemic writing 49, 51, 59f, 65, 78, 80f, 86f, 99,
    101, 108, 110, 117, 124, 129, 137, 156,
    161, 167, 197
Central Institute of Indian Languages 200
Chadwick, J. 219
Chafe, W. 39
Champollion, F. 61, 214–16
Chang, K. 91
Chao, Y. R. 52, 107, 109, 110
Chatterjee, S. 196
Chiera, E. 29, 35, 73, 90
Childe, G. 15f, 70, 156
Chinese 30, 43, 46, 49f, 199
Chinese characters
    adaptation of 114, 123
    number of 94, 98, 100f, 110
    number of strokes 95
    order of strokes 97
    phonological poverty of 105
    processing of 134
    simplification of 245f
    see also Hanzi
Chinese empire 8, 91
Chinese orthography 37
Chinese paleography 94
Chinese script
    reform of 244f
    spread of 112
Chinese scripts 95f
Chinese texts 111f, 117
Chomsky, N. 170
Chou En-lai 245
chu nôm, 114
Civil, M. 80
civilization 4, 6, 8–10, 15
Classical Chinese 111f, 113, 115, 117, 123, 200
    see also wényán
classifier 98–102, 104, 107f, 109, 219
clay tablets 35, 74
Cohen, M. 107
communication 7, 12f, 35, 106, 135, 160, 247
    international 174
Confucianism 113

consonant clusters 41f, 85, 183, 187f, 190, 192,
    220
consonant roots 67, 98, 145, 148, 150
consonant script 139–41, 162, 185
context 22f, 65, 144, 149, 217, 230
convention 9, 22
Copperman, P. 21
Coptic 71, 214f
Coptic alphabet 166, 243
Cottrell, L. 86, 216
Coulmas, F. 10, 14, 23, 35f, 95, 98, 195, 200,
    239, 262
Cowgill, W. 53
Coyaud, M. 127f
Creel, H. G. 105, 109, 110
Crofts, A. 113
cult, 58f, 79
    see also religion
cultural contact 124
cultural diffusion 112
cuneiform alphabet 88, 138f
cuneiform signs 36, 125, 137
    adaptation of 84
    decipherment of 208, 216–19
    expressive power of 77f
    invention of 72
    number of 73, 100
    spread of 88
cuneiform texts 76
cursivization 69, 95
Cypriot syllabary 220
Cyrillic 37, 166, 233, 237, 243

Dani, A. H. 180
de Casparis, J. G. 191
de Rooij, J. 169
De Silva, M. W. Sugathapala 195, 197f
Dead Sea Scrolls 157
decipherment 33, 62, 86, 140, 205f
deep orthographies 169f
DeFrancis, J. 8, 104f, 106, 110, 245, 262
demotic script 69, 121
Deshpande, M. M. 194, 199
determinatives 63, 65, 67, 70, 78f, 82, 87, 100f,
    137
Devanagari 38, 112, 172, 186f, 199, 237
Dhorme, E. 139, 156
diacritics 42, 44, 114, 120, 149, 150, 153, 176,
    183f, 190, 231, 250, 256
dialects 79, 106f, 112, 165, 198, 228f, 238, 247
dictionaries 39, 73, 98, 103, 106, 107, 109, 186,
    244, 246, 252
    monolingual 268
digital code 9
diglossia 80, 200, 249

Arabic 151, 195, 200
  in India 194–8
digraph 51f, 235, 246
direction of scripts 211f
Diringer, D. 36, 44, 70, 138–41, 153, 156, 159, 161, 181, 197
distinctive features 48, 120
distribution analysis 216f, 219
divinatory texts 92
double articulation 98
Downing, J. 251
Dravidian languages 192, 196
Dressler, W. 39
Driver, G. R. 137, 156
Duggan, J. J. 14
Dutch 174f, 228
  spelling reform 260, 263
dyslexia 239

Easter Island script 199
economy of writing systems 45f, 48, 52, 60, 100
Egyptian hieroglyphs 61, 137–9, 140
  decipherment of 214–16
Egyptian language 61
Ehlich, K. 9
Ehri, L. C. 230
Eisenberg, P. 172
Elamite 72, 84f
Ellis, A. W. 239
Elsasser, N. 239
English 49, 51, 106, 228, 250
  orthography 37, 107, 170, 228, 253
  spelling reform, 250–6
Ethiopic 137, 145, 166
Ethiopic script 152–4, 181
etymological spelling 170f, 191, 256
Evans, A. 141, 207

Faeroese 228
Falkenstein, A. 72f, 76, 78, 79
Farsi 150
Feldbusch, E. 26, 35, 228
Ferguson, C. A. 200, 228
Fiore, K. 239
Firth, J. R. 5
Fishman, J. A. 200
Fleckenstein, J. 249
Follik, M. 262
Franklin, B. 254f
French 49
  orthography 46
Friedrich, J. 11, 35, 57, 63, 67f, 78, 85, 86, 107, 139f, 155f
Fries, C. C. 39
Frith, U. 52, 230, 232

function of writing 7, 11–15
  aesthetic 14f
  distancing 12
  interactional 14
  mnemonic 11f
  reifying 12
  social control 13f
function words, 132

Gardiner, A. H. 139f
Garvin, P. 227, 234
Ge'ez 155
Geerts, G. 262
Gelb, I. J. 19, 34, 43f, 62, 63, 67f, 86, 90, 159, 161, 177, 181
general literacy 249, 260
German 41, 228
  orthography 37, 171, 174
  orthography reform 257–9
Gibson, E. J. 169
Goody, J. 9–11, 40, 54, 158, 197
Gordon, C. H. 222
Graff, H. 10
Grantha script 192
Greek 122, 147, 214, 220
  alphabet 143
  epigraphy 177
  orthography 165
  society 16
Greek, modern 200
Green, M. W. 29, 74
Gregersen, E. A. 261
Gudschinsky, S. 230, 233
Gupta, R. S. 236
Gupta, alphabet, adaptation of 190

Haas, M. 200
Haas, W. 37, 41, 49, 54, 169, 262
Halle, M. 170
Hamito-Semitic languages 67
Han'gul 38, 54, 118–22, 134, 135, 242
hànyǔ pīnyīn 245f
Hanzi 95, 113, 122, 133, 134, 262
  adaptation of 114, 115, 123
  internal structure of 245
  literacy 129, 247
Harappan seals 180
Harris, R. 39, 268f
Haugen, E. 229
Havelock, E. 160
Hayashi, O. 128
Hebrew 137, 145
  alphabet 143
  orthography 149
  script 143f, 148f, 157
Hembram, N. 180
Henderson, L. 47, 52, 178

Hentai–Kanbun 123, 135
Henze, P. B. 237, 243, 261
Herdner, A. 90
Herodotus 57, 70, 213
Herslund, M. 178
Hevesy, M. G. de 199
Heyd, U. 243
hieratic script 69
hieroglyphic alphabet 63f
Hindi 188, 193, 196, 199, 237
Hiragana 129, 131
history 4, 12, 16, 58, 122, 160, 208
   of linguistics, 268f
Hittite 42f, 72, 85, 90, 138
Hittite hieroglyphic 90, 141
Hjelmslev, L. 49
Ho F. 93
Homer 14
homophony 30, 46, 63, 99, 101, 105, 114, 127f,
   136, 173, 232
Horappolo 214
Householder, F. 178
Hun Min Jong Um 118
Hurrian 72

iconicity 17, 21f, 29f, 34, 74f, 88
ideogram 26, 28f, 62, 104f, 107
ideographic principle 99, 110, 111
Ido 116f
illiteracy 21, 159, 194f, 199, 239
   in Turkey 243
Indic scripts 132, 155, 181f
Indo-Aryan languages 181, 196
information load 52, 103
Initial Teaching Alphabet (ITA) 251f
inner form
   of Chinese characters 98f
   of Egyptian hieroglyphs 61f
   of Han'gul 119, 121
   of Indic scripts 184f
   of North Semitic alphabets 144
   of Sumerian cuneiform 76f
intonation 270
invention of writing 3–6, 58, 86, 120, 272
IPA 48, 231, 234, 239
isolating language 108, 112

Jacobson, T. 73
Jalaluddin, A. K. 233, 240
Japanese 42, 109
   orthography 132
   phonology 127
   writing 36, 122f
Javanese 191f, 193
Jensen, H. 5, 8, 31f, 34, 63, 67f, 86, 107, 141,
   156, 177, 181

Johnson-Laird, P. 53
Jordan, J. 35, 73

Kadamba script 192
Kahane, H. 262
Kana 126, 129–33, 134
   orthography 132
Kanbun 123, 124
Kang Xi 98
Kanji 122–9, 134
Kannaiyan, V. 185
Karlgren, B. 94, 102, 110
Kashmiri 150
Katakana 129f
Kavi script 190, 191f
Kazakh 150
Kemp, J. A. 234
Kennedy, G. A. 105, 106, 110
Kharosthi script 155, 182f
Khubchandani, L. 199, 200, 201
Kindaichi, H. 39, 127
Klima, E. S. 48
knot-strings 18
knowledge 4, 6, 135, 179
   societal 28f
Kohrt, M. 262
Kokuji 129
König, F. W. 84
Kôno, R. 120
Konrad, N. J. 245
Korean 43, 115f, 129
Krishnamurti, B. 195, 198
Krummbacher, K. 200
Kugyol 117
kun reading 123–5 128

Labahn, T. 239
language, units of 34
language 11, 13, 15, 18, 22, 27, 37, 62, 88
   acquisition 207
   analysis of 41, 120, 270
   attitude 227
   contact 80, 82, 133, 136, 138
   cultivation 80, 191, 194, 198
   inflecting 81
   scholastic 194, 198
Larfeld, W. 177
Latin 122f, 147, 200, 249, 262
   alphabet 166
law 4, 13, 16
Ledyard, G. K. 118
Lee, S. 118, 120, 121
Leibniz, G. W. 104, 110, 223
Levenson, J. R. 109
Levin, A. 169
Lévi-Strauss, C. 13, 16

Levitt, J. 178
Lewis, G. 261
liaison 172
Linear, B. 219–21
Linell, P. 39f, 269
linguistic awareness 45, 79, 135, 171, 231
lists 11, 16, 73, 259
literacy 6, 10, 90, 135, 179, 236
    promotion 197, 247
    restricted 180, 197, 249
    spread of 155
literary language 194, 198
literary tradition 181, 193, 242, 244, 251
literate society 9, 13, 252, 257
literature 14, 80, 113, 160, 186, 194
Liu S. 111
loan words 82, 85, 112, 122–3, 124f, 127, 132f,
    147, 157, 173, 259
    identity of 174
    spelling of 174
logogram 78, 80f, 83, 100, 104, 107, 110
Lüdtke, H. 40
Ludwig, O. 35
Lyons, J. 53
Lyu Shuxiang 247

McCarter, P. K. 158
McCarthy, P. A. D. 224, 262
McIntosh, A. 35
McLuhan, M. 4, 44, 159–61, 177, 197
Mahadevan, I. 180
Makita, K. 134
Malay 150
    spelling reform 259
Mallery, G. 19f
Malone, J. 251
Mandarin 247f.
    see also Chinese
Manyôgana 129f
Mao Zedong 247
mapping relation 52, 101, 107
Marçais, W. 200
Marcus, J. 36
Martin, S. 115
matres lectionis 129, 146–50, 164
Maya hieroglyphs 31, 210
    decipherment of 223
meaning 12f, 22f, 29, 46, 51, 63, 78, 99f, 103f,
    123, 161, 208, 222
Meinhof, C. 21 237
memory 11, 18, 20, 28, 134
metaphor 77, 135
Miller, G. A. 53
Miller, R. A. 125, 132, 136
Miyajima, T. 136
monoconsonant sign 67f

monogenesis theory 71
monosyllabism 79, 105, 113
mora 132
Morais, J. 54
Morioka, K. 128
morpheme 128
    grammatical 116, 117, 124, 132f
Morse code 48
Mulugeta, S. 155
Mycenaean writing 158
myth 5, 10

Navon, D. 149
Nayanak, H. M. 200
Needham, J. 93, 109
Nida, E. 227
norm 241, 248, 254, 256, 269
    written 169, 171, 178, 197, 241, 257
numbers 25f, 99, 104

O'Donnell, R. C. 39
Ol Chiki 240
Old Persian 72, 85f
    decipherment of 217
Olson, D. 13, 161
on readings 125–8
Ong, W. J. 4, 11, 14, 135
onnade (women's hand) 130
Oppenheim, A. L. 72
oracle bones 91, 110
oral societies 6f, 179, 194
oral tradition 179, 194
order of alphabet 88, 159, 186
orthographic word 172, 230f
orthography 37–9, 47, 108, 132, 225
    design 226
    linguistic adequacy of 238
Oxenham, J. 4, 6

Pali 186, 190f
Palmyran script 143
Panini 186, 194, 200
Paradis, M. 136
Park, S. 134
Pattanayak, D. P. 189, 198, 236, 243, 261
Pawley, A. 39, 238
Persian alphabet 151
Perso-Arabic 189, 199
Phaistos disk 212
Phoenician 139, 141f
    alphabet 141f, 159, 163f
    letter names 163f
phoneme 40, 170
phoneme–grapheme correspondence 50, 169,
    174, 230, 250

phonemic analysis 168
phonemic orthography 229, 232, 246
phonemic representation 134, 138, 155, 161,
    171, 230
phonetic alphabet 160
phonetic complements 83
phonetic decoding 109
phonetic interpretation 51
phonetic principle 105
phonetic system 54
phonetic writing 33
phonetization 26, 28–30, 33, 100
phonological poverty of Chinese 105
phonological system 44, 147, 222
phonology 185
pictogram 25, 34, 75
pictographic characters 98f, 100
pictorial signs 23, 70, 99f, 219
picture 19, 23, 93f
Pitman, J. 251
places of articulation 119, 185
plene writing 147
pleremic writing 49f, 59f, 65, 78, 80f, 94, 99,
    101, 108, 117, 137, 156, 170
Plotinus 61
poetry
    Classical Chinese 106
    Japanese 124
    Javanese 191
    oral 14
    Telugu 195
Pope, M. 61, 209, 214, 223
Powell, M. A. 29, 36, 90
Praetorius, F. 141
Prem, H. 18, 31, 210, 223
Pritchard, J. B. 90
proper name 30, 33, 116, 147, 157, 191, 213f,
    216f, 223, 258f
    importance for decipherment 223
Proto-Sinaitic script 139f
Pulgram, E. 44
punctuation (Tiberian system) 148f
Punic script 142, 147
Pǔtōnghuà 247

quipus 18

radicals 98
Ray, P. S. 189
Read, K. 251
reading 52, 120, 133, 134, 150, 167, 205f, 230,
    232, 239, 258
    disabilities 134, 239
rebus principle 30–2, 59, 65, 77, 98, 129
record keeping 8f, 24f, 73
Reiner, E. 80, 83, 90

religion 4, 58, 132, 148, 150f, 155, 166, 190,
    194, 197, 199f, 261
Renou, L. 199
reparatio 249
representation of speech 226, 228, 237, 249
Riese, B. 18, 31, 210, 223
Romanization 243, 246, 261
Rosetta Stone 214, 223
Rubin, J. 260
Russell, B. 105, 110, 111
Rüster, C. 85

Sacy, S. de. 214
Sampson, G. 35, 54, 107, 120, 169
sandhi 172, 188f
Sanskrit 186f, 192, 194, 217
    literature 199
    orthography 189
Sansom, G. 122
Santhali 189, 193, 240
Sasanuma, S. 134
Sato Habein, Y. 123
Saussure, F. de 28, 35, 267
Sayce, A. H. 141
Scharlipp, W. E. 190
Scheerer, E. 169
Schmandt-Besserat, D. 4, 23–5, 27, 35, 90
Schurmann, F. 109
schwa 148, 185
Scragg, D. G. 250
script, social significance of 226
script reform 242
    Chinese 244–8
    Turkish 243f
script selection 225, 234
scriptio plena 147
secret code 5, 205, 208, 222
Segert, S. 87, 139, 222
segmentation 47, 221, 230, 268
semantic decoding 104, 109
semantic–phonetic compound principle 99,
    102f
Semitic consonant writing
    adaptation of 145, 162, 185
    origin of 141, 159
Semitic languages 137
sentence 53
    notion of 39, 189, 270, 272
Sethe, K. 70
shallow orthographies 169, 175
Shang dynasty 91, 94f
Shaw, G. B. 251, 262
Sheets, B. 199
Shimron, J. 149
Shuo wen jiezi 98
Shuy, R. 238

sign
  linguistic 26, 28, 33
  surrogational 19, 35
sign inventory 52, 60, 73, 84, 100, 211
sign transfer 78
simplification of Chinese characters 94f, 245f
Sinhalese 190, 195
Sjoberg, A. F. 227
Slavonic 150
Smalley, W. A. 226f
Smith, F. 52
Smith, P. T. 171
Snow, E. 247
Sobelman, H. 139
social control 5, 8, 13f
Somali 150, 239
Sommer, F. E. 157
Soothill, W. E. 110
sound stream of speech 52, 189, 232, 268
South Arabic script 152
Spanish 150
speech, mapping of 47
speech recoding 134
speech sound 29, 34, 46, 63, 100, 120, 155, 167, 219
Speiser, E. A. 72
spelling, externally motivated 227
spelling pronunciation 171
spelling reform 224, 248f, 259f
Srivastava, R. N. 233, 236
standard language 14
Steinberg, D. D. 239
Steuerwald, K. 261
Stratton, J. 16
Street, B. V. 10, 21
Stubbs, M. 13, 250, 262
Sumerian 29, 42, 72
  cuneiform 25, 57
  pictograms 73
Sumerograms 84f, 89
Suzuki, T. 120, 136
Swahili 150
Syder, F. H. 39, 238
syllabary 78, 83, 129, 139, 161
syllabic signs 81, 83, 117, 145, 153, 220
syllabic writing 33, 41, 43, 48, 51, 68, 106, 120, 124, 134, 138, 219
syllable structure
  of Akkadian 81
  of German 41f
  of Japanese 42
  of Korean 117
  of Sumerian 78
Syriac 137, 143, 145, 148
Sznycer, M. 156

tally sticks 9, 18
Tamil 192, 195
Taylor, Insup 178
Taylor, Isaac 177
Telugu script 192
Thai script 190f, 200
Thompson, J. E. S. 31
Tibetan script 190, 193
tone 44, 47, 103, 113, 176, 190, 191, 200, 234, 246
transcription 54, 167, 219, 226, 229, 252
transfer of scripts 88f, 112, 138, 156, 162, 233f
Tsuen-hsuin, T. 92
Tuareg 11
Tucker, A. N. 234
Turkish 150, 243f
  orthography 244
Tzeng, O. J. 134

Ugaritic 72, 87f, 139, 156
Uighur 150
Underwood, G. 239
Underwood, J. 239
Ungnad, A. 93
UNIFON 251f
universal alphabet 234, 239
universal language 105
unwritten language 198f, 225, 228, 236
Urdu 150
  alphabet 151
Uruk 72f

Vachek, J. 178, 250, 256, 262
Van der Plank, P. H. 228
Vargha, D. 212
varieties of language 79, 194f, 198, 239, 249
Venezky, R. 169f, 228, 256
Ventris, M. 219f
Verhoeven, G. 169
Vietnamese see Annamese
Virolleaud, C. 156
Voegelin, C. F. 177
Voegelin, F. M. 177
Vollemaere, A. L. 31
vowel indication 147f, 149, 150, 153, 155, 162, 164, 166, 181, 183, 185f, 190
vowel length 132, 146, 165, 172

Wabun 124, 132
Wakankar, L. S. 200
Wallerstein, N. 239
Wang Li 247
Wang, W. S.-Y. 93
Watanabe, K. 120
Watt, I. 9f, 158, 197
Webster, N. 252–4

Wen-Pu, Y. 93
wényán 113, 115, 122, 198
   see also Classical Chinese
Whiteman, M. F. 238
Wieseman, D. J. 73
Wijk, A. 256
Wilhelm, G. 224
Willcox, W. B. 254
Winter, W. 227
word 29f, 189
   notion of 39f
word boundary 53, 85, 142, 165, 172f, 188f,
   212, 220
word formation 127, 129
word memory 134

word order 135
word sign 31–3
writing, definitions of 34f
written language 27, 53, 76, 79, 84, 89, 106,
   113, 116, 117, 122, 123f, 128, 132f, 151,
   155, 172, 178, 197, 228, 249, 262, 267,
   269, 270
written *Sprachbund* 133
Wurm, S. 227

Yoruba 19

Zachrisson, R. E. 254
Zapotec writing 35